THE YEAR OF JULIUS AND CAESAR

WITNESS TO ANCIENT HISTORY

Gregory S. Aldrete, *Series Editor*

Also in the Series

Jerry Toner, *The Day Commodus Killed a Rhino: Understanding the Roman Games*

Debra Hamel, *The Battle of Arginusae: Victory at Sea and Its Tragic Aftermath in the Final Years of the Peloponnesian War*

Robert Garland, *Athens Burning: The Persian Invasion of Greece and the Evacuation of Attica*

THE YEAR OF JULIUS AND CAESAR

59 BC and the Transformation of the Roman Republic

Stefan G. Chrissanthos

Johns Hopkins University Press
Baltimore

Printed in the United States of America on acid-free paper
2 4 6 8 9 7 5 3 1

Johns Hopkins University Press
2715 North Charles Street
Baltimore, Maryland 21218-4363
www.press.jhu.edu

Library of Congress Cataloging-in-Publication Data

Names: Chrissanthos, Stefan G., author.
Title: The year of Julius and Caesar : 59 BC and the transformation of the Roman Republic / Stefan G. Chrissanthos.
Description: Baltimore, Maryland : Johns Hopkins University Press, 2019. | Series: Witness to ancient history | Includes bibliographical references and index.
Identifiers: LCCN 2018046671 | ISBN 9781421429694 (hardcover : alk. paper) |
ISBN 9781421429700 (pbk. : alk. paper) | ISBN 9781421429717 (electronic)
ISBN 1421429691 (hardcover : alk. paper) | ISBN 1421429705 (pbk. : alk. paper) |
ISBN 1421429713 (electronic)
Subjects: LCSH: Rome—History—First Triumvirate, 60–53 B.C. | Caesar, Julius.
Classification: LCC DG263 .C47 2019 | DDC 937/.05—dc23
LC record available at https://lccn.loc.gov/2018046671

A catalog record for this book is available from the British Library.

Johns Hopkins University Press uses environmentally friendly book materials, including recycled text paper that is composed of at least 30 percent post-consumer waste, whenever possible.

For Dawn, Korena, and Nikolaos, who make it all worthwhile

CONTENTS

ACKNOWLEDGMENTS

I would like to thank Johns Hopkins University Press, especially Matt McAdam, my editor Jacqueline Wehmueller, and editorial assistant William Krause, who worked so diligently on the book's behalf. Thanks too to copyeditor David Goehring. Series editor Greg Aldrete has provided much valuable advice during the course of this project. In addition, I would like to thank the anonymous readers, as well as Dr. D. Brendan Nagle, whose insightful comments helped a great deal. It goes without saying that for the book's remaining faults, I bear complete responsibility.

MAPS

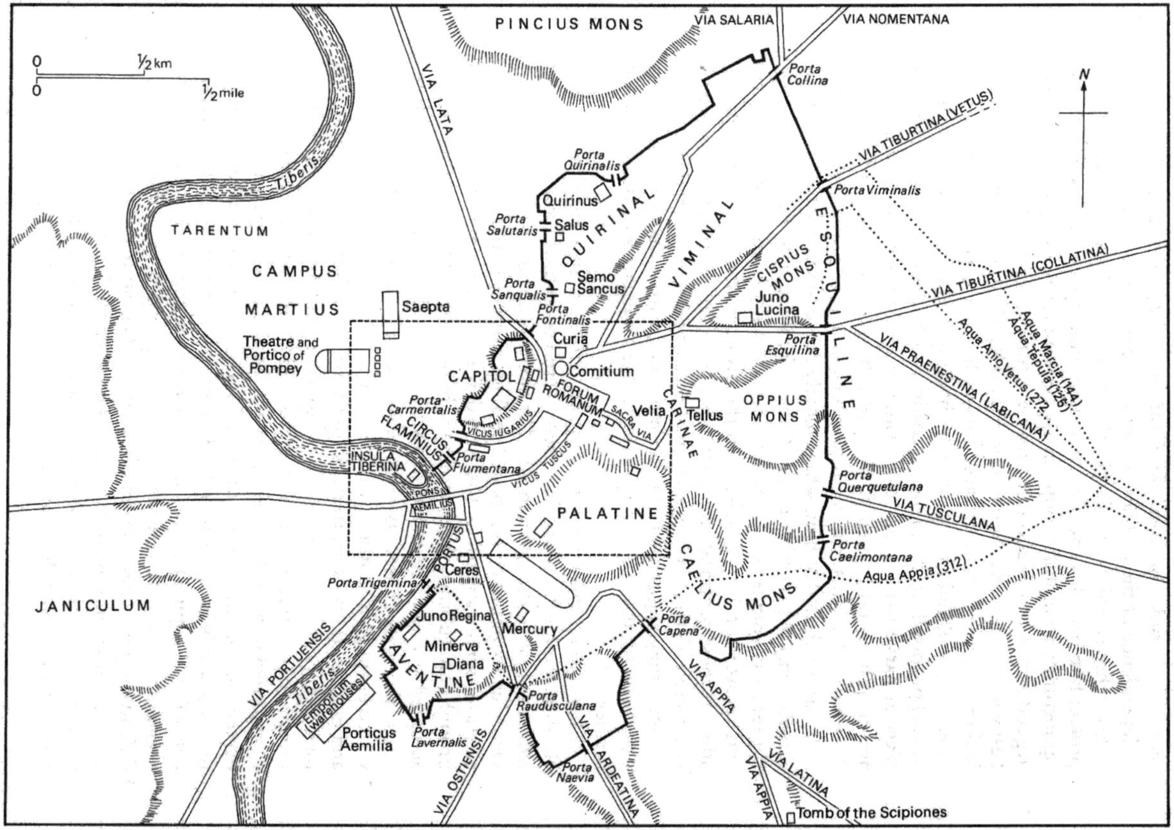

Rome in the Late Republic. Courtesy of Cambridge University Press

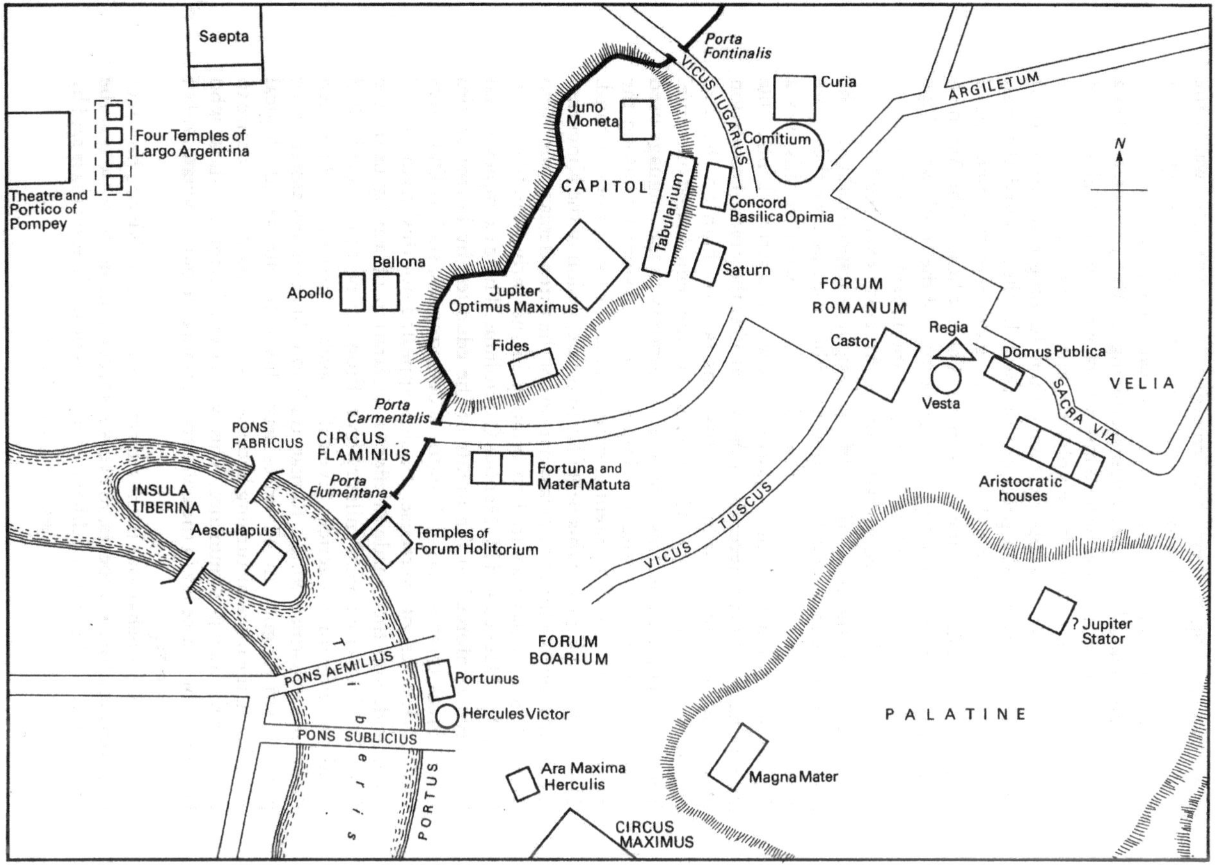

The Center of Rome in the Late Republic. Courtesy of Cambridge University Press

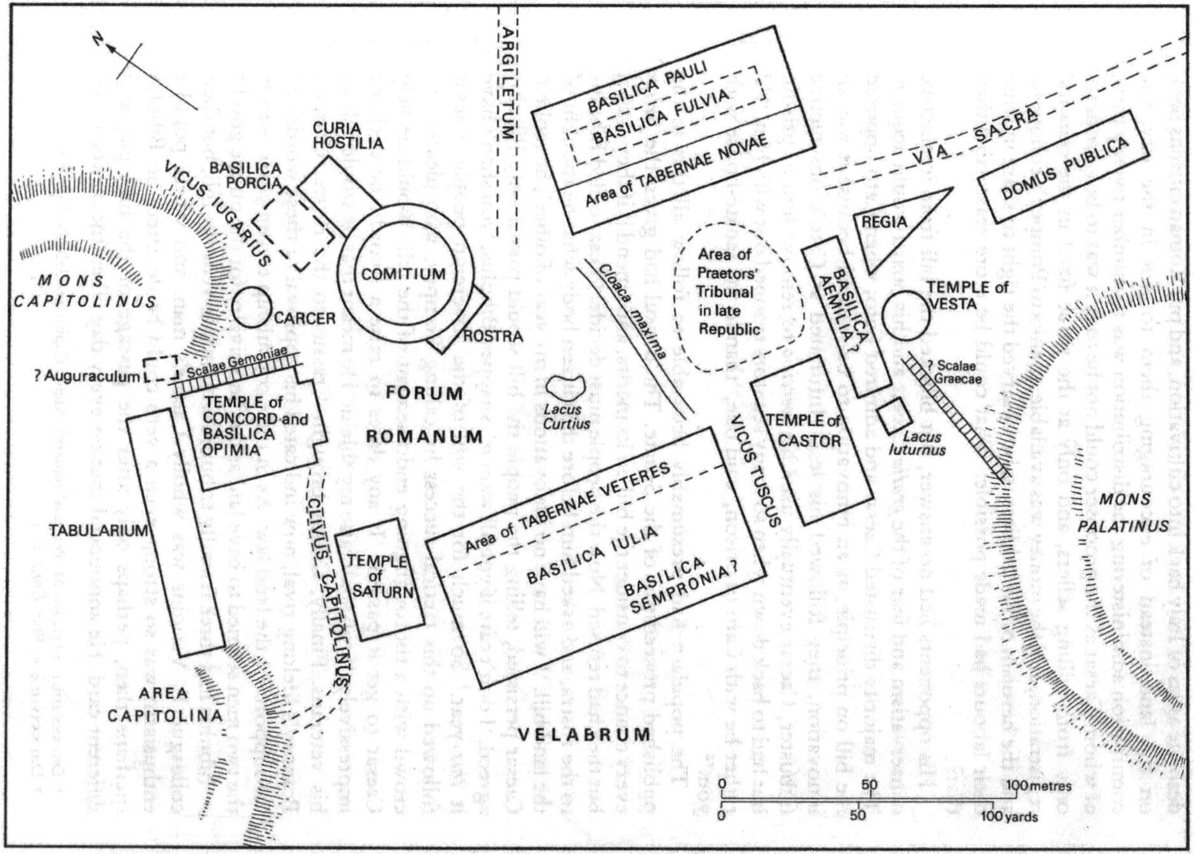

The Roman Forum in the Late Republic. Courtesy of Cambridge University Press

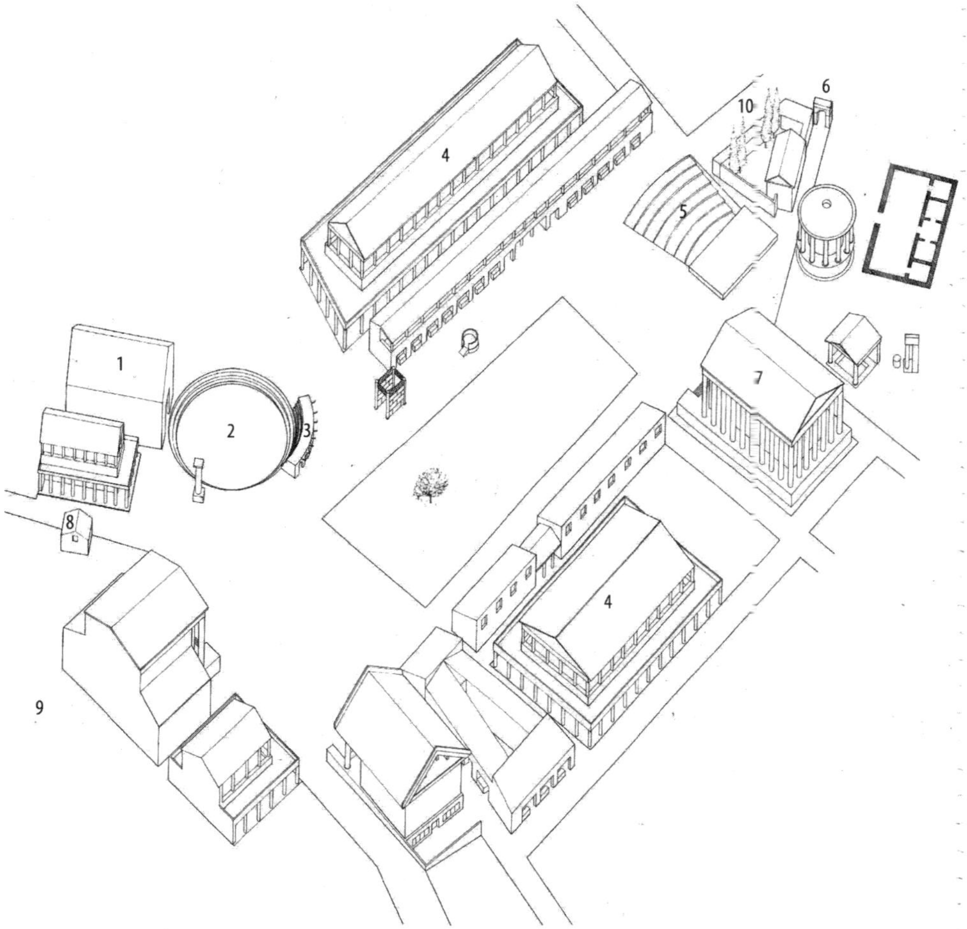

The Roman Forum in the Second Century BC
Key: 1. Senate 2. Comitium 3. Rostra 4. Basilica 5. Aurelian Steps 6. Fornix Fabianus 7. Temple of Castor and Pollux 8. Carcer 9. Capitoline Hill 10. Via Sacra. Courtesy of Johns Hopkins University Press

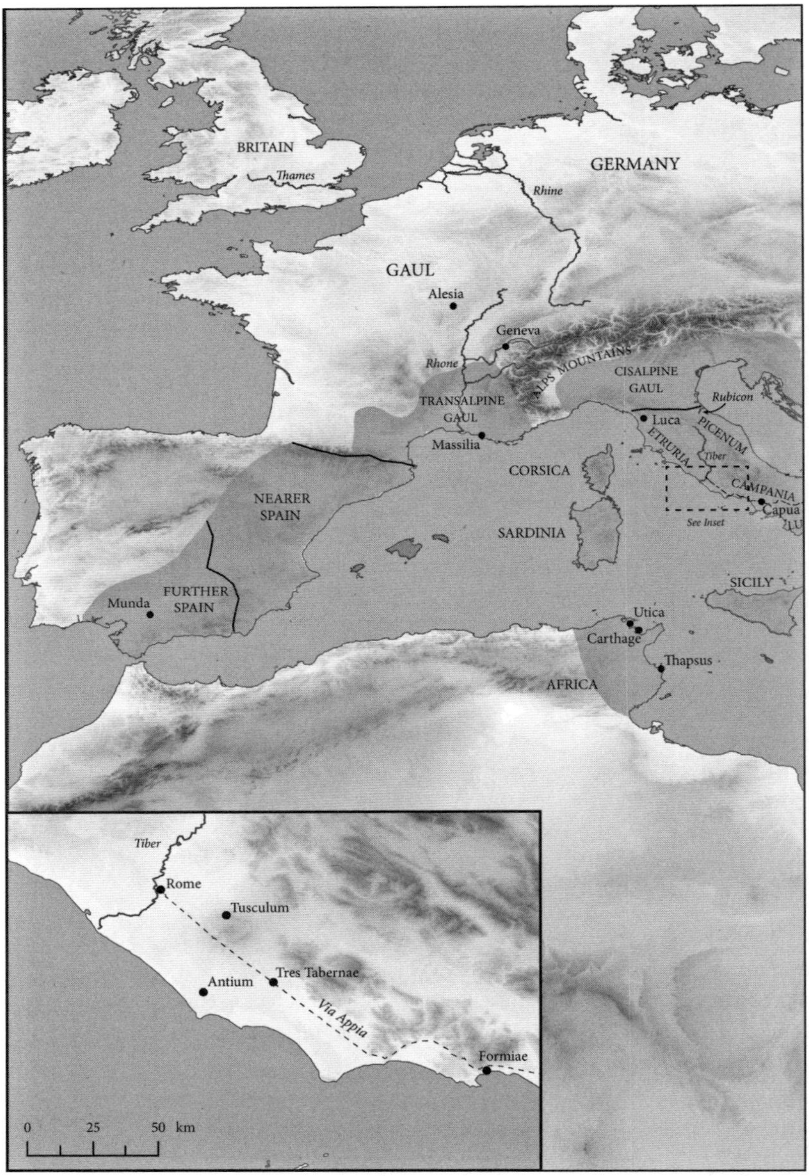

The Roman Empire in 60 BC. Courtesy of Ancient World Mapping Center

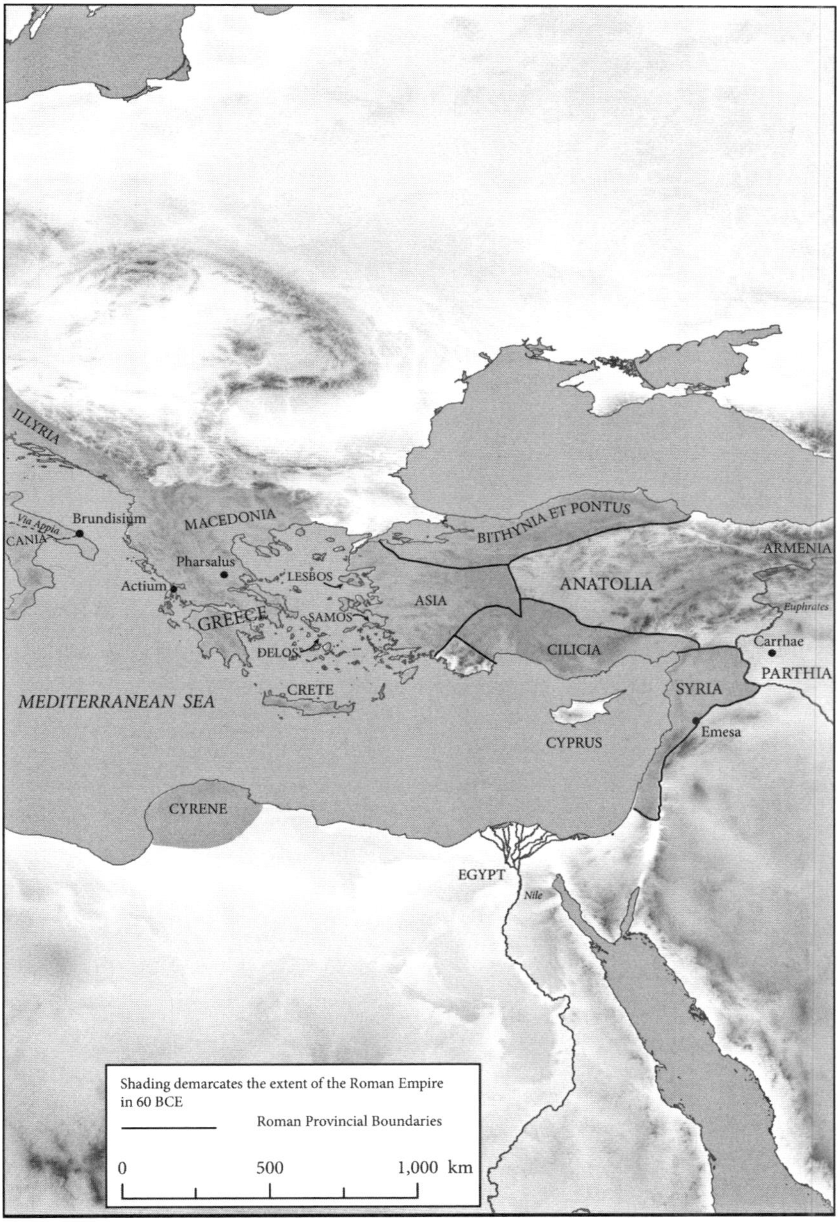

ILLYRIA
Via Appia
CANIA
Brundisium
MACEDONIA
Pharsalus
Actium
GREECE
LESBOS
SAMOS
DELOS
CRETE
MEDITERRANEAN SEA
BITHYNIA ET PONTUS
ASIA
ANATOLIA
ARMENIA
Euphrates
CILICIA
Carrhae
PARTHIA
SYRIA
Emesa
CYPRUS
CYRENE
EGYPT
Nile
Shading demarcates the extent of the Roman Empire in 60 BCE
Roman Provincial Boundaries
0
500
1,000 km

THE YEAR OF JULIUS AND CAESAR

PROLOGUE

Caesar and Bibulus

April 4, 59 BC/695 AUC

BY 59 BC, the year of the consulship of Gaius Julius Caesar and Marcus Calpurnius Bibulus, the Roman Republic ruled most of the known world, controlling an empire that stretched across Mare Nostrum (the Mediterranean—literally "our sea").[1] The city of Rome proper was home to as many as a million citizens, foreigners, freedmen, and slaves who inhabited six of its seven hills and many of the valleys in between. Rome was enclosed in the *pomerium,* a religious boundary that separated it from the surrounding countryside, and by the Servian Wall, seven miles of fortifications that were no longer needed, because Rome's empire was so large and its frontiers extended so far that an attack by a foreign foe was all but unimaginable.[2]

Although the empire was secure from outside enemies, many internal problems augured a turbulent future. Hanging heavily over the year 59 were the memories of the recent past, especially the political violence and civil wars that had been set into motion by the assassination of the tribune Tiberius Sempronius Gracchus in 133 and the recent horrors of the dictatorship of Lucius Cornelius Sulla Felix (82–79). Sulla's willingness to lead his army against Rome itself inspired similar acts by other commanders; five civil wars and a series of massacres followed. The republic had weathered these storms, but 59 marked a turning point in its history and in the continuing Roman "Revolution," whose significance was recognized even at the time.[3] It stands out as a momentous year of political intrigue, bloodshed, and murder, featuring some of the largest personalities ever to grace the Roman stage, including Cato the Younger, Clodius, Pompey, Crassus, Cicero, and, especially, Caesar.

Darkness enveloped the city of Rome in the hour before dawn on April 4, 59.[4] From the Tiber River to the Viminal Hill, from the Quirinal to the Aventine, many in the city still slept. Yet it was far from quiet. The ancient Mediterranean's greatest metropolis was notoriously noisy, especially in the densely populated valley of the Subura, home to *insulae*—apartment towers reaching thirteen stories high. People were already making their way to work or preparing their businesses for the coming day. Less reputable characters committed petty crimes or worse in the narrow, bewildering, and unpoliced city streets. And there was the continuous talking and laughing and cursing and shouting of those engaged in their various pursuits, along with the sounds made by the many animals living and dying in the city.

In the predawn darkness one group of men gathered in the fashionable Carinae district on the western tip of the Esquiline Hill's Oppian spur, at the mansion of Rome's best-known general, Gnaeus Pompey Magnus ("the Great"). These men were not ordinary citizens; rather, they were mostly veterans of Pompey's eastern campaigns (67–62) that had ended in victory and the addition of four new provinces to the Roman Empire.

Since the men's return in 62, Pompey had attempted to persuade the Roman senate to provide an allotment of land and a secure retirement for each veteran as a reward for his military service. Repeatedly blocked in his efforts by his political enemies (notably, a group of conservative senators, the *optimates,* led by Marcus Porcius Cato), Pompey had joined an alliance in 60 with his old rival Marcus Licinius Crassus, Rome's wealthiest man, and Caesar, one of Rome's two newly elected consuls. Theirs was a formidable new faction known as the First Triumvirate. But even after Caesar took office in January 59 and proposed new legislation, the *lex Julia Agraria,* which would grant allotments to the veterans and the urban poor, obstruction continued under the leadership of Cato and Bibulus, Rome's other consul and Cato's son-in-law. The *optimates* obstructed the *lex Julia Agraria* via the filibuster and religious manipulation while refusing to offer any constructive criticism of the proposal, merely repeating endlessly that they would not allow any revolutionary measures to be passed or any innovations to be made to the traditional structure of Roman government and society. The stalemate dragged on for more than two months. At a public assembly, or *contio,* held to discuss the measure, Bibulus told the crowd that even if *every* Roman desired the bill he would nonetheless use the powers

Caesar in Rome Today. ©iStock.com/Bill Perry

of his office to see to its defeat. An exasperated Caesar finally set a date to vote on his land law at a meeting of a legislative assembly to be held at the Temple of Castor and Pollux in the Roman forum on April 4, 59.

The night before the vote, the conservatives held a strategy session in the house of Bibulus on the Palatine Hill. Even without a modern poll they were convinced that the overwhelming popularity of Caesar's land law would result in its passage. The city's poor, its equestrians (businessmen who hoped to realize huge profits from deals the bill would generate), and its veterans (who expected at last to be rewarded for their military service) were all in favor of it. The assembled conservatives therefore decided that the next morning Bibulus would either exercise his consular authority, which included the use of religious objections, or employ the veto of one of the three friendly tribunes to object to the law and prevent a vote on it indefinitely.

Caesar and his allies expected their enemies' parliamentary maneuvers and, since Cato and the others had resorted to violence in 62, they also expected that they might employ violent tactics again. Accordingly they recruited Pompey's veterans from all over Italy to gather in the darkness at his mansion in the Carinae. The men were clad in white togas, the attire male Roman citizens were required to wear to participate in a formal political function such as a legislative vote. Carrying torches, they moved from Pompey's house following the city's stone-paved streets down the Velian slope, which connected the Esquiline and Palatine Hills, to the region known as the Upper Sacra, home to fashionable shops and bordering some of the wealthiest neighborhoods in the city. There the group turned northwest on Rome's greatest and earliest thoroughfare, the Via Sacra. On the south side of the street stood the Domus Publica, the official residence of the Pontifex Maximus, a position Caesar had held since 63. At the Domus Publica the group joined more of the triumvirate's supporters who had gathered there. Caesar led the entire party into the forum, a large open space shaped like an irregular rectangle. Long ago a marshy home to wandering animals, this area was now the political heart of the city and its vast Mediterranean empire.

Near the southern boundary of the lower forum stood the Temple of Castor and Pollux. Commemorating Rome's great early victory at the Battle of Lake Regillus in 496, the temple was one of the most magnificent in the city, with columns rising nearly fifty feet high. It looked out over the large area used as a venue for speeches, trials, and legislative assemblies. Thrusting out from the front of the temple was a podium that stood almost twenty feet above the forum floor. Stairs ran parallel to the front of the temple on two sides of the podium, each stairway connecting to a temporary bridge on which the voting would take place. In the darkness, the triumvirate's supporters filled the open space in front of the temple, while the veterans, experienced soldiers that they were, occupied the strategic elevated points of the forum and the temple podium. When the sun rose, the First Triumvirate controlled the voting area.

The Roman Forum Today
Looking northwest across the Roman forum today from the Palatine Hill. The three columns in the left foreground mark the remains of the Temple of Castor and Pollux. The events of April 4 took place on the temple podium and in front of the temple in the center of the picture; the Capitoline Hill is on the far left; the imperial senate house is straight ahead fronting the Via Sacra; Caesar's residence in the Domus Publica would have been on the far right of the photo. ©iStock.com/marcorubinophoto.com

At dawn a herald called the *togate* citizens together. As presiding magistrate, Caesar conducted the religious ceremonies, being careful to avoid negative omens that could lead to the cancellation of the vote, and he delivered a final speech in support of the land law. Caesar came onto the podium wearing the white *toga praetexta* with a purple border denoting his consular office, complete with long fringed sleeves and a loosely fitting belt. He also wore the scarlet and purple tunic of the Pontifex Maximus and a crown of oak leaves he had received in recognition of bravery in battle. Forty years old, tall, with intense, dark eyes and a receding hairline but still with the good looks that had made him a notorious womanizer, Caesar was one of Rome's great orators. The crowd hushed, and Caesar began to speak, most likely repeating many of the arguments he had employed in numerous addresses during the previous months. The proposed law was designed to strengthen the state by acquiring land in Italy to divide among the veterans of the eastern wars and the neediest citizens of Rome. Funds for purchasing the land would come not from the treasury but from the plunder and new tribute procured by these same veterans during those eastern campaigns. The land would be bought only from willing sellers at fair market value. All transactions would be administered by a board of twenty commissioners from which Caesar would be excluded. This law was just, benefiting those soldiers who risked their lives to expand the power of Rome. The bill would also give land to the urban poor so they would turn to labor and agriculture, and the desolate parts of Italy would be colonized afresh. And although Caesar probably did not mention it publicly, supporters of the law hoped that gainful employment for the city's destitute might reduce crime and chronic rioting. Caesar noted that while the *optimate* opponents of the bill argued that no innovative or revolutionary laws should be passed, they had never put forward any measure to help veterans or the poor. In the past, not only had they used all their formidable power and wealth to block such measures; they had resorted to violence, even murder, to see to their defeat. They had not found any defects in this law, but they opposed it nevertheless—out of pure conservative ideology.

One of the republic's two highest elected magistrates, Caesar, was about to be joined by the other, Bibulus. Before the voting could begin, twelve *lictors* led another group into the forum. The *lictors* were Bibulus's bodyguards, assigned by the state to protect the consul and provide him with the physical power of compulsion over Roman citizens. In their left hand they each carried a bundle of wooden rods about five feet long and held together by red rope. These were the *fasces*, the symbols of consular authority. Bibulus, his loyal tribunes, many senators, and a large group of supporters followed. Although Bibulus quickly realized that Caesar's group vastly outnumbered his own, he was unconcerned. He intended to use the consular *intercessio* or the tribunician veto to halt the proceedings. The Roman constitution did not require a majority vote for these actions—or the support of even one other Roman citizen or magistrate. Bibulus and the tribunes made their way through the crowd, the twelve *lictors* clearing a path, and then Bibulus climbed the stairs to the podium, planning to stop his consular colleague.

He never got the chance. The men standing around Caesar immediately grabbed Bibulus, threw him down the temple steps, and dumped a bucket of manure on his head. Caesar's adherents quickly overwhelmed the twelve *lictors* and hurled them from the podium. In the process they broke the *fasces* into pieces, a symbolic act representing an end to Bibulus's power to block legislation that was desired by the Roman people. They pummeled the tribunes (a position considered *sacrosanct* under Roman law), who thereafter were unable or unwilling to interpose their vetoes to officially prevent a vote. On the forum floor the pro-triumvirate multitude threw rocks and other projectiles at Bibulus's followers and then surged forward to beat and batter their opponents. Their rage was genuine: Caesar's first act as consul, passed on his first day in office, was to begin publishing a report of senatorial proceedings, so the citizens of Rome knew who was responsible for blocking the land law and other popular measures in the senate, and they were getting revenge. Cato alone tried to defy the hostile crowd, using his great resolve to force his way through to the podium to verbally abuse Caesar. To no avail: Caesar's men picked him up and tossed him from the platform. The conservative senators and their followers were beaten and thrashed, their snow-white togas in tatters and stained with blood. They were driven southeast out of the forum and up the Velian slope, where they took refuge at the Temple of Jupiter Stator on the Via Sacra.

The violence erupted suddenly and was carried out with military precision; it lasted only a few minutes. The veterans in Caesar's entourage not only vastly outnumbered Bibulus's supporters but also possessed superior fighting skills due to their years of army service. Still, Pompey's men were clearly under orders not to kill but only to terrorize and humiliate the triumvirate's adversaries, especially Bibulus, for whom the bucket had obviously been prepared in advance. The attack's immediate purpose was to prevent any constitutional maneuvers that would block passage of the land law; in the longer term, it would stifle further opposition.

Once the forum had been cleared of the opposing party Caesar was free to start the voting. The herald again read the law in its entirety, and Caesar proclaimed that the people would now be asked to decide the matter: "The law has been read, go and the ballots will be handed out."[5] The ballots were then brought in and distributed by the *custos*. Each was made of wood and wax; the letter *V* would be used for a yes vote, *A* for a no vote. To participate, citizens lined up at one of the two bridges linked to the temple steps; ascending one by one they moved to the middle of the bridge, filled out a ballot in secret, then dropped the completed ballot in a *cista* at the other end of the bridge. The process took hours, but eventually the law passed—the veterans and the poor would get their land. For the first time since the dictatorship of Sulla twenty years before, a land law was approved and would be implemented.

Of far greater importance than the passage of one law, the violent scene in the forum resulted in the April 5 retirement of Bibulus to his house, where he spent the rest of the year watching the skies for religious omens. Thus, the events of April 4 and the subsequent absence of his colleague allowed Caesar and his allies to govern Rome almost unopposed. Since Caesar was now in effect sole consul, the year 59 BC came to be referred to by the Romans not by the names of the two consuls ("the Year of Caesar and Bibulus") as was customary, but sarcastically as "the Year of Julius and Caesar." No matter how it was labeled, the year would have a tremendous impact on the course of Roman history, ultimately leading to massive violence in the city, the conquest of Gaul, civil war, the dictatorship and assassination of Caesar, the rise of Augustus, and, finally, the fall of the republic.

-1-

Caesar and Cato

60 BC/694 AUC

The political divisions were so bad because politicians were motivated more by hatred than by patriotism . . . When parties do anything to defeat their opponents . . . they destroy great states.

Gaius Sallustius Crispus, *circa* 41

THE ROMAN REPUBLIC—constitution, citizens, calendar, magistrates, assemblies, senate—had existed for four and a half centuries. For most of that time this government provided Rome with internal stability that in turn helped to contribute to its imperial expansion. Unfortunately, in the late republic (133–31) Rome's political structure revealed itself to be susceptible to the type of violent coup that Gaius Julius Caesar and his allies pulled off in the forum on April 4.

After Rome was liberated from the rule of foreign kings in 509, the Romans decided that no man could be trusted with absolute power.[1] They therefore established a new government, the *res publica* (literally, "public thing"). This "mixed" constitution created a system of checks and balances that distributed power among magistrates and assemblies.[2] Sovereignty in the republic ultimately lay with male Roman citizens, however, who at the time were the only citizens permitted to participate in the political process, and then only if they were in Rome on the day of the voting. By the late republic there may have been as many as 910,000 male citizens in Rome and Italy.[3] Each was either a patrician or a plebian. In the early republic the patricians monopolized political, economic, and religious authority, but the Conflict of the Orders (494–287) ushered in significant reforms that dramatically improved plebian fortunes. Although the patricians still enjoyed certain prerogatives, there was very little difference between the patrician and plebian orders in the late republic. The father's order determined the order of his children, and membership was usually for life.[4]

Whether patrician or plebian, all Roman citizens enjoyed certain legal protections from coercion, summary judgment, and punishment by the state and its magistrates.[5] All enjoyed freedom of speech.[6] They voted by secret ballot in the centuriate assembly and in the two tribal assemblies, the *comitia tributa* and the *concilium plebis*.

All political activity in the city was strictly regulated by the pre-Julian calendar of 355 days. A signal element in the calendar was the cycle of *nundinae* (market days). A nundinal period ran for eight days, beginning with the market day. By the late republic no legislative or electoral assemblies could be held on a market day. Furthermore, no measure could be voted on by an assembly until at least a *trinundinum* (three market periods, or twenty-four days) had passed since the measure was first officially proposed. Each day on the calendar was marked with a letter. *Comitial* days, denoted with the letter *C*, were the most common, but the 195 *C* days were not apportioned evenly from month to month. Voting on legislation or in elections for city magistrates could take place only on *C* days. The days were inviolable and backed by divine authority: it was against the will of the gods to hold assemblies on any other type of day. Usually, the senate could convene on any day *except C* days and market days. There were only 139 days on the calendar on which the senate could meet, and these dates were also spread unevenly during the year. *Contiones,* which did not involve voting for legislation or candidates, could apparently be held on any letter day. A rare form of voting assembly, the *comitia curiata*, was apparently not restricted to *C* days.[7]

The Magistrates

For each city office, a minimum age was specified and a strict sequence of magistrates had evolved called the *cursus honorum* ("ladder of honor"), which dictated the order in which each office could be held.[8] Each magistrate held office for one year, from January 1 until December 29 (the last day on the Roman calendar), except the tribunes, who were inaugurated on December 10 and served until the following December.

The consuls, Caesar and Bibulus, elected by the centuriate assembly, were co-presidents of the Roman republic and occupied the top rung of the political ladder. After the expulsion of the last king, the consuls were given some of the king's executive powers, but because there were two of them, neither could accumulate too much authority. Each consul had the power to call the senate into session, to convene the *comitia tributa*, and to call an assembly of citizens (a *contio*), to speak directly to the people in the forum. They could also be invested with the *imperium* to lead a Roman army into battle or to govern a Roman province.

Second on the political ladder were the eight praetors, also elected by the centuriate assembly. These officials were in charge of Rome's permanent standing courts, which adjudicated offenses ranging from extortion in the provinces to embezzlement, electoral bribery and fraud, treason, and violence. The praetors decided which cases would be allowed to come to trial, oversaw the selection of the jurors, and presided over the proceedings. Next came the four aediles, two plebian and two curule. They were responsible for the city of Rome and the welfare of the urban population and also organized the annual games staged in and around the forum. At the bottom of the ladder were the twenty quaestors responsible for the treasury. Senate membership was conferred for life on those who won election to the quaestorship, which meant that most senators entered the house between the ages of twenty-seven and thirty.

The office of tribune had been created during the two-hundred-year-long Conflict of the Orders to protect the rights of Rome's plebian citizens and to give them a voice in the government. Restricted to members of the plebian order, the ten tribunes were inviolable—making it a religious sacrilege to harm them. Each had the power to convene the senate and set the agenda for discussion. Only a tribune could call the *concilium plebis* into session and propose laws or other resolutions to be voted upon. Each tribune had the authority to call a *contio* to speak directly to the people on any matter he chose. The most significant power a tribune possessed may have been the right of veto (literally, "I forbid!"), which could be used to block any act by any city magistrate (including other tribunes), by any electoral or legislative assembly, and even by the senate. Each of the tribunes had this power of veto, and a majority of them did not have to agree before it was implemented. One tribune alone, then, could effectively obstruct any political action by anyone in Rome.

The Assemblies

The centuriate assembly elected most of Rome's magistrates: two consuls, eight praetors, the two curule aediles, and two censors. All male citizens were allowed to vote in the centuriate assembly by secret ballot. Each citizen was assigned to one of the 193 voting groups called centuries based on his wealth. However, there were not an equal number of citizens in each century; instead, ninety-eight centuries were reserved for the wealthy. Therefore, since each century had one overall vote, and since there were only 193 total votes in any election, Rome's richest citizens controlled 51 percent of the vote in the centuriate assembly. This system accorded a richer man's vote far greater weight than a poorer man's and generally allowed the wealthy few to decide elections. On occasion, though, despite the system, the votes of citizens from the lower ninety-five centuries could decide close contests.

Rome's democracy lay in its two tribal assemblies. In each, citizens voted by secret ballot and were divided roughly evenly into thirty-five tribes, rather than centuries, so the votes of poor and wealthy citizens were similarly weighted. One, the *comitia tributa,* elected two curule aediles and twenty quaestors. The *comitia tributa* occasionally was called into session by a consul to pass laws and make decisions regarding the Roman state. Only plebians could participate in the second tribal assembly, the *concilium plebis*; patricians were excluded. This assembly elected the ten tribunes and the two plebian aediles. Only the tribunes could convene and preside over the *concilium plebis*; after 287 it passed most of Rome's laws and made most determinations about war and peace and other significant issues.

There was also a distinctive nonvoting assembly, the *contio*, Rome's bully pulpit, which figured prominently in the events of 59.[9] Only a magistrate, usually a tribune or a consul, could summon the *contio*. After saying a prayer an official spoke directly to the populace in the forum, usually from the rostra or a temple podium. The magistrate who called the *contio* or someone he designated were the only persons who could address the crowd. Used as political rallies for or against pending legislation or specific candidates, the *contiones* also provided dramatic settings for debates and audience participation by means of cheers, boos, and catcalls.

The Senate

Beyond the assemblies and the city magistracies, which constituted the official government of Rome, one other element played a significant role in the political functioning of the republic: the senate, which drew its members from those who had won election to the quaestorship.[10] By 59, the senate had roughly five hundred members—who served for life. The senate was required to assemble in Rome or within one mile of the *pomerium*, either in the Curia Hostilia or in other consecrated temples. Except for the New Year's Day gathering in the Temple of Jupiter on the Capitoline, the senate did not have regularly scheduled meetings and could gather only when convened by a consul, praetor, or tribune. Typically, the magistrate who summoned the senate would make an introductory speech concerning a law or issue confronting the Roman state and would then ask each senator for his opinion. The opinions of the older, more experienced members customarily carried the most weight in any senate debate. Rather than rigid affairs governed by strict and precise rules of seniority and decorum, as they are sometimes portrayed, debates were in fact often hectic, loud, and unstructured, taking on issues well beyond the topic initially proposed.[11] Senatorial influence was partly based on the ability of a speaker to hold the floor during tumultuous meetings and if necessary to humiliate an opponent in front of his peers.[12]

Officially the senate's main function was to advise the city's magistrates as it had once advised Rome's kings. Technically, it could not pass laws. Instead senators could vote to authorize a *senatus consultum* (*s.c.*), a decree that formally expressed a decision made by the senate. Even this could be vetoed by one of the ten tribunes or ignored by the city magistrates. The senate's structure and rules and the variety of stalling tactics available to its members made it far easier to block a measure than to force one through. As a result, gridlock was constant.

Despite the limits on its power, over the course of time the senate had managed to accumulate unofficial prerogatives which, in addition to the collective weight of its powerful members, allowed it to influence city officials and through them the assemblies, courts, and treasury, and thus to maintain a predominant position in the state. An essential aspect of senatorial authority was the elaborate religious structure that had developed in Rome to mediate between gods and men. There was no separation between church and state, so individual senators played a significant role in the religious process.[13] Because Romans generally attributed their success in conquering a vast empire to the gods, it was imperative that they maintain good relations with them by performing all the proper religious rituals, festivals, and sacrifices. It was also imperative that the Romans accurately interpret the portents sent by the gods through bird signs and other omens and act accordingly. Before any senate meeting, assembly vote, or military action, the auspices had to be checked and interpreted. Almost all the eminent priests in the Roman religion were senators, many of whom used their religious authority to enhance or defend their political power.

Empire and Army

The republican government was responsible not just for one city. By the first century BC Rome had conquered a vast empire that stretched across most of the known world. Thus, the actions of the various magistrates and assemblies in the capital often had a profound effect on the roughly fifty million people living around the Mediterranean Sea. In 59 Rome controlled a total of fourteen provinces; each was governed by a senator, usually with the title of proconsul or propraetor, who performed both political and military functions.[14] Each governor administered his province, collected taxes, and enforced Roman law. Half of these officials also commanded Roman armies to conduct wars against foreign enemies, to defend their provinces in case of attack, and to prevent rebellions by the local subject population. Overall there were fifteen legions stationed in seven provinces in 59.[15]

The Roman "Revolution"

Unfortunately, the peace and stability provided by Rome's government during the middle republic (287–133) eventually began to fail. Problems produced by crushing urban and rural poverty jeopardized domestic peace. Senatorial unity and the senate's monopoly on power were threatened by the corrupting pressures of the tremendous wealth and power created by an expanding empire. This pressure produced a new propensity on the part of individual senators to use tricks or technicalities, ignore laws, flout constitutional precedents, and even resort to violence to secure political victories. This danger was made worse by the willingness of senators to disregard such transgressions if they were perpetrated by political allies pursuing similar political goals. These stressors brought about a political cataclysm known as the Roman Revolution, which exploded during the tribunate of Tiberius Sempronius Gracchus in 133.[16] In the tribal assembly Gracchus defied his fellow senators by passing laws economically favorable to the masses and intervening in matters of foreign policy, previously the senate's exclusive domain. For perhaps the first time a Roman tribune exercised the independent authority of his office and demonstrated the potential power of Roman citizens voting in opposition to the senate. Tension mounted throughout 133 until Gracchus announced he would run for reelection for 132—a move that, although not illegal, had not been attempted by a tribune in more than two centuries. Senators feared that Gracchus would win and continue to run Rome from the tribal assembly. Unwilling to stand by while the people and their patron usurped senatorial authority, some senators and their supporters clubbed Gracchus and three hundred of his followers to death and dumped their bodies into the Tiber River under cover of night. Because the senate controlled the courts, no one was ever prosecuted for these crimes; only Gracchus's adherents were brought to trial, charged with attempting to make him tyrant of Rome. For the first time since the expulsion of the kings and the foundation of the Roman Republic 376 years earlier, a city magistrate had been assassinated.[17] It would not be the last.

Partisan Politics

With the consensus among Rome's ruling class shattered, there developed what Romans in the late republic called *duas partes*: *optimates* and *populares*.[18] These were not organized political parties, for in Rome there were no permanent political entities possessing an established leadership, hierarchies, treasuries, or slates of candidates. Furthermore, many of Rome's political alliances were transient, and personal motives often trumped "party" politics, as senators sometimes switched allegiance due to rivalries, alliances, or family considerations. Women frequently played a role in the formation—and dissolution—of alliances. Nevertheless, it can be said that *optimates* worked through the senate to achieve their goals while the *populares* looked to the people for support in the assemblies. The senator Cicero defined the two kinds of politicians in Rome: "Those who wanted to be popular with the people were *populares*; but those who wanted the support of the *boni* ["good men"] were considered *optimates*."[19]

The *optimates* generally shared an ideology based on three critical beliefs: the collective primacy of the senate in the republic, faith in the gods, and the rule of law that protected their power and the inviolability of their property rights.[20] Any attack on the senate's primacy was literally an attack on Rome and the gods and therefore had to be resisted. In addition, the sanctity of private property had to be protected against any efforts, legal or illegal, to tax or seize assets in order to bestow them on other segments of Roman society. Cicero argued that in fact the principal function of any government was to protect private property.[21] All men must "control their own property" and the state must never grow so powerful as to threaten that control.[22]

Optimates were usually unsympathetic to the plight of poor laborers in the city or farmers in rural Italy. Even employed citizens were often disparaged, and craftsmen and merchants were lumped together with the worst elements of the city. Cicero repeatedly labeled the urban poor as "leeches of the treasury, wretched and hungry."[23] Once these citizens had worked on farms, but now, thanks to misguided government programs, they had been lured to Rome to live idly on handouts from the state, contributing nothing but children and demanding public support, rather than working to support their families. Their main goal, Cicero said, was to take from the treasury until the state sunk under overwhelming debt. He opposed any law that provided government handouts to reward them for their behavior, and he worried that humbler citizens would follow demagogic leaders, such as Gracchus, who would use their popularity and power to pass laws designed to redistribute wealth through taxation and redistribution of the land.[24] He argued that all property taxes and agrarian laws were evil since they robbed people of wealth and land they had long possessed.[25]

The *optimates*' faith in the rule of law was not limitless, however. They did not hesitate to employ violence to maintain their power, beginning in 133. And while *optimates* complained bitterly about the masses draining the treasury, they were often willing to use the treasury, the government, and its officials for their own economic advancement. For well-connected citizens with government contacts, the treasury in Rome made unauthorized monetary grants and either refused to collect monies owed to the state or agreed to cancel tax debts altogether.[26] Senators often "drew handsome allowances from the treasury" for dubious "official" business.[27] They could even receive a commission to travel around the empire on personal business or pleasure at the state's expense.[28] As the *optimates*' rivals often pointed out, they were seemingly concerned about the health of the treasury only when it involved popular legislation.

Although the most ardent *optimates* were wealthy citizens, segments of Rome's population further down the social and economic ladder may have shared some of their views. This was true of Romans who, although not rich, prospered in various enterprises or as smaller rural landowners and may have had more in common with those above them than those below. They may have agreed with Cicero's attitudes concerning Rome's lower classes and may have been unwilling to use government money, their tax dollars, to provide relief for what they saw as the lazy rabble while they themselves worked so diligently.

Power to the People

Unlike the *optimates*, the *populares* attempted to gain power through appeals to the people in the tribal assemblies.[29] Thus represented, the power of the people increased in the late republic, as popular leaders intervened in almost every aspect of the state's operation. These politicians became engrossed in financial issues, proposing and sometimes passing laws involving the disposition of "public funds, of public property and its possible distribution, and of the right form of the management of resources."[30] They intruded in matters of foreign policy, claiming that the empire belonged to all the people of Rome, and that the people therefore had the right to dictate how that empire was administered. With few exceptions, in the early and middle republic the senate chose Rome's governors. Their selections then governed for a short time, usually one year. However, during the late republic the tribunes and the people in the tribal assembly increasingly intervened by deciding who governed Rome's provinces and who led Rome's armies, appointing proconsuls and propraetors who often served longer periods. There was also an increase in what were known as extraordinary commands, when the people provided governors with extraordinary powers, sometimes for years, to deal with a specific crisis or crises. For example, Pompey's great commands and subsequent military successes in the east (67–62) were made possible by two laws proposed by tribunes and approved by the people against the will of the senate. For the generals, these extended terms produced greater opportunities to win wealth and military glory, which translated into increased political power back in Rome. They also tended to engender a closer relationship between a commander and his soldiers, and often late-republican generals were able to retain the loyalty of their men long after the conclusion of a campaign. For the people, the wealth generated by these commanders and their soldiers was often used to finance legislation that provided them with economic assistance, land distribution, or basic necessities, such as food. Tiberius Gracchus had articulated this new political doctrine in 133 by declaring that the people, not the senate, had the right to legislate such issues.[31] In the late republic, although the people and friendly city officials by no means triumphed in all instances, they were able to pass many laws in the face of senatorial resistance in matters over which the senate formerly had possessed unchallenged authority.[32]

Popular politicians missed no opportunity to attack their *optimate* rivals. While speaking at a *contio,* Gaius Memmius (tr. 111)* labeled the *optimates* "wicked" and provided detailed references to religion and the gods, Roman law, constitutional history, and current political events, all in support of a popular ideology.[33] Gaius Marius (cos. 107) argued that the *optimates*' power was undeserved because it was based not on talent or hard work but on the luck of birth. He denigrated their lavish lifestyles, claiming that *they* were lazy, relying on the wealth and reputation bequeathed to them by their ancestors, and interested only in "love-affairs, alcohol, and their stomachs."[34]

Populares were by definition politicians who "defended fundamental popular rights and powers" even "in the face of senatorial infringement, indeed especially in the face of such opposition."[35] Claiming that these rights were under *optimate* assault, the *populares* argued that the people must resist the "tyranny of that faction" and its encroachment on their liberties.[36] *Optimates,* they reminded, were willing to do anything to protect their power, even murder the people's tribunes.

It hardly needs saying that tribunes and other politicians, whether *optimates* or *populares,* did not always act for altruistic reasons. Sallust, echoing Thucydides's appraisal of rival politicians during Greece's Peloponnesian War (431–404), cynically declared that all politicians, whether defending the rights of the people or the authority of the senate, usually wished only to augment their own personal power.[37]

Violence and Civil War

The best illustration of the poisoned partisan atmosphere of the late republic was the dramatic rise in the frequency and scale of violence in the Roman political process. Before 133 there were seven instances of political violence, yet all were cases of "coercion" or "formalized violence" involving no actual bloodshed.[38] Between 133 and 59 there were thirty-four violent incidents, as the use of physical force became part of the political landscape. Assassinations began

*In this book the highest office attained by each Roman senator is provided within parentheses the first time he is mentioned, to indicate his political success and thus his importance. The abbreviations used are: cos. = consul, pr. = praetor, tr. = tribune. Because of the minimum age requirements for each office, an estimate of a senator's age can be gleaned by knowing the highest office he attained.

in 133 with the attack on Tiberius Gracchus and his adherents and continued with the slayings of many others during the years that followed.[39]

Worse was to come. Through most periods of the republic citizens were required to possess a certain amount of wealth to be eligible for military service. During the second century BC many factors had triggered a decline in the number of Romans who still possessed that wealth, thus reducing the number of citizens eligible for the army. Rome needed more soldiers. In an attempt to solve the problem, Tiberius Gracchus had passed a land law in 133, but the remedy had failed. In 107, the consul Gaius Marius set a new precedent by abolishing this property requirement and accepting *proletarii* (men without property) into his army. As a result, during the late republic most soldiers were poor volunteers. Though Marius's actions alleviated Rome's soldier shortage, having poor citizens serve did change an important dynamic within the army. Now, for the first time, veterans who had concluded their military service could not simply return to their farm or business, since many had no livelihood to return to. Like Pompey in 62, some commanders believed that the state should reward such men for risking their lives for the empire with a grant of land that could support a veteran and his family. *Optimate* senators vigorously opposed these efforts. Thus, soldiers no longer looked to the senate but to their generals, not only for effective leadership and plundering opportunities while on campaign but for help in acquiring land at discharge. This close relationship combined with the longer tenure of some governors to create in certain cases an incredibly strong bond between leaders and those they led.

Thanks to the changing political climate after 133 and Marius's reforms in 107, some senators, willing to do almost anything to protect or expand their power, now commanded loyal armies. Consequently, in 88 after an attempt by his political rivals to strip him of his command, the consul Lucius Cornelius Sulla Felix became the first Roman general to lead his army against Rome itself. After capturing the city, he held power long enough (88–87) to outlaw and execute some of his enemies. After returning control to the state, he left to fight a war in the east, but his departure and absence could not make men forget his example. Similar acts of violence followed, until for the first time in Rome's history Roman generals commanding loyal Roman soldiers led their armies into battle against each other, resulting in five civil wars between 87 and 62, the first such conflicts in Rome's long history.[40] The horrors of civil strife were sometimes followed by brutal dictatorships and ghastly massacres.

This all represented very recent history to the generation of Romans who played central roles in the events of 59. Crassus was twenty-four when Sulla first marched on Rome; Pompey and Cicero were both eighteen; Caesar was twelve, Cato seven. Crassus's father and brother were both killed by Marius's supporters, and he was forced to flee with only a few friends to Spain. Pompey spent much of the 80s in Picenum hiding from his enemies and dodging assassination attempts. After Sulla's return from his eastern war, Pompey's bloody role in his second conquest of Rome and ensuing dictatorship (83–79) led to the enduring hatred many still felt for him in 59. Caesar was obliged to escape from Rome during Sulla's rule, and later was nearly killed by a group of Cicero's bodyguards during the Catilinarian crisis. The last civil war had ended barely three years before Caesar and Bibulus entered the consulship.

These traumatic near-death experiences had a profound effect on these men, as the shadow of recent events hung heavily over the late republic. The actions of Roman politicians during this period can be understood only in this context. The divisions were so deep, and made deeper by the trials of civil war, that senators were willing to bend or break the laws, employ violence, and on occasion resort to civil war to protect themselves and their power. It became progressively easier for senators to employ extreme tactics, and increasingly easier to convince themselves that these tactics were justified, given what had gone before and given the possible motivations and designs of their rivals. The proper environment had been created in which the events of 59 and ultimately the republic's collapse could transpire.

The Rise of Caesar

Gaius Julius Caesar was born on July 13, 100, into an ancient patrician family that claimed descent from the gods and Rome's founder, Romulus. His clan first held a consulship in 489, just twenty years after the republic was established. Unfortunately, his branch of the family had fallen on difficult times. Its last consul was a Sextus Julius Caesar, who held office in 157. Caesar's grandfather Gaius's career is unknown, while his father Gaius had risen to the praetorship (c. 92) but no further before dying, in 84. Caesar, on the other hand, worked his way up the political ladder, holding the office of quaestor (69), curule aedile (65), and praetor (62); he was elected Pontifex Maximus in 63. He was popular among Rome's lower classes, partly because he had been raised in the Subura, the most densely populated area in Rome, which exposed him to Rome's diverse population. He championed popular causes. During the seventies he repeatedly spoke in favor of restoring the powers of the tribunate that Sulla had temporarily abolished, and on the Capitoline Hill he restored the images and trophies of Sulla's rival, Marius, the popular general and seven-time consul. A gifted public speaker, Caesar early on made a name for himself in the courts, prosecuting enemies of the people and helping his fellow citizens.[41] In the litigious society that was Rome, many nobles such as Caesar provided gratis legal services to poorer citizens in return for political support.

Caesar adroitly employed vast amounts of money to increase his popularity.[42] As curator of the Appian Way he combined cash earmarked by the state with his own funds to refurbish the highway. As aedile he staged theater performances and religious processions, as well as gladiatorial shows that exhibited the unprecedented (and expensive) number of 320 matched pairs fighting to the death in honor of his late father. He spent lavishly on Rome's citizens, offering loans and paying for large public banquets. He sponsored funerals and games in memory of his first wife, Cornelia, and his aunt Julia, using those occasions to remind the people in the forum of the august lineage of his house.[43]

Like many Roman senators, Caesar borrowed heavily to finance his political ambitions and was therefore deeply in debt.[44] Bankers or private lenders might continue to loan money if a politician's career moved forward and they saw some hope of repayment, whereas lost elections and political stagnation might not only sour them on lending cash but also lead them to begin legal proceedings against him. Conviction in court could lead to expulsion from the senate or exile. During an especially expensive campaign for the office of Pontifex Maximus, a rival candidate offered to pay Caesar's debts if he agreed to drop out of the race.[45] Caesar refused, remarking to his mother on the morning of the election that by sundown he would become either the Pontifex Maximus or an exile.[46] Substantial bribes saved him as he defeated two more experienced opponents.[47] After his year as praetor, Caesar owed his creditors a staggering 830 talents.[48] When he attempted to leave to govern his province in Spain, the creditors sought to bring him to trial and even to seize his baggage. Only Crassus's willingness to provide security for his debts allowed Caesar to depart.

Once established in his province, Caesar defeated the Callaici and Lusitani tribes while extending Roman territory to the Atlantic Ocean; these successes represented the first military victories of his career as a commander. His men saluted him as *imperator*, and the senate awarded him the right to celebrate a triumph—a parade in Rome to commemorate a military victory.

By the time he reached forty years of age Caesar was already seen as hardworking, brave, and ambitious—an able politician, advocate, orator, soldier, and military commander. His career was off to a promising start and, although no one could have predicted what was to come, two incidents foreshadowed the future. First, while passing through a tiny village in the Alps on his way to Spain, his officers laughingly remarked that even in this small community, as in Rome, the inhabitants must struggle fiercely to become the leading citizen. Caesar replied, in all seriousness, "I would rather be the first man here than the second man in Rome."[49] The other incident occurred in Spain, when Caesar happened upon a statue of Alexander the Great. Weeping, Caesar noted that while barely twenty-five years old Alexander had conquered the largest empire the world had yet seen, while he, nearly forty, had accomplished nothing.

Now, in the first days of June 60, he returned to Italy to celebrate a triumph and to campaign for the following year's consulship.[50] Caesar's intention to run for Rome's highest office was already common knowledge: in December of 61 Cicero mentioned Caesar as one of three potential candidates for 59.[51] While in Spain, Caesar had presumably corresponded with key senators, writing home to keep his name in the public eye, to publicize his achievements, and to prepare an organization for his expected run. Many Romans who knew about his Spanish exploits believed his successful governorship enhanced his electoral chances.

Caesar, like all contenders for office, had to make a formal declaration of his candidacy in person in the forum in Rome before the presiding magistrate at least three market cycles ahead of the election. Voting was scheduled for mid-July, shortly after the Games of Apollo, so Caesar had to be in Rome by June 26 at the latest. As proconsul (or propraetor), however, he still possessed the *imperium* of a provincial governor. By law, if he crossed Rome's *pomerium* and entered the city, he forfeited that *imperium*. Unfortunately for Caesar, a triumph could be celebrated only by someone holding the *imperium*, so if he entered the city to declare his candidacy, he would surrender his right to a triumph. The highlight of many a senator's career—something he would have waited his entire life for—a triumph would also provide invaluable publicity for a consular candidate. Much of the city's population turned out to watch the procession, which doubled as a priceless political advertisement. To secure his right to his triumph, Caesar forwarded an entreaty to the senate requesting that he be allowed to declare his candidacy *in absentia*—a favor that apparently had been granted to others in the past—and when the matter came up for debate, many senators supported his appeal.[52] But Caesar's political adversaries wished to stop or delay his candidacy. If he could not run in 60, he would have to wait at least a year for another opportunity, possibly providing his enemies with time to drag him into court and indict him for real or imagined crimes. They may have hoped that his mounting debts would provide an avenue of legal attack.

Furthermore, if they could prevent Caesar's run, the odds for their favorite candidate, Marcus Calpurnius Bibulus, would increase.

Spearheading the opposition to Caesar was Marcus Porcius Cato, also known as Cato the Younger or Cato Uticensis (due to his suicide in the North African city of Utica in 46).[53] The great-grandson of Marcus Porcius Cato ("the Censor") (cos. 195), he was just thirty-five years old and had held only the offices of quaestor (64) and tribune (62). Despite his youth, the hard-drinking Cato had already become a major political figure since he demanded the death penalty for the Catilinarian conspirators in a speech in the senate that eventually carried the day.[54] Afterward he became a powerful spokesman for the *optimate* cause, opposing any measures that might infringe on senatorial authority or the sanctity of private property. He led a faction of likeminded men united by *optimate* ideology and admiration for their leader; in many cases the bond was cemented by a marriage tie.[55] His faction supported Cato unconditionally through the decades of the 60s and 50s, and he thus cared little if he offended people outside his immediate circle. Enriched by a large inheritance and committed to a frugal lifestyle, he was able to lend significant sums of money to senators at no interest and thereby secure a wider network of supporters.[56] His wealth meant he did not need to seek loans or accept bribes like so many other senators who were deeply in debt from political ambition and lavish living. Because he was under no financial obligations to other senators or equestrian bankers, they could not control him, as they could so many others in the house. Always the first to arrive and the last to leave, he never missed a senate or assembly meeting. He mastered Rome's laws and customs and used his superior knowledge of obscure political procedure or little-known religious technicalities to great advantage.[57] Cato's personal determination and force allowed him to ignore the will of senate, equestrians, and the people for months if necessary; in the end he often simply outlasted his opponents. This type of political method would later be termed "porcupine power"—"the politics of confrontation, stalling, filibustering with marathon speeches, tying the senate up in knots, and frustrating others to achieve his own ends."[58]

Although Cato built his reputation on his incorruptibility, even many allies were often exasperated with his rigidity and unwillingness to compromise. Cicero famously remarked that Cato acted as if "he were in Plato's Republic, not amongst the dregs of Romulus."[59] Cato did little to solve the many problems facing the Roman state and especially those that affected the average Roman citizen. And, in numerous cases, Cato did not hesitate to ignore his principles or even break the law to further his political goals. For example, as tribune he publicly swore to prosecute any consular candidates he suspected of employing bribery to secure election, but he made an exception for his brother-in-law Decimus Junius Silanus, whose crimes during a victorious but corrupt campaign were conveniently overlooked.

Cato had always hated Caesar, not only because of their opposing political views but also because Caesar carried on a long affair with Cato's sister, Servilia.[60] Once, while Cato spoke in the senate during the Catilinarian crisis, a messenger delivered a note to Caesar. Suspecting that this communication somehow linked Caesar to the conspiracy, Cato demanded that Caesar read it to the house. But when Caesar handed the note to Cato, he discovered to his embarrassment that it was a love letter from his sister.

Knowing that a senatorial majority favored Caesar's petition to declare his candidacy for consul *in absentia,* Cato could not allow the matter to come to a vote. To injure his rival and help Bibulus in the process, Cato blocked Caesar's request with his most effective weapon, the filibuster.[61] Because senate meetings usually convened at dawn and had to conclude by dark, and because all senators enjoyed unlimited speech on any topic they wished, a bill's opponents could simply continue talking until the meeting had to be adjourned. The next meeting of the senate represented an entirely new session, so all the senators from the first *consularis* down to the lowest back bencher (senators who had held no higher office than quaestor and wore the plain white toga) would be allowed to speak again. The United States Senate has a procedure called *cloture,* whereby sixty senators (three-fifths of the total membership) can vote to force a fellow member to stop talking. This is "the only procedure by which the Senate can vote to terminate debate and bring a proposal to a vote, thereby overcoming a filibuster."[62] The Roman senate, however, did not have any procedural method to stop a member from speaking. Because senatorial meetings could be held only on certain days on the calendar, an obstructionist senator was usually relieved from filibustering day after day.

When a senator filibustered a proposal, all other proposals became trapped behind it as senatorial business ground to a halt and pressure began to build.[63] Urgent matters involving foreign policy, especially the appointment of governors to Rome's many provinces, might be delayed. With so much pending business and pressure from fellow senators to drop the affair and move on, it would be difficult for supporters of a measure to bring up any filibustered matter continually. After a few frustrating sessions, proponents of a bill often capitulated and withdrew their proposal.

Cato was a master of the technique.[64] In the summer of 60 he promised to continue to filibuster indefinitely to block Caesar's request from ever coming to a vote, a vow people believed, given his previous history. Caesar had only a few days before the deadline to appear in the forum to declare his candidacy, so Cato would not have to filibuster very long. The triumph represented a milestone in a senatorial career—and few men ever passed up the opportunity to celebrate one. Some spent years outside of Rome waiting for their chance. Caesar's enemies assumed that he would never give up his triumph and would therefore be forced to wait to run for the consulship. But, as he did many times later on the battlefield, Caesar employed an unexpected maneuver to take his enemies by surprise. Figuring that becoming consul was of greater political importance than waiting outside the city indefinitely for his triumph, and confident that he would have more opportunities to celebrate additional triumphs in the future, he decided to forgo the parade and enter Rome.[65] The presiding magistrate accepted his petition, published the list of satisfactory candidates in the city and around Italy, and chose the date for the vote.

There were two other known contenders for the consulships of 59. One was Lucius Lucceius (pr. 67), a wealthy ally of Pompey who had been planning to run since at least December of 61. Caesar and Lucceius had already made a pact either by letter while Caesar was in Spain or in person once he had returned: they would run together, with Caesar contributing his larger base of support while Lucceius employed his enormous wealth on behalf of the ticket. The third aspirant was the *optimates*' candidate, Cato's son-in-law, Marcus Calpurnius Bibulus (pr. 62).

With the slate of candidates set, the campaign for the two consulships for the year 59 could begin.

The Making of the Consuls

The result of a Roman election was never a forgone conclusion, because public opinion could change repeatedly before a vote.[66] Time spent attempting to forecast election results was often spent in vain. The campaign for the consulship was normally a long and difficult process, but Caesar had barely three market cycles (twenty-four days) before the vote. He had much to do in a very short time.[67] Although the sources provide scant details about his campaign, a few years earlier Quintus Tullius Cicero wrote a long letter to his brother Marcus to guide him during his campaign for the consulship for the year 63.[68] This document, which came to be known as the *Commentariolum Petitionis*, provides valuable advice about winning elections and, combined with other evidence, offers insight into Rome's electoral process. Written only four years before Caesar's campaign, it may offer some hints about his campaign.

In a typical senator's home the *tablinum* was adjacent to the atrium and represented the closest thing to a campaign headquarters a Roman politician possessed. The *tablinum* provided the setting for meetings of a candidate's inner circle: relatives, close friends, and senatorial allies. The candidate would choose one of these trusted associates to perform as something like a campaign manager, while the rest would serve as officers in the campaign organization.[69] Besides regularly attending on the candidate while he campaigned, members of the organization acted as campaign surrogates, carrying news to and from the candidate and speaking to groups or to influential individuals in public or private.[70] According to Quintus Cicero there were more than two dozen constituencies in Rome and Italy whose support a candidate needed to secure a victory.[71] The inner circle mapped out a strategy to win their support, mobilize them, and induce them to go to the polls to vote.[72]

Personally or through surrogates, the candidate worked diligently to attach prominent senators to his organization to add "luster" to his candidacy.[73] The candidate's organization sought out even young nobles, senators' sons, who stood high in the centuriate assembly and whose enthusiasm could attract others in and around the forum. More vital were the current city magistrates, especially the consuls and the tribunes. By virtue of their offices these men wielded great power; they could call *contiones* on a candidate's behalf, reminding the audience of the exploits the candidate had accomplished for Rome and of his ancestors' great deeds, and inviting the candidate up to the rostra to address the crowd. A candidate could, if he chose, use this opportunity to negatively campaign against his rivals. Praetors could also call *contiones*, and more importantly could make valuable allies in the courts either by helping prosecute political rivals or by providing protection against a legal attack. A campaign could not neglect to secure the support of the equestrians;[74] they were among Rome's wealthiest citizens and their money was key in the service of any campaign. In addition, they were members of the higher centuries, so their votes were extremely valuable, and they controlled Rome's most efficient postal service, which a candidate could use to correspond with supporters elsewhere in Italy and around the empire.

Yet the campaign could not court just the wealthier citizens. Even though the structure of the centuriate assembly generally meant that elections were decided by the wealthy, poorer Romans could provide the swing votes in a close contest. To win the support of these citizens, a candidate began each day of his campaign with the *salutatio*.[75] The morning salutation functioned as a campaign rally. Moving around the atrium, the candidate normally spoke to his followers, communicating his campaign "message" and offering specific promises concerning the programs he would enact once elected to office. He exhorted his base to work energetically in his campaign. For a poorer citizen, the gatherings provided access to an important Roman senator and offered an opportunity to ask a favor, for instance a loan, legal representation, or merely sage advice. In return, the candidate expected their help and their vote.

Every day in late June and early July before the sun rose at just after 5:30, people from all over Rome began making their way to Caesar's home on the Via Sacra. A successful campaign depended on the size and diversity of those in attendance; it was vital that a candidate's house be full long before dawn with men from every segment of Roman society. The hopeful received and entertained his many guests in the rectangular peristyle atrium, the heart of the dwelling, usually decorated with marble columns, floor mosaics, and wall paintings.[76] An atrium typically contained a small pool and a fountain that opened to the sky, allowing sunlight and a cool breeze to penetrate. It accommodated the family shrine and acted as a repository for all the cherished family heirlooms. Military trophies earned by a candidate and his ancestors, such as decorations, armor, weapons, or spoils captured from Rome's enemies were exhibited here. Caesar had won the civic crown of oak leaves in 81–80, awarded for saving the life of a fellow soldier in battle, and he enjoyed the right to wear the crown at festivals in Rome to remind people of his achievement.[77] No doubt this award was prominently displayed. Most significantly, the atrium housed the family's *imagines*, depicting dead ancestors.[78] Each sat on display in a small wooden temple, with a plaque containing the name of the ancestor and a concise record of his political and military exploits. In Caesar's case, the likenesses of eleven consular ancestors, six praetors, and one dictator stared out from their temples at his guests. Like any senator's, Caesar's atrium advertised the illustrious history of his family and its long service to the city.

In addition to these loyal supporters, any political hopeful had to win the votes of the undecided citizens in the forum. Therefore the critical "motorcade" followed the morning rally.[79] At the beginning of the third hour of the day (just after eight in the morning) a candidate's followers, now thoroughly galvanized by his atrium exhortations, escorted him to the forum.[80] His staff, senatorial allies, and those who were unemployed or who took time off from work would attend him throughout the day while he campaigned. Caesar, dressed in a blindingly white toga made so by the application of special chalk, along with his running mate, Lucceius, led the convoy on the short walk from the Domus Publica onto the Via Sacra. After only a few steps they would pass under the Fornix Fabianus, Rome's first great triumphal arch commemorating a victory in Gaul in 121, which marked the entrance to the forum. Straight ahead reared the Capitoline Hill on the forum's western border. To right and left stood the great basilicas on the forum's northern and southern boundaries that housed the offices of various banks and financial institutions and possibly a number of casinos. Temples dotting the forum landscape between the basilicas provided the setting for senate meetings and for *contiones* or voting assemblies. As Cicero observed, the gods watched over the political drama from their temples to protect Rome from ignoble candidates.[81] Events from Rome's past were commemorated in the forum by monuments, statues, and other structures of propaganda or public utility. There stood the fig tree that supposedly sheltered the twin brothers Romulus and Remus while they were suckled by the she-wolf. Hanging nearby was the armor of the hero Horatius Cocles, who, according to Roman legend, singlehandedly saved the city from an Etruscan attack in 508. Other monuments to more recent military victories were scattered about the forum: Gaius Duilius (cos. 260), who won a great naval victory over the Carthaginians during the First Punic War (264–241), celebrated this achievement by erecting a column with the beaks of the enemy ships prominently represented. A painting on the south wall of the senate house immortalized another victory from that war. Important historical records were still displayed, such as the Cassian Treaty of 493 inscribed on a bronze pillar. Before the Flavian Amphitheater (Colosseum) and permanent theaters were built, the Roman forum also provided the setting for gladiatorial shows, games, and theatrical productions.

In the early summer of 60 the forum provided the stage for a different type of actor; it was here that the candidates spent most of their time campaigning. Anyone entering the political heart of Rome would see a vast crowd, for a total of forty-four city magistracies would be filled by the voters that summer. In these days leading up to the elections the forum was packed with as many as a hundred candidates and their even more numerous supporters. To make sure that plenty of undecided voters showed up in the forum, a campaign's representatives would fan out all over Rome, even to the "remotest parts of the city" (which were not very remote, since the city encompassed a relatively small area), and invite people to come meet the candidate.[82] A politician's ability to win support of the undecided often depended on the size, diversity, and enthusiasm of his forum following, which visibly advertised the extent of his popularity. A large throng moving with a candidate under the Fornix Fabianus and into the forum would create a great impression on the people and would allow the candidate to stand out in the crowded field, exerting an enormous influence on potential backers.[83] A candidate's performance, supported by a large and enthusiastic crowd, was all part of Rome's political theater designed to generate positive publicity that could spread around the forum and then to voters in every corner of the capital.[84]

Presumably a candidate's reputation would have preceded him into the forum. By the time Caesar ran for the consulship in 60 it is very likely that he had already established his credentials, and his public benefactions and services would be well known. Many of the traits necessary for election are noted by the sources: a man should be approachable, polite, and charming; he must keep his house open to all and be hospitable to his friends, clients, and other citizens; and he must live with a certain "splendor."[85] Descent from the gods, Romulus, and a noble family like Caesar's definitely helped.[86] More significantly, Caesar had already demonstrated the two foremost qualifications for electoral success. First, he had the ability to speak with "eloquence and good sense" in the senate, assemblies, and courts.[87] Second, he had a vital prerequisite for political office: a record of distinguished service in the Roman army.[88] As an officer he had won awards for bravery in battle. As a commander, he had led the Roman army to victory in Spain (61–60), had been saluted by his troops, and had been awarded a triumph that, thanks to Cato, he had been unable to celebrate.

Accompanied by his entourage, a candidate moved through the forum among the monuments to Rome's illustrious history, shaking hands, demonstrating an ingratiating and approachable manner, and reminding the people of his record. Addressing citizens by name always made a good impression.[89] And, since voters judged a campaign's status from the expression and body language of the candidate, he exuded confidence. A candidate who appeared dejected or looked as if he despaired of winning only convinced potential supporters that his chances were low and that they were better off voting for another.[90] Even worse, people would then spread stories about his negative attitude, leading to certain defeat.

While a contender extolled his own virtues, he also did not miss any opportunity to sling mud at his rival and his rival's supporters. Like all candidates, he assured his audience that the election of his opponent would be an unmitigated disaster for the republic. Apparently campaign organizations worked diligently to uncover any damaging information about their adversaries concerning their crimes, attempts at bribery, alcoholism, and sex scandals.[91]

It has often been argued that a platform played no role in the campaign for political office in Rome, an assumption largely based on Quintus Cicero's admonition that to avoid alienating key constituencies, a candidate should not make any political statements or take a stand on any issue either in the senate or in the forum.[92] Quintus makes it clear elsewhere, however, and other sources agree, that most politicians crafted a political program to bolster their campaign. Many a candidate tailored his political message to each person or group he met, reminding them of earlier positions he had taken on their behalf as well as his intention to act similarly in the future. He told senators that he would defend them against the people.[93] He convinced the equestrians that he would work for peace to create a calm environment in which business would flourish.[94] He reminded the people of his unwavering support for their favorite politicians and of the many speeches made and votes cast on their behalf.[95] In this last cohort of voters Caesar had an advantage. He had grown up not on the Palatine Hill or another wealthy enclave of the city but in the Subura and was therefore one of them. Unlike his rival, he understood their problems.

Political support often derived from *gratia*, or favors. Consequently an aspirant must always be ready to employ his connections, wealth, and power on the voters' behalf.[96] A valuable favor was legal advice and representation in court.[97] During the campaign a candidate had to remind people repeatedly and forcefully of the kindnesses he had done for them in the past,[98] because "the coin of political gratitude is a currency subject to rapid devaluation."[99] He had to make it clear that if they valued his assistance they must reciprocate, and that there was no better time than the present to return the favor. He had to assure his fellow citizens that he would never forget this favor and that being in office would provide him with even greater power to help his supporters. For anyone he had not assisted in the past and anyone who was not under any obligation to him, the diverse crowds attending him would attest to his ability and willingness to help his friends. Hope for future favors created a far stronger bond than gratitude for favors already conferred. However, as Quintus Cicero cynically assured his brother, a candidate could make almost any promise during a campaign, even if he would never have the opportunity or the intention of fulfilling it.[100]

A candidate had to persuade not only individual voters but also the various organizations in the city to join his campaign. After blood ties and marriage connections, group membership represented the strongest bond for a Roman citizen.[101] Quintus Cicero listed no fewer than six different types of associations that had an impact on the electoral process. The candidate held numerous campaign meetings to try to discover what the leaders of these associations wanted in exchange for their backing—or, to put it more bluntly, to find out their price.[102] The campaign compiled extensive lists registering the names and locations of these leaders and the groups they represented; detailed maps could be created as well to pinpoint their location in the city.[103] A hopeful or his surrogates then had to meet with these men. Each tribe had a headquarters in Rome, run by officials called *curatores*. The campaign contacted these tribal leaders who, along with their assistants, the *divisores*, could act as liaisons between their constituents and the candidate. The campaign canvassed the leaders of the religious, professional, and social clubs (the *collegia*), and worked to convince the neighborhood chiefs in the city and the suburbs beyond to win over their districts on a candidate's behalf.

A candidate could meet with leaders at his house or, as a sign of respect, he could travel to their apartments or headquarters. Although a time-consuming ritual, this exercise was essential to securing not just these chiefs' votes but their willingness to act as political operatives and persuade their members to work and vote as well. These leaders possessed detailed membership rolls with names and "addresses," information the candidate could use to canvass these members, street by street. Clubs could help with political propaganda by publishing honorific decrees that were posted around the city and expressed support for individual candidates.

While speaking to so many people, candidates had to avoid gaffes that could lose them the election. Every politician knew the cautionary tale of Publius Cornelius Scipio Nasica Serapio (cos. 138).[104] As a candidate for the curule aedileship (c. 145), Scipio and his retinue strolled through the forum greeting citizens and shaking hands. One farmer had rough and calloused hands due to a lifetime of hard toil. The noble Scipio, unused to manual labor, jokingly asked if the farmer's hands were so coarse because he "walked on his hands." The crowd heard the remark and quickly broadcast it around the city and beyond. Rural citizens did not take kindly to Scipio's jest, which they saw as mocking their difficult lives and devastating poverty. They voted overwhelmingly against Scipio, who lost the election. Scipio discovered that even a famous family name could not provide defense against an unfortunate remark to the voters, because public opinion could indeed have a powerful impact on an election.

That a noble like Scipio even had to be in the forum pressing the flesh gives some idea of the importance of campaigning.[105] Lazy, distracted, or overconfident contenders had no hope, even if they descended from distinguished families,[106] and even if they were already popular. A candidate had to repeatedly stump and at regular times each day, continuously campaigning personally to meet and talk at least once to *every* citizen who frequented the forum and therefore demonstrated an interest in politics. He must "approach the people as a suppliant" to ask for their votes.[107] Someone like Marcus Juventius Laterensis, who declined to pander to the people, invited defeat.[108] Similarly, in 52 Cato refused to humble himself or offer favors and thus lost the election for the consulship.[109]

The campaign organization worked hard to magnify the power of the candidate's message through campaign literature, graffiti, and posters that commended a candidate, presented a candidate's life story, or slandered a rival.[110] The campaign publicized a candidate's military successes; pictures, posters, and even floats representing his exploits were paraded through the forum. They were also exhibited along major highways leading into the city to appeal to Italians on their way into the capital to vote. It was illegal for a candidate to provide free gladiatorial shows, chariot races, or other entertainment for the people while officially campaigning for office but, of course, there were loopholes. The death of a relative served as a pretext for candidates to hold funeral games—even if that relative had died years or even decades before.[111]

Elections were usually held in conjunction with key festivals or games (such as those of Apollo), which made it easier for citizens from nearby Latin cities and wealthier Italians from farther away to plan a trip to Rome to vote. With the expected arrival of citizens from beyond the city, a candidate and his campaign had to reach out to voters beyond Rome. Campaign organizations identified each tribe, city, and praefecture on the peninsula and drafted maps clearly showing their locations. More strategically, the leading men in these regions were identified. No doubt candidates had already spent years cultivating men of influence throughout Italy.[112] On his way to Spain in 61 or on his way back to Rome in 60 Caesar may have stopped in Italian cities to publicize his candidacy. After his return to the city Caesar had less than a month before the election, however, so trusted campaign deputies might have been assigned to visit other districts on the peninsula. Once these surrogates had secured a man's support, that man could promise his own vote and then stump in his hometown or in neighboring districts to encourage his friends and associates to vote for the candidate as well.[113]

Follow the Money

Polybius once claimed that the Romans considered furnishing or accepting bribes to be shameful, but it is clear that bribery was involved in almost every consequential political episode of the late republic, even though numerous laws were passed to combat the problem.[114] Cicero complained that the late republic witnessed the "worst bribery and corruption" in Roman history.[115] Bribery played a role in trials, legislative assemblies, and senatorial resolutions. Even foreign states and rulers employed bribes to gain favorable rulings from Roman politicians.[116]

Corruption had an impact on elections involving all city magistracies from the quaestorship to the censorship, and the consular campaign of 60 was no exception.[117] Caesar had effectively employed bribery many times during his rise up the political ladder; now he had access to the great wealth of his running mate, Lucceius, and presumably that of other supporters as well.[118] To distribute the money, Caesar may have brought citizens to his house to dispense the cash directly,[119] or he may have used his campaign subordinates as intermediaries to funnel funds to recipients.[120] Links he had previously forged with the leaders of the city's organizations, such as the tribes, may have helped transfer the funds.[121] Bribes to potential voters were provided both in cash and in commodities such as amphorae of wine.[122] Food items, tickets to the baths, and oil could be "donated," as well.[123] Campaign organizations also illegally paid people to follow a candidate around the city or attend his speeches; for a little extra cash they would pretend to like everything that they heard.[124]

To combat the massive amounts of money employed by Caesar and Lucceius, Bibulus's noble supporters contributed to a campaign war chest to be used for bribery and other electoral purposes.[125] Even the normally virtuous Cato supported the illegal effort in the name of the *optimate* cause. Although he had prosecuted so many others for violating Rome's bribery statutes, he now argued that sometimes the law must be ignored in order to save the republic.

Voting took place in mid-July of the year 60 on a *comitial* day. Before dawn the candidates and their entourages walked by torchlight out of the city to the Campus Martius, about a hundred yards northwest of the Capitoline Hill, to a rectangular wooden structure called the Saepta.[126] After sunrise, citizens interested in participating followed. The proceedings had to take place on a single day, which meant that only a small part of the population would have time to vote; estimates of the number of citizens able to participate in the time and space available range from fifty-five thousand to seventy thousand, although in practice probably fewer attended.[127] The presiding magistrate sat on his distinctive ivory curule chair that had no back and low armrests. The other city officials and the candidates were also present on the tribunal. A brief assembly preceded the vote, which usually consisted of a set speech whereby the presiding magistrate asked the voters to choose among the candidates. Prayers were offered to the gods, and the priests examined the auspices. An evil omen such as thunder represented a warning from the gods to postpone the assembly.[128] If all religious, political, and military rituals had been satisfied, however, a lottery determined the (wealthy) century that would begin the voting. The Romans believed that ultimately the gods, not luck, chose the first century that would vote, so when the herald announced the first century's decision, others were influenced.[129] Every century from each of the five classes would follow, from the richest to the poorest. An individual citizen joined his particular century, and when the herald called his group he lined up and received a ballot made of wood and wax. He would then walk through the long enclosure of the Saepta and privately mark the wax with the candidates' names or initials. When finished, he dropped the ballot in a box and exited. The votes would be under the control of the *custodes,* who counted them. Guards were present to make sure that no one returned to vote again. The process usually continued until two candidates had a sufficient number of votes to mathematically eliminate their rivals or, rarely, until all 193 centuries had voted.

In the end the *boni* failed to stop Caesar; he was elected first and would therefore be senior consul. He had the support of most elements of the urban population thanks to his long residence in the Subura, his munificence, his advocacy of popular causes, and his backing of popular leaders. Caesar most likely received the votes of the equestrians as well, since they would never choose Bibulus, married as he was to Cato's daughter Porcia and most likely a supporter of his father-in-law's attacks on their order. Bibulus, however, took the second spot. Lucceius's loss ensured that there would be no accommodating partner in the junior consulship alongside Caesar. Instead, Bibulus would be in a position to block any legislation Caesar wished to propose.[130]

Planning

For Caesar the consulship was merely a step (albeit an essential step) toward his ultimate goal of acquiring a perpetual position of power in the state. He had to pass laws to reward the various individuals and constituencies who had elected him and whose support he would require during his year in office and beyond. Above all else he required a proconsulship of a Roman province after 59, a position that could bring him military glory and wealth, and that would most definitely translate into increased authority in Rome. In addition, the proconsulship, as all Roman magistracies, provided immunity from prosecution for any crime—insurance that Caesar might be in need of after his consulship. Thus, once he was elected to Rome's top city magistracy in July 60, Caesar immediately began to plan the agenda for his term, which would commence in barely five months.

Caesar's enemies, however, could not allow his power to increase and therefore planned to stop him from passing any meaningful legislation. Most of all they could not permit Caesar to segue from the consulship in 59 to the governorship of a lucrative province in 58. Bibulus and his allies were already designing methods to frustrate Caesar. On his side Bibulus had three tribunes who possessed the veto as well as senators who were determined to employ multiple techniques in the curia and in the forum to block Caesar's schemes. At some point in 60 the senate passed a resolution directing both of the next year's consuls to administer Italy's paths and forests after their terms concluded.[131] This resolution effectively precluded both Caesar and Bibulus from obtaining a command abroad. Bibulus, who had no military aspirations, happily sacrificed a proconsulship for the good of the cause. For an ambitious senator like Caesar, on the other hand, no assignment could be less welcome. He understood that this resolution represented only a first tactical salvo from a formidable faction resolved to stop him.

Caesar needed powerful allies, and one potential partner was Cicero. Author, lawyer, and consul in 63, Marcus Tullius Cicero exercised enormous influence in the forum and in the senate thanks to his oratorical abilities. In mid-December of 60, Caesar sent one of his most valuable surrogates, Lucius Cornelius Balbus, to meet with Cicero in Tusculum, a city in the Alban Hills away from the prying eyes and gossips in the capital.[132] At Cicero's villa, possibly in the library of which he was so proud, Balbus offered Cicero an alliance with Caesar, pledging that Cicero would have great influence in the new consul's administration and that Caesar would always follow his advice.[133] No doubt Balbus played to Cicero's well-known vanity, assuring him that Caesar would need the guidance of such a wise elder statesman, the "father of his country," who had saved the republic during the Catilinarian conspiracy of 63. Cicero realized that Balbus offered not only an alliance with Caesar but also reconciliation and peace with the people.[134] Although it is unlikely that Balbus used threats, he certainly made clear what Cicero's rejection might bring. Without an alliance with the new consul, Cicero would be open to political attack by his enemies. Actions that Cicero had taken as consul, including executing the Catilinarian ringleaders without trial, made him vulnerable to potential reprisals in court. Cicero certainly understood the implications, but he apparently gave no answer to Balbus. Later he informed his friend Titus Pomponius Atticus that he intended to reject the offer and to chart an independent course. Quoting Hector in Homer's *Iliad,* he said this would allow him to fight for "my country."[135]

Efforts to secure Cicero's support had failed, but in the last days of December Caesar enjoyed better luck with Rome's two most influential senators, Gnaeus Pompey Magnus and Marcus Licinius Crassus, who were at that moment in need of the assistance of Rome's highest magistrate.

A Roman Alexander

In 67 and 66, the Roman people in the tribal assembly had approved the *lex Gabinia* and the *lex Manilia* in defiance of the senate to give Pompey extraordinary military commands in the east. His great victories clearly justified their faith in him, and in 61 they would turn out in the thousands for his triumph.[136] September 28, the first day of the celebration, was a spectacular success, as the spoils of Pompey's wars were paraded throughout the city. Horse-drawn carriages and litters conveyed gold, silver, works of art, captured enemy arms, and the rams of captured enemy ships. Great placards recorded the names of the defeated countries and peoples, noted the addition of four new eastern provinces to the empire, and tallied the great financial rewards for Rome. Images of Roman gods vanquishing the strange gods of the east were displayed along with trophies representing every battle won by Pompey and his lieutenants. Paintings and models illustrated the crucial moments of the campaigns and portrayed the many rulers Pompey had defeated as well as his victories over the Cilician pirates on land and sea, which ended a threat that had plagued Rome's shipping and grain supply for more than forty years. A series of vivid images depicted the greatest of Rome's enemies during this period, King Mithridates VI of Pontus, as he fought against, lost to, and fled from Roman forces before ultimately committing suicide. A gold statue of Mithridates standing nearly twelve feet high was paraded through the city along with his throne, his scepter, and his priceless library. The Roman people had fought three wars against Mithridates during a twenty-five-year period, so surely they found it sweet to view abundant evidence of his final defeat.[137] Spoils, floats, paintings, placards, and models, all were later displayed in the forum for the people's admiration.

The first day of Pompey's triumph was only the beginning; the main event would come on day two. On September 29, 61, a huge crowd assembled by torchlight just before dawn outside Rome, in the Circus Flaminius. Pompey addressed the crowd and in particular his soldiers, thanking them for all their efforts during the war and for their participation in the festivities. As the sun rose over the eastern hills just after seven o'clock, the greatest triumphal procession of the last century of the free republic set out.

Leading the parade were the dancers, drummers, and trumpeters whose thunderous music announced the main body's imminent approach to the throngs waiting ahead on the route. Next walked 324 captives and hostages from the countries Pompey had conquered. Wearing not chains but the exotic and colorful costumes of their homelands, members of this group included five sons and two daughters of Mithridates, the wife and son of King Tigranes II of Armenia, Cilician pirate chieftains, the female potentates of the distant Scythians, and countless other rulers from beyond the eastern frontiers of the Roman world. To the watching Romans, the sheer number and variety of these captives represented living proof of the incredible victories of Pompey and the dramatic extension of the empire. Next in the parade marched those Romans who had been liberated from captivity or slavery by Pompey's victorious armies, who now proudly wore the caps signifying their newfound freedom. The many animals that were to be sacrificed to the gods followed, along with the priests who would conduct the religious ceremonies at parade's end. After the animals came Pompey's *lictors,* wearing the traditional red and carrying the *fasces* complete with axes, signifying that their commander still held the *imperium*. Then came the great general himself, riding in the tall triumphal chariot pulled by four horses inlaid with gold, gems, and ivory.

Pompey wore a magnificent embroidered tunic and purple toga and, tellingly, a cloak taken from Mithridates that supposedly had once belonged to Alexander the Great. Already known as Magnus ("the Great") because he physically resembled Alexander and held a similar record of youthful military success, Pompey highlighted his connection to the Macedonian king by donning the cloak.[138] Pompey carried a laurel branch in one hand and an ivory scepter in the other. His face was painted red to imitate the statues of Jupiter in the city. He shared his chariot with a slave, who held a gold crown over his head while constantly reminding the conquering general that despite his great success he remained mortal. Pompey's youngest son, Sextus, about six years old, also accompanied his father in the chariot. His oldest son, Gnaeus, who was eighteen, rode on horseback alongside. Also on horseback following behind were the officers from Pompey's army, and then, coming along on foot, strode Rome's city magistrates and senators. Finally came Pompey's soldiers, crowned with garlands, singing victory songs and bawdy songs to inspire and amuse the crowd.

This cast of thousands followed the ancient triumphal route from the Circus Flaminius through the Triumphal Gate into the city and the densely populated region of the Velabrum. Following the Vicus Iugarius under the cliffs of the Capitoline Hill, the parade passed along narrow streets in a man-made canyon of towering apartment buildings. Even at this early hour people jammed the roads or hung out of windows to secure a view of the spectacle and cheer the victorious general. Turning, the procession slowly headed toward the Tiber River and the Vatican and Janiculum Hills beyond, before making its way into the Forum Boarium, a commercial district normally crowded with shoppers and merchants but closed for the holiday and crowded with revelers. Turning southeast, the trumpeters and drummers led the procession away from the river and into the Circus Maximus, the greatest of Rome's chariot racetracks. Seven hundred yards long, the arena normally held more than one hundred thousand spectators when they congregated to watch chariot teams, all named after colors, race seven times around the track. On September 29, however, the stadium was full for Pompey's triumph, its seats providing what was likely the most comfortable vantage point in the city for viewing the parade. After leaving the track the procession moved northeast between the Palatine and Caelian hills, upon which more citizens had gathered to watch, before it turned northwest onto the Via Sacra. Coming down the Velian slope between the Palatine and the Carinae, the procession finally emerged into the Roman forum where images and floats from the previous day still stood. Citizens thronged the large open space in the heart of Rome, either standing on the forum floor or perched on the temples and basilicas that ringed it.

At long last the paraders arrived at the foot of the Capitoline Hill. Pompey then made his way up to the Temple of Jupiter Optimus Maximus to thank Rome's supreme god. Pompey and the senate would enjoy a large feast in the temple while banquets for the victorious soldiers and Rome's urban population were held in the forum and around the city. Food and wine flowed as the Romans celebrated more victories over yet more foreign enemies. The festivities came to an end only after dark, when to the sound of flutes the victorious general was escorted to the Carinae, returning to his house for the first time in six years.

It had been an extraordinary day for Pompey, and in retrospect it represented the zenith of his military career. He had established himself as Rome's greatest general and in the process accomplished something no other commander had ever achieved by winning three triumphs over three different continents, Africa (79), Europe (71), and now Asia (61). He had defeated Mithridates VI, destroyed the pirate threat, restored the capital's food supply, and added four lucrative provinces to the empire. If all that were not enough, September 29, 61, was Pompey's forty-fifth birthday.

Pompey intended to leverage his military glory and popularity into political victories. He had two targets in his sights. First, he had promised his soldiers that after their service was complete the state would reward them with land allotments in Italy; now he wanted the senators to honor that vow. Second, he wanted the senate to approve the arrangements he had made in the east involving the organization of the new provinces he had conquered and the grants he had made to independent cities and rulers.

Thus far Pompey had enjoyed remarkable, almost uninterrupted, success. That changed abruptly, as he immediately encountered strong opposition. Regarding his first goal, numerous senators were philosophically opposed to using the treasury's money to provide land for the poor, even for citizens who had risked their lives fighting in Rome's wars. Others argued that such a land-distribution program was so costly it could bankrupt the state. Regarding the second goal, many senators were unwilling to accept Pompey's eastern arrangements because the senate normally dispatched a commission of ten of its members to organize new provinces, but Pompey had acted alone, without senatorial guidance. Above all, due to his unconventional and in many ways unlawful rise to power, Pompey remained a polarizing figure; many senators remained unalterably opposed to him personally. At the age of twenty-three he had sided with Sulla during the civil war of 83–82 and helped him win the dictatorship. Pompey was therefore seen as sharing in the blame for Sulla's reign of terror, which led to hundreds of senators and equestrians being executed. Pompey had also received several unconstitutional commands during a series of civil wars that led to victories over his fellow Romans, not over foreign enemies.[139] The last of these civil wars had concluded barely ten years earlier. People whose relatives had died at Pompey's hands could neither forgive nor forget his early career.[140] His rise to the consulship in the year 70 violated electoral law because he was too young (only thirty-six), had never held any preliminary offices, and was still not a member of the senate. He had in fact never won a free Roman vote—his election to the consulship occurred while his devoted army camped outside the city walls. His eastern commands had come not from the senate but from the people voting in the tribal assembly. While in the east Pompey had received unprecedented honors for a Roman: the people of Samos hailed him as a savior, the Delians dedicated a cult in his honor, and in Mytilene, on the island of Lesbos, the populace named a month after him. Senators found especially galling the sight of Pompey continuing to wear the triumphal insignia and the specially embroidered toga, something no other Roman was legally permitted to do once a triumph had been completed.[141] This "intolerable distancing" of Pompey from his peers enraged many of his senatorial colleagues.[142] Furthermore, Pompey's early crimes, the unconstitutionality of his career, his spectacular eastern victories, and his incredible triumph provoked fears among his enemies that he might attempt to follow in Sulla's footsteps.

Many senators, unwilling to allow him to enjoy his preeminent position unchallenged, blocked his every effort in the senate and the assembly. Pompey responded by supporting candidates for the year 60 who he hoped would pass his laws when they entered office. One was his former deputy, Lucius Afranius.[143] Pompey used his considerable popularity to campaign on Afranius's behalf, greeting voters in the forum, making speeches praising his military successes in Spain (for which he received a triumph), and extolling the crucial role he played in Rome's (and Pompey's) victories in the east. According to rumor, Pompey also brought tribal distributing agents to his gardens outside the city and provided them with money to be disbursed to the voters. Afranius won election to the consulship for 60 while another ally, Lucius Flavius, secured election to the tribunate.

Unfortunately for Pompey, his enemies continued to fight. Afranius's consular colleague was Quintus Caecilius Metellus Celer, Pompey's bitter enemy. Celer and his brother Quintus Caecilius Metellus Nepos (cos. 57), descended from one of the republic's eminent plebian families, had been staunch supporters of Pompey when he had been married to their sister Mucia Tertia (c. 79–62).[144] But while Pompey campaigned in the east his wife had apparently been unfaithful, and consequently he sent her a notice of divorce (62).[145] Unwilling to accept this slur on her or on their illustrious family name, the brothers Metelli stood by their sister, although they wisely waited until after Celer's election before openly breaking with Pompey.[146] The Metelli now became Pompey's antagonists. As consul Celer would use the powers of his office to block Pompey's legislation. They were joined by Cato, their enemy when they supported Pompey but now an ally.[147] Lucius Licinius Lucullus (cos. 74), an *optimate* stalwart, a political ally of Cato, and husband to Cato's niece Servilia, emerged from his luxurious retirement seeking revenge on Pompey.[148] Lucullus loathed

Pompey after Pompey had replaced him in command against Mithridates VI in 66, overridden his provincial arrangements in the east later that year, and apparently played a role in postponing his triumph, forcing him to remain outside the city for three years (66–63).

First Pompey's foes prevented ratification of his decrees in the east. Lucullus led the opposition, demanding that every single one of Pompey's acts in the east be debated by the senate individually rather than as a collection. He also convinced the senate to discuss his own eastern acts as alternatives to Pompey's. Discussion of the counterproposals took time, and a vote on Pompey's decrees was postponed indefinitely. Pompey's ally Afranius offered no help; after serving abroad for years, he showed little political acumen and endured constant abuse in the senate.[149] Apparently he was a much better dancer than politician.[150]

While one of Pompey's measures stalled in the senate, another stalled in the assembly. His ally, the new tribune Lucius Flavius, had proposed a law designed to provide land for Pompey's soldiers as well as for some of the poor citizens of Rome.

Since 133 similar agrarian laws had been a part of the popular political agenda. And since 133 *optimate* ideology ensured powerful opposition to these types of proposals. Just three years before Lucius Flavius put his measure forward, the disheveled, unshaven Publius Servilius Rullus (tr. 63), a throwback to the tribunes of early Rome, had proposed using public money and the booty from the eastern campaigns to buy land in Italy and the provinces to distribute to veterans and the poor.[151] In this case Cicero led the opposition, using his consular authority to call numerous *contiones* at which he delivered orations condemning the law. Like so many politicians in Roman history and beyond, Cicero exaggerated and lied outright in order to persuade his fellow citizens that the Rullan law was wicked and would harm the very people it purported to help. Feigning concern for their interests, he urged his audience to oppose the bill because if it passed and they received land, they would have to leave Rome. He begged them not to abandon the many amenities of city life for the dreadful backwaters of Italy. Swiftly contradicting himself, Cicero then beseeched the urban populace to reject the measure because all the land would in fact go to rural citizens, not citizens of the capital. Pivoting again, he proclaimed that there would be no land at all, because the bill would allow the *decemviri*, the board of ten men appointed to administer the law, to embezzle most of the money earmarked for land acquisition. Lastly he tried to scare his listeners by exaggerating the potential power of the *decemviri*: so great would be their authority, he said, it would destroy republican liberty.[152] Cicero went on to postulate conspiracy theories, warning his audience of sinister forces, the real promoters of the law who were working behind the scenes "at night in dark and secret places" to implement the law and through it seize power.[153] One historian has suggested that Cicero's speech "should be studied by all politicians who aspire to become proficient in the art of misrepresentation."[154] Although his analysis of the Rullan bill was contradictory, hyperbolic, and often completely false, Cicero helped create enough confusion and fear that public opinion turned against the proposal and it never passed. Cicero later justified his actions, bragging that his dishonest speeches had saved the state from a wicked land bill.[155]

In 60, at a *contio* in the forum, the selfsame Cicero, possibly due to his friendship with Pompey, expressed limited support for Flavius's new law as long as specific amendments were incorporated that protected private property in Italy.[156] Cicero's moderate stance apparently led to friction with *optimates* who wished to oppose the measure (and Pompey) at all costs. Cicero bemoaned the death of Quintus Lutatius Catulus (cos. 78), which, he said, had deprived the *optimates* of a wise leader; now they obstructed merely to obstruct, without offering alternative solutions, and they resisted anything connected to Pompey even if in some ways it might be beneficial to Rome and the *optimate* cause.

For months the consul Celer directed the opposition to the Flavian law.[157] The conclusion of this political struggle began on the rostra when Flavius, tired of the constant obstruction, had Celer hauled off to the *carcer* (prison), barely fifty yards northwest of the stage. A large crowd of Celer's supporters escorted him, while Flavius's adherents watched and applauded the move. Celer then attempted to convene the senate at the entrance to the prison. Flavius responded by putting his tribune's bench in front of the door to prevent the meeting from being held. Because the tribune was *sacrosanct*, law and religion declared it a sacrilege to remove him by force. Celer then had the wall of the prison knocked out so the senate could meet with him there. The "people," citizens who supported the senate and who might have seen Flavius's actions as an attack on *libertas*, were upset. This political drama made Pompey realize he was losing in the court of public opinion, and he privately convinced Flavius to release Celer.

Flavius proposed his land law sometime between December 10, 61, when he took office, and January 20, 60, when Cicero mentioned the law in a letter.[158] In another letter, written on March 15, 60, Cicero informed his friend Atticus that Flavius, supported by Pompey, continued to "energetically" push his law in the teeth of stiff opposition. Even though three months had passed, there had been no resolution. In a third letter, from June 3, 60, in answer to an inquiry from Atticus, Cicero reported that it now appeared that the law would not pass—apparently it had never even come up for a vote. Six months after Flavius first proposed the bill, it appeared dead.

Eighteen months after Pompey's return from the east and nearly a year after his triumph he stood no closer to accomplishing his legislative agenda. Despite his enormous wealth and prodigious military achievements, and even with supporters holding two key city magistracies, he could not overcome the obstruction of his senatorial adversaries. Thanks to their obstinate resistance to (and in some cases bitter hatred of) Pompey, and to the nature of the Roman constitution, these senators exercised greater power to hinder Pompey's measures than Pompey and his allies could muster to force them through. To conquer the opposition the great general would need more powerful and resolute associates in the future—a need that would provide Caesar with a splendid opportunity.

Marcus Licinius Crassus

Marcus Licinius Crassus, an eminent Roman who had been stymied in his efforts to pass legislation, was another potential ally for Caesar. Crassus had never won (and never would win) the military glory associated with a triumph. Instead, on a December morning in 71 this member of a noble plebian family had celebrated an *ovatio* for his victory over the slave army of Spartacus.[159] Crassus's consolation prize was a far less prestigious affair than Pompey's spectacular third triumph in 61. Crassus did not ride in the triumphal chariot dressed in impressive robes but led the procession on foot wearing a regular toga. An *ovatio* consisted of relatively few soldiers and senators; flute players, not trumpeters, accompanied the procession. Making his way through the city, Crassus undoubtedly noted the low turnout compared to the size of triumph crowds. Nevertheless, as he walked across the forum and then alone up to the Capitoline Hill to give thanks to Jupiter, he could take comfort in the knowledge that there were alternative paths to power that existed beyond military glory.

Crassus was perhaps Rome's wealthiest man.[160] Through acute business deals and profiteering during numerous civil crises, he had parlayed an inheritance of 300 talents into an enormous fortune of 7,100 talents. He employed this wealth to acquire great influence. For Rome's poor he provided free dinners in his home, sponsored huge banquets around the city, distributed free grain, and dispensed loans. Crassus also gave freely of his time. He kept his house open to any and all callers and provided sage advice. He greeted all citizens by name without the help of a *nomenclator*. Acknowledged as one of Rome's best orators, he appeared regularly in court representing citizens of all classes. He campaigned often on behalf of friends. He paid off the debts of potentially useful politicians such as Caesar, frequently lending money without interest.[161] He did his duty to the gods, on one occasion donating one-tenth of his wealth to Hercules.

Crassus's power derived not only from the popularity generated by the many favors and services he performed in Rome and Italy, but also from the fear his willingness to use this power inspired. One politician, the tribune of 76, Gnaeus Sicinius, famously remarked that although he gladly assailed other senators, he did not attack Crassus because of the "hay on his horns," referring to a practice by which Romans tied hay on the horns of particularly dangerous bulls to warn people to keep their distance.[162] Reckless politicians such as Publius Clodius Pulcher (tr. 58), who harassed even the great Pompey, avoided attacking Crassus. And when Lucius Tarquinius, a participant in Catiline's conspiracy, implicated Crassus in the plot, senators were outraged—not at Crassus but at Tarquinius, shouting him down and accusing him of lying.[163] Some senators believed the charges were false, but many who judged that Crassus was probably involved were unwilling to confront him, because they had private business dealings with him or they owed him money. Some feared alienating him in a moment of national crisis, while others feared retribution. Consequently, a serious allegation that might have destroyed another senator did no damage to Crassus. Instead, the senate threw Tarquinius into prison for making false accusations.

A pragmatic rather than a partisan politician, Crassus acted in his own interests to increase his power.[164] He became a master of the political game, preferring "the reality of power to the show."[165] According to many he became more influential than Pompey.[166] Cicero, a contemporary, called him "extremely powerful."[167] A younger contemporary, the senator and historian Gaius Sallustius Crispus (pr. 46), described him as a man of "enormous wealth and power."[168]

The powerful Crassus had a problem in 61–60, however—a problem that involved the equestrian order, which had always represented a distinct class in the Roman state.[169] The order's influence derived in part from the Aurelian Law (70), which, by mandating that equestrians make up two-thirds of every jury, provided them with great influence in the courts.[170] The *publicani* represented the most powerful element within the equestrian order.[171] They had always enjoyed unique economic rights under Roman law, which provided them with certain advantages over other businessmen. They alone had the right to form long-term companies.[172] The *publicani* ran Rome's banks. They controlled an elaborate mail system, Rome's "only efficient postal service," which brought information from all over the empire and beyond.[173] They had long been the recipients of government contracts awarded by the censors,[174] the most lucrative of which involved a system known as tax farming. Publican companies submitted bids to the censors, and the highest bids received government approval to collect taxes in the provinces. The amount stipulated in the contract had to be turned over to the state, but all the money collected above that sum could be pocketed by the publican firms. Usually backed by the provincial governors and their soldiers, companies were able to extort enormous amounts of money from the unfortunate provincials and realize enormous profits.

Their extraordinary wealth, elaborate business operations and preponderant role in the courts allowed the equestrians, and especially the *publicani,* to influence the political process. The many senators who were in need of funds to finance both their rise up the political ladder and their lavish lifestyles were dependent on publican cash for legitimate loans and illegitimate bribes. *Publicani* often worked behind the scenes generating support for measures or candidates they favored while using their wealth and influence to produce speakers at *contiones* to sway public opinion.[175] Occasionally they even used the courts to punish senators who worked against their business interests.[176]

Although laws prohibited senators from investing in equestrian firms, and senatorial society frowned upon those engaged in business in the pursuit of profit, Crassus and others participated as silent partners.[177] Through his numerous business enterprises, Crassus worked closely with the *publicani*, probably owning shares in one or more publican companies that bought the contract from the censors of 61 to collect the taxes of the province of Asia.[178] Peace had finally been restored after the three Mithridatic Wars, and the tax farmers had submitted an extremely high bid. Unfortunately, it quickly became apparent that their tender was excessive; they had been unable to raise sufficient revenues in the war-devastated province to cover the payment they made to the state for the contract and still realize their typically hefty profit. In November 61 the firms, encouraged and backed by Crassus, petitioned the senate to cancel the contract so they could avoid huge losses. Theirs was a legal request, and the senate had granted similar appeals in the past.[179] Crassus spoke out forcefully in the house on behalf of the *publicani*. He had allies; although Cicero asserted in a private letter that the *publicani* had behaved "disgracefully," he nonetheless feared a rupture between the senate and the equestrians.[180] He too had long-standing ties with the equestrian order and needed their support in the future, not only for himself but also for his son and for his brother Quintus, who at the time governed Asia as proconsul and therefore dealt constantly with publican companies. Despite his private reservations, Cicero spoke out in favor of canceling the contract. On December 1 and 2, 61, he addressed a packed curia on his favorite theme, the two pillars of the republic, which he immodestly pronounced he alone had established. Those foundations rested on the unity of the senatorial and equestrian orders to protect private property and the Roman state.[181] Cicero argued that the senate must placate the equestrians and restore concord between the two orders by approving their request concerning the tax contract.

Some senators, however, resented the equestrians' rise and were unwilling to accommodate this new power in their midst, believing that the *publicani* in particular threatened the senate's natural position atop the state's hierarchy. Leading the opposition were Cato, Celer, and Lucullus, whose command against Mithridates had been transferred to Pompey in part because of complaints by the *publicani*, who objected to Lucullus's unwillingness to allow them to extort money from the Asian provincials. These and other senators may have sensed an opportunity to educate the equestrians as to who truly governed the state. As the minority, though, they could not allow the matter to come to a vote. Luckily for them, in the senate majorities were unimportant: beginning in late 61, Cato used the filibuster to prevent a vote on the publican appeal.[182] The resulting gridlock meant that no other business could be conducted—senators' pet projects languished, critical domestic and foreign policy decisions remained unresolved, foreign embassies were kept waiting, and magistrates were not given their provincial assignments.[183] In June of 60, with pressure mounting, the equestrians' senatorial supporters were finally forced to let the matter drop. Cato's attempts earlier that year to pass a law against bribery in legal proceedings had already caused the order to resent the senate.[184] Now Cato's stubborn obstruction prompted an angry outburst from the venerable equestrian leader and publican company chairman of the board, Gnaeus Plancius. Plancius decried the senate's actions, bitterly stating that envoys from hostile foreign states were granted audiences in the house but the equestrians were not even permitted the courtesy of a vote.[185] As a result of this dishonor the equestrian order was now "at war" with the senate.[186]

Crassus, who had sponsored equestrian interests, stood to lose a vast amount of money due to the unprofitable contract. Even worse was the enormous amount of prestige he lost because of his inability to help his partners. To reverse this defeat the great plutocrat would need powerful and determined associates in the future.

Alliance

In a significant twist of fate for Caesar's consulship—and for the course of Roman history—Crassus's setback coincided with the other momentous developments of the summer of 60. At almost the same time, to the disappointment of veterans and poor citizens, the conflict between Celer and the tribune Flavius finally played out to its dramatic conclusion at the *carcer*, leading to the defeat of Pompey's cherished land law. In addition, ratification of Pompey's eastern acts had been postponed indefinitely.[187] As these events proceeded to their conclusion, Caesar arrived home from Spain in the first days of June to run for consul.[188] Caesar was handed a tremendous opportunity by the defeats suffered by Pompey and Crassus in 61–60, for both men desperately needed the help of the consul, a city magistrate, to achieve their respective goals. But Caesar saw even greater possibility in a triple alliance among himself, Pompey, and Crassus. Procuring the aid of only one of these men might not deliver the clout Caesar needed to help his partners and, more crucially, safeguard his future prospects. Worse, it might beget the enmity of the other. To succeed in his consulship and beyond, Caesar needed both Pompey and Crassus.

It would not be easy. Pompey and Crassus had helped Sulla win the civil war (83–82) and had worked together in their joint consulship (70), but in the decade following they had become bitter rivals.[189] Having celebrated only an *ovatio*, Crassus expressed envy at Pompey's military reputation and saw him as a "hated rival."[190] Cicero reported tension between the two after a senate meeting in February 61.[191] In 60 Crassus operated openly against Pompey, siding with Lucullus in the latter's efforts to block senatorial approval of Pompey's eastern acts.[192]

Although they disliked each other, Pompey and Crassus were both friends of Caesar, had benefited from his support during the 60s, and had strong incentives to back him during the consular campaign.[193] By mid-December, as Balbus informed Cicero at their meeting, the newly elected Caesar had begun the delicate task of reconciling the two men. Both in person and through surrogates, he urged them to join with him against their enemies. Caesar had numerous arguments available to him. For one thing, he probably pointed out to both men that their antagonism merely increased the power of rivals such as Cato.

Caesar may have informed Pompey that he had begun to devise a new agrarian law that he believed would succeed where the Rullan and Flavian laws had not. Pompey may even have joined Caesar in designing the legislation to benefit his veterans. At some point Caesar made public his intention to propose the land law once he took office in January of 59.[194] Caesar possibly informed Pompey that he would use the power of his office to have Pompey's arrangements in the east approved as well.

It was said of Crassus that "he easily ended an alliance or a quarrel" if doing so increased his influence.[195] Caesar must have spelled out to him the potential advantages in a political union with Pompey, although an astute politician like Crassus would have known them already. Caesar no doubt promised Crassus he would help solve his problem with the tax contracts. He may have promised Crassus a place on any board created to oversee the distribution of land; such a position would provide opportunities for incredible wealth, patronage, and power. An alliance with Pompey would help Crassus achieve his own goals, while having a hand in Pompey's legislation would earn Pompey's gratitude.

The lobbying effort eventually bore fruit: in late 60, sometime after the mid-December meeting between Cicero and Balbus at Tusculum, and before Metellus Celer's term as consul had ended on December 29, the three men swore an oath to work together to pass desired legislation and oppose any measure not agreeable to each.[196] Caesar had thus secured the support of two of Rome's most influential senators who nevertheless had no position in the government that would allow them to introduce and push forward legislation. Both needed an energetic chief magistrate with the power of initiative to pass their laws. Caesar's alliance with Pompey and Crassus also increased his support among the equestrians, veterans, and wide segments of the urban and rural population. Caesar could have confidence that he would be able to ratify legislation, even in the teeth of bitter political resistance from Bibulus and his allies.

The coalition of Gaius Julius Caesar, Gnaeus Pompey Magnus, and Marcus Licinius Crassus would become known to history as the First Triumvirate, or as Varro called it, the "Three-Headed Monster."[197] In many ways a typical pact among Roman senators, an informal agreement designed to further one another's individual interests, this union was far from typical, in that it would play an enormous role in the history of the late republic. The alliance was so important that ancient Roman historians such as Gaius Asinius Pollio began their chronicles with its formation.[198] It was not only ironic but hugely consequential that Cato and his allies' efforts in 61–60 to limit the power of the three drove them together.[199] Conservative elements had managed to win tactical victories to stymie their opponents in the curia and in the assembly, but their temporary triumphs would prove Pyrrhic. Cato and his allies had alienated two of Rome's most powerful senators and some of Rome's most powerful constituencies. Cicero admired Cato's integrity and considered his stands on the issues to be just, but he also believed they were potentially dangerous. He remarked privately to Atticus that for all Cato's love of Rome he "sometimes harms the republic."[200] He blamed the *optimates* and especially Cato for shortsighted policies that deprived them of the support of much of the senate, the equestrians, the people, and Pompey. That they refused to budge on these issues and, especially, that they were unwilling to provide any economic relief to the veterans and to the poor, ultimately led to the disaster they had worked so hard to avoid.

-II-

Caesar, Pompey, and Crassus

59 BC/695 AUC

The alliance formed by Gaius Caesar, Gnaeus Pompey and Marcus Crassus proved so evil for the city, for the world, and later for each of the three men themselves.

Velleius Paterculus

Winter 59 BC/695 AUC

Inauguration Day

The ceremonies to install the Roman Republic's new city magistrates and formally launch the new year began early on the morning of January 1, 59. Caesar spent the predawn hours outside the Domus Publica staring up at the night sky, watching for omens. As the sun rose just after 7:30 he took the auspices. Fortunately, all signs were positive: the gods had bestowed their favor on his term of office and on the Roman state. After Caesar completed these religious duties, he dressed, facing the shrine of the household gods and the images of his ancestors, including Aeneas, Romulus, and Roman consuls dating back to a Gaius Julius in 489; his family's history surrounded him as he prepared to take up his position in Rome's highest office. He donned the *toga praetexta*, the crimson tunic of the Pontifex Maximus, the crown of oak leaves awarded for bravery in battle, and his senatorial ring. Caesar's colleagues, friends, and supporters arrived at his residence to offer congratulations for his electoral success, and Caesar then led this group in a procession onto the Via Sacra.[1] Nearby, the

Palatine Hill reared high above the surrounding valleys. To the north it overlooked the Via Sacra and the forum, to the west the Tiber River, and to the south the Circus Maximus. A replica of Romulus's original hut still stood, supposedly at the very spot where Rome's founder had once lived. Only the very wealthy could afford to live in a house on the Palatine, and it remained Rome's most exclusive address, home to some of its most powerful politicians.[2] Cicero, Publius Clodius Pulcher, and Metellus Celer were neighbors, living on the hill between the Via Sacra and *Clivus Victoriae* just above Caesar's residence. In his home on the Palatine Bibulus performed the same religious ceremonies that Caesar had performed and, joined by his friends and supporters, made his way down the hill and onto the Via Sacra to join Caesar and his entourage.

The two crowds merged, and the convoy moved on into the forum, with the equestrians, twenty-four *lictors*, and new consuls leading the way. Next came the members of the senate, organized by rank: the *consulares* first, wearing the purple-bordered toga, followed by other former magistrates, the back benchers, and, finally, Roman citizens who were attached to one of the consuls or who merely wanted to witness the pageantry of the inauguration. Thousands of Romans thronged the streets and hills throughout the city to watch the spectacle. The procession moved past the large crowds perched on the great basilicas on the northern and southern borders of the forum. At the forum's northwestern end, on an outcrop thirty feet above the forum floor, stood the renovated Curia Hostilia. A few steps to the south, past the Greek steps, were the circular well of the *comitium*, where public meetings had once been held, and the rostra, a curved platform that faced out onto the forum and that derived its name from the rams or beaks taken from enemy ships in 338 during the Latin War. The bench of the ten tribunes sat on the rostra as well.[3]

The procession then moved up from the west side of the forum along the Clivus Capitolinus to the top of the Capitoline Hill, passing the Temple of Saturn (which contained Rome's treasury), the Tabularium (which housed Rome's archives), and the Temple of Concord, which had been built to commemorate plebian successes during the Conflict of the Orders and the resulting harmony that followed between Rome's two orders. Jutting out from the Capitoline Hill was the Tarpeian Rock, a cliff from which the Romans threw traitors and murderers to their death. Crowning the hill was an enormous statue to Jupiter constructed in 293 by the consul Spurius Carvilius Maximus from the armor taken from defeated Samnite soldiers; the glint from the statue could be seen for miles.

Rome's provincial governors swore their oath at Jupiter's feet before departing to their provinces.

Rome's most important sanctuary for the Roman pantheon's supreme god was the Temple of Jupiter Optimus Maximus. Here on January 1 Caesar and Bibulus each sacrificed a young white ox. Caesar's died without a struggle, a good omen; Bibulus's took some time to die, portending difficult times ahead for the junior consul. A meal celebrating the inauguration of the new consuls was held in the temple with the other city magistrates and senators. After the inauguration procession, ceremonies, and banquet, the senate held the first meeting of this new year, as they did every new year, in Jupiter's temple, symbolically in the presence of Rome's greatest deity.[4] The heralds called the senators to order, and as senior consul, Caesar presided over the gathering. With his back to the gods' statues he faced southeast with a view straight across to the Palatine Hill; the forum was to his left and the Tiber River to his right. Caesar made the customary vows for the welfare of Rome and designated a date for the commencement of the Latin Games. As his first act as consul, he announced that written records of senatorial debates would now be posted around the city and Italy so the people could keep abreast of senatorial proceedings.[5] This was a shrewd move on Caesar's part; henceforward members who resisted popular measures would not be able to hide behind claims of senatorial privilege, and the people would quickly learn who opposed laws they favored.

As senior consul Caesar determined the ritual order in which members would speak in the senate for the coming year. The rankings were a telling indicator of the dignity and power possessed by specific individuals.[6] First came the *consulares*, then the praetors, then the aediles, down to the most junior members. Caesar gave Crassus the great honor of speaking first at any future senate meeting. This choice may have come as a surprise to many senators, who probably expected Pompey to receive this distinction, but no doubt the matter was negotiated beforehand. It is highly unlikely that Caesar would have passed over Pompey in public without discussing the subject with him first, and Crassus may have made this privilege part of his price to join the coalition—a small victory over his old rival and future ally Pompey. Caesar's pick made it clear to those in the temple that he and Crassus would be working together. Even if Cicero or others had not leaked the news about Caesar's December negotiations, some in the temple, aware of Caesar and Pompey's already close relationship, may have suspected something even more ominous at work on January 1: the possible reconciliation of Pompey and Crassus.

As was traditional, Caesar ended the New Year's Day meeting by delivering a speech on the state of the republic. He discussed foreign affairs and the roster of governors and legions in the provinces. He may also have noted that as the year 59 dawned the empire was relatively peaceful; no foreign state threatened the supremacy of Rome, and no major conflicts were ongoing. Caesar finished by making a plea to his colleague and rival Bibulus. He declared that Rome faced many critical problems and that government gridlock would prevent a cure. He called on Bibulus and Bibulus's allies to put aside past grievances and partisanship to work with him to repair the republic.[7] A new year, Rome's six hundred and ninety-fifth, had officially begun.

The Julian Land Law

Sometime very early in January (January 2, 5, and 6 all were appropriate calendar days), Caesar convened the senate in the Curia Hostilia and formally proposed his highly anticipated land law. Senators sat on benches along the east and west sides of the building, with the consuls Caesar and Bibulus seated on their curule chairs on the north platform. As always, the building's doors remained open and spectators crowded around the entrance or sat on the Greek steps or in the *comitium* nearby. After the introductory prayers Caesar rose to call the session to order and then read from a prepared text explaining the nature and purpose of his law.[8] The *lex Julia Agraria* provided land in Italy to Pompey's veterans and to poor Roman citizens, land that would be divided up into small parcels that the recipients could farm. The land could not be sold by the recipients until twenty years had passed. To provide the plots, the republic would divide and distribute public land already owned by the state (except for territory in Campania) and would buy land from private property owners willing to sell at the fair market price established in the previous census. Plunder, tribute, and taxes derived from Pompey's eastern conquests would provide funds to purchase land. Two boards would be created to oversee the administration of the law. The Board of Twenty would oversee the acquisition and assignment of the land while the Board of Five would provide legal counsel. By the terms of the law, Caesar could not hold a position on either board. Caesar had clearly learned from the failures of the Rullan and Flavian land laws, and he avoided controversial clauses in his legislation.

In his speech Caesar described the main provisions of the bill and emphasized its merits.[9] It seemed only fair that the new provinces and the wealth they provided should benefit the soldiers who had risked their lives to expand the power of Rome and had been promised economic rewards upon discharge. The law would also benefit Rome by draining the swollen population of the city to repopulate desolate areas of Italy. These poor unemployed citizens would now possess farms on which they would work to support themselves and their families. Because these people so often rioted and caused many of Rome's urban ills, removing them would be beneficial to the city. And, although he did not comment on this benefit in public, Caesar may have already pointed out to the *optimates* in private that thousands of citizens who usually voted for popular causes would no longer be in Rome.

Like most agrarian legislation, the bill was lengthy, so Caesar probably did not recite it in its entirety at this meeting.[10] He did, however, see to it that written copies of the complete law were distributed to the senators for their inspection; later he had copies posted around the city and in Italian municipalities. After he finished summarizing the law's key provisions in the senate, he dismissed the senators to allow them time to study the law.

The consul Bibulus, the senator Cato, and three of the ten tribunes (Quintus Ancharius, Gnaeus Domitius Calvinus, and Gaius Fannius) led the opposition, even though after carefully examining the proposal they found little to criticize.[11] The law confiscated no land, forced no landowner to sell, and used money from the eastern provinces to pay for the program. Yet they resisted any innovation or challenge to the status quo, which had been handed down from their forefathers and which institutionalized the senate's primacy and power.[12] Nor were they willing to use Rome's wealth to help the poor with government handouts, thus rewarding lazy citizens. By their reasoning, if the provincial tribute could not cover these new public expenditures, then the treasury would have to supply the rest, possibly leading to a huge deficit, a dramatic rise in property taxes, and the bankruptcy of Rome.[13] And they had another reason to resist: as pragmatic politicians they understood what the bill's passage could mean for their enemies. It would mean victory for the hated Pompey after two years of *optimate* obstruction. It would be a political boon for Caesar, who, even though he was excluded from the two boards, would benefit from the power this law could bestow—for example, Caesar would gain the patronage by appointing board members. Anyone seated on one of the two boards would have great opportunities for profit (legally or illegally) and patronage in his own right. All those who received land would be indebted to those who passed the law, which meant that these new landowners or their descendants, wealthier thanks to Caesar's law, might one day be able to afford to return to Rome and vote for Caesar and his allies. Citizens granted land would rise into higher centuries in the centuriate assembly, enhancing the weight of their votes. Providing land for Pompey's soldiers meant that Pompey would have a loyal army that could spring to his defense if civil war once again threatened the state. Crassus's equestrian friends would also support the law, as equestrian expertise would be needed for the lucrative financial transactions involved in the state's acquisition of so much land; the equestrians would provide bankers, accountants, clerks, scribes, and surveyors to implement the law. Equestrian companies may already have bought Italian land in anticipation of hefty profits—when the law passed, they would sell that land to the state.

Caesar's enemies could not allow the matter to come to a vote because, despite *optimate* opposition, it became clear that a majority of the senate favored the law.[14] In the senate, though, the power to block a vote on a measure often proved greater than the power to pass a measure, and the bill's opponents were prepared to use any constitutional weapons available to them for this purpose.

Later in the month Caesar reconvened the senate, most likely on the earliest possible day. January 7, 8, 10, and 12 were marked with a *C* on the calendar, so the senate could not assemble on any of these days; January 9, 11, 13, 14, and 15 were available. Probably on January 9, then, after the usual preliminary festivities, Caesar rose on the north platform of the curia and made a brief speech reiterating the strengths of his plan and inviting house members to make suggestions or criticisms.[15] Caesar promised to alter or even delete any clause to which a senator objected. Caesar sat down in his curule chair and called on the senators seated to his left and to his right to speak on his proposal. He began with Crassus: "Speak, Marcus Crassus, what do you think we should do?" He then invited the other ranking members of the house to speak, before moving on to each senator in the ritual order he had established on New Year's Day. Many spoke in favor of the law; none spoke in opposition. Eventually Caesar turned to Cato; "Speak, Marcus Porcius, what do you think we should do?" Conspicuous in bare feet and with no tunic under his toga, Cato rose and began to employ the filibuster. Voicing no objection to specific clauses in the bill, he nevertheless repeatedly said that the proposal should be rejected as an attack on the republic, and that the senate should make no move to change Rome's current system.[16] He then talked on and on, not only about the matter at hand but about any subject that came to mind. When darkness fell, Caesar, who had remained silent during the monologue, was forced to adjourn that day's meeting. The next gathering of the senate (presumably January 11) would constitute an entirely new meeting, forcing Caesar to start again at the top of the roll with

Crassus before eventually making his way down to Cato. Cato could easily maintain his filibuster, since there were many days on which the senate could not meet. After January 11, only three more days in the month (13, 14, 15) could be used for senate meetings; January 16 through January 29 (the last day of the month) were all *comitial* days, on which the senate could not lawfully convene.[17] Once Cato talked out those last three days, Caesar lost his chance in January to gain senatorial approval for his measure.

Since possession of the *fasces* alternated between the consuls each month, on February 1 Bibulus took the rods and axes and along with them the power to call the senate into session. That month had twenty-two days available for senate meetings, but the *lex Pupia* required the house deal first with matters of foreign policy before moving on to any other issues.[18] While the senate discussed the disposition of governorships in the provinces, the reception of foreign envoys, and the state of the empire, the land law languished.[19]

By March the bill still had not come up for a vote in the senate. Caesar resumed possession of the *fasces* and convened a meeting on March 1 or March 2. The stalemate continued, as Cato once more exercised his right to unlimited speech.[20] It quickly became clear that he intended to speak until dark to prevent a vote on Caesar's motion. As Cato continued to talk out another session, Caesar finally could endure no more.[21] He called to his *lictors* and ordered them to arrest Cato. The dozen men converged on Cato and escorted him out of the chamber for the very short walk to the prison, just a few yards away.[22] On this day many in the crowd of people listening to the proceedings just outside the senate's open doors apparently were supporters of Cato, possibly stationed there for just such a moment. Sensing an opportunity to embarrass Caesar, Cato happily departed while calling out to his followers to continue the fight against the bill. Infuriated at seeing their hero emerge from the curia under arrest, the *boni* signaled their support by providing him an escort to the *carcer*.[23]

Caesar's enemies had forced him to adopt an extreme course of action to break the gridlock in the senate, but Caesar's exercise of consular power turned Cato into the victim, because he had been well within his sacred rights as a Roman senator to filibuster. The right of all senators to speak freely, to speak for whatever length of time deemed necessary on whatever topic deemed worthy, and to disagree with fellow senators and presiding magistrates, characterized true liberty. To force a senator to stop talking was intolerable; the consul's actions lent credence to the charges that Caesar and his allies planned to impose some sort of tyranny.

Cato had not exited the curia alone. Many senators, even some who normally opposed Cato, accompanied him out of the chamber. At first Caesar may have been surprised that so many were heading for the exits, but he was even more surprised that some of Pompey's backers were leaving in protest, including his former legate Marcus Petreius (pr. 64). Becoming angry, Caesar called to Petreius, saying that the meeting of the senate had not ended and that he as presiding officer had not properly dismissed its members. Petreius replied defiantly that he would rather go to jail with Cato than stay in the senate with Caesar.[24] Caesar may have initially expected Cato to appeal to a friendly tribune to gain his release but now, watching the house empty, Caesar realized that Cato would exploit the occasion and that as a result he, Caesar, was losing the propaganda war. Caesar could not allow Cato to use this potent political weapon to sway senatorial and public opinion, so he quietly ordered one of the tribunes to intervene by using the power of his office to free Cato.[25]

This episode proved analogous to that in 60, when the consul Celer allowed himself to be arrested and dragged to the *carcer* in an attempt to block a land law. In 60, Celer's continued resistance resulted in the matter being dropped. In 59, with a more determined proponent, the delay was only temporary. Caesar reconvened the senate and announced that he would waste no more time in trying to gain the senators' assistance and approval.[26] He had not wished to take his plan to the people and instead had invited the senate to work with him to improve the law. The senate's obstructionist conduct now left him no choice.

Caesar adjourned the meeting and, trailing his *lictors*, left the curia. He walked the few yards around the rim of the *comitium* and mounted the rostra directly south of the senate house. The rostra acted as the great stage from which city magistrates or their designees addressed the Roman people. It was the "point of intersection between senate and people."[27] Now standing on the twelve-foot-high podium crowded with monuments to Rome's illustrious heroes, Caesar symbolically faced south toward the people, with his back to the senate house (where many senators no doubt watched from the senate steps), and announced that he would convene a *contio* later that day on a matter of the utmost importance to his fellow citizens.[28] His heralds then went around the forum before fanning out to all corners of the city—to the densely populated Subura and Velabrum, and to the Aventine Hill. Caesar may have expected Cato's filibuster and may already have used his contacts in the city to warn those interested in the law's passage of a potential meeting. Advance notice would have allowed his poorer followers to make arrangements to be absent from their places of employment. Because Rome covered a relatively small piece of land, nearly everyone in the city lived within a mile of the forum, making it convenient for citizens, whether they lived on the Palatine, in the Carinae, or in the Subura, to participate in the Roman political system. The larger the crowd that materialized, the greater the popular pressure on the senators and therefore the greater the hope that they would be unwilling to oppose the measure out of fear of the multitude.

When the *contio* convened, Caesar invited his consular colleague Bibulus to join him on stage. This was not an unusual request; politicians often willingly faced their rivals on the rostra to argue their case. Bibulus accepted, and what followed was an open, public exchange between the two consuls who stood before the forum crowd. Caesar asked Bibulus to explain which of the law's provisions he found unacceptable, promising that they would be amended or eliminated. Bibulus did not respond directly, and in fact made no mention of the law itself. Instead he repeated the *optimate* mantra, proclaiming that he would tolerate no innovations during his year as consul.[29] Caesar encouraged the crowd to cheer for the measure, to demonstrate its popular support. "Do you want my law?" he asked.[30] The crowd loudly voiced its approval. Putting the pressure squarely on his colleague, Caesar informed the people that "you will have it if only Bibulus would end his opposition."[31] Bibulus refused to yield. Defiantly addressing the hostile mass, he reasserted his unwillingness to allow innovations during his consulship. Then, simultaneously demonstrating the obstructive powers of a senior magistrate in spite of massive public support and the limitations of Roman democracy, Bibulus stated, "You will not have this law this year, not even if *all* of you want it."[32] He descended from the rostra and left the forum with his entourage and supporters, undoubtedly accompanied by the jeers and taunts of his opponents.

Caesar now turned to Pompey and Crassus and called them up to the rostra to speak on behalf of the law.[33] There had been recent hints of a possible reconciliation between Pompey and Crassus and an alliance of both with Caesar, but now, standing on the rostra and speaking together in favor of legislation, the three, maybe for the first time, publicly manifested their new faction. Presumably each had prepared an oration for the occasion. Pompey began, providing a thorough examination of the law in a speech containing the detailed and complex information often furnished in addresses at *contiones*.[34] He began by appealing to justice. It was only fair, he said, that the soldiers who risked their lives to expand and defend the power of Rome should be rewarded for their efforts. In the process he clearly articulated major planks in the *populares*' "platform": the state must provide for society's less fortunate members and to that end the empire's wealth should be used to help not just the soldiers but also the poor in the city of Rome and in the Italian countryside. As Caesar had been doing since January, Pompey tried to demonstrate that this law was not innovative or unconstitutional and had even been supported by the senate in the past. He listed historical precedents for the law, referring to the *lex Plotia Agraria*, passed in the assembly and approved by the senate in 70 to provide land for his soldiers who had fought in Spain.[35] The soldiers had never received their rewards, likely because after being outvoted the bill's opponents had claimed that there was no money in the treasury for the project, thereby devising a way to block its implementation. Pompey made it clear to the crowd and to the bill's enemies that the same maneuver would not succeed in 59. Due to the influx of wealth from the east, an influx made possible through his and his men's efforts, there would be plenty of money to fund the new law. He drew cheers when he informed the assembly that he approved of each of the law's specific clauses and of the law as a whole.

When Pompey concluded, Caesar asked him a series of questions. Given his support for the bill, would he actively work on its behalf and against those obstructing its passage? Pompey replied that he would. If the opponents of the law employed violence to block the measure, would Pompey come to the aid of the people? Pompey, delighted with the crowd's obvious enthusiasm for the bill and support for himself, made another, shorter speech that ended with a vow: "If anyone raises a sword against this law, I will defend it with my sword and my shield too."[36]

Crassus followed, also voicing his support for the law. Caesar then formally announced that he would bring the measure before the people in the *comitia tributa*, which as consul he could summon.

Official promulgation of a law did not automatically mean that the people would get the chance to vote. In this instance, Bibulus refused to capitulate and employed the powers of his office to prevent a vote.[37] Using religious weapons for political purposes, he scheduled movable religious holidays and festivals on *comitial* days to prevent the assembly from meeting. If mistakes were made in the religious rituals during those celebrations, or if Bibulus claimed mistakes had been made, he could demand that the festival and religious procedure be repeated on future *C* days. He declared thanksgiving days to commemorate military victories, and such days precluded any political business. One thanksgiving was granted by Bibulus to Gaius Pomptinus (pr. 63) for a victory over the Allobroges in Gaul.[38] At the dinner the tribune Publius Vatinius (cos. 47) appeared in mourning to protest Bibulus's continuing obstruction. Finally, Bibulus employed what in modern politics would be called the "nuclear option" by pronouncing that all of the year's remaining *comitial* days were to be sacred and therefore political business could not be conducted.

Caesar could not allow this legislation to die as previous land laws had in the face of *optimate* opposition. If he proved unable to push this law through, its death would most likely be accompanied by the breakdown of the triumvirate and the destruction of his hopes for future political and military success. Accordingly, he decided to ignore Bibulus's obstructions and scheduled a vote on the *lex Julia Agraria* to take place in the *comitia tributa*. At least a *trinundinum* (twenty-four days) had to elapse from the time a magistrate officially proposed a law until the vote was taken.[39] Because a *comitial* day was necessary for a vote, the wait usually proved somewhat longer. Considering that the vote on Caesar's law took place in early April, the last day it could have been proposed was March 9, meaning 66 days after Caesar became consul. There were only two *comitial* days at the beginning of the month: April 3 and April 4. There followed a long gap before the next *comitial* day of April 24, by which time, Cicero informs us, the law had already been passed. April 3, however, was a market day (which could not be used for legislative assemblies), so the vote would take place April 4—at the Temple of Castor and Pollux.[40]

Lessons

In preparing for the crucial day Caesar demonstrated that he had learned from recent Roman history and from his own past mistakes. Between 133 and 59, blood was shed and people were murdered at assemblies, *contiones*, senate meetings, and trials on no fewer than thirty-four occasions.[41] In at least half of these instances politicians from both sides of the aisle forcibly seized control of the voting area, either to exclude or drive out their rivals before a vote took place or to stop the proceedings altogether. It became clearer with each new instance of violence that political decisions were often predetermined by tests of physical power between rival political groups.

Caesar had a ringside seat for a number of these violent episodes. On one occasion, while he was praetor in 62, he supported the efforts of the tribune Quintus Caecilius Metellus Nepos (cos. 57) to pass legislation directing Pompey to return from the east to complete the war against Catiline.[42] On the day of the vote, in January 62, Nepos came down into the forum escorted by mercenaries, gladiators, and slaves.[43] Nepos took a seat on the podium at the Temple of Castor and Pollux next to Caesar while his followers surrounded the temple and guarded its steps, as opponents of the bill, led by the tribunes Cato and Quintus Minucius Thermus, appeared. Nepos's men permitted only Cato, Thermus, and Cato's friend Munatius Rufus to mount the platform.[44] When Nepos ordered the clerk to read out the law, Cato, sitting on the tribunician bench between Nepos and Caesar's praetor's chair, interposed his veto by commanding the clerk to stop. Nepos took the text and continued to read, but Cato grabbed it out of his hands, at which point Nepos began to recite the decree from memory. When Thermus clapped a hand over Nepos's mouth, Nepos signaled his followers to attack with sticks and stones. A fight erupted in the forum, and initially Nepos's gang drove his enemies out. Cato took refuge inside the temple. Believing himself to be victorious, Nepos sent his mercenaries, gladiators, and slaves home (not being Roman citizens, they could not vote). When Nepos commenced the preliminary rituals necessary for a legislative assembly, his enemies returned with an even larger gang and forced Nepos, Caesar, and their followers from the forum. Nepos fled to the east to join Pompey. The normally law-and-order-minded Cato emerged from the temple and delivered a speech in praise of his supporters' violent actions.

But the senate was not finished. Later that same afternoon it passed the *senatus consultum ultimum* ("ultimate decree") proclaiming a state of emergency. Used at least four times since 121, an *s.c.u.* allowed the senate to declare martial law, which suspended liberties and judicial procedure and permitted the magistrates to use any means necessary to quell turmoil in the city.[45] In 62 this move not only retroactively provided legal cover for the tribunes' use of violence in the forum but also enabled the senate to move against Caesar by depriving him of his praetorship. At first Caesar attempted to ignore the decree by continuing to exercise his office, but after the senate threatened to use force he theatrically dismissed his six *lictors*, removed his praetor's insignia, and retired to his home. The next day Caesar's supporters arrived and vowed to stand with him against the senate. Throughout his career Caesar would demonstrate that he was willing to use any means necessary to acquire political power. Now he hesitated. Realizing that the senate at that moment possessed greater forces in Rome than his own and that its loyal consular army was stationed just north of the city, Caesar decided not to resort to a test of strength. Instead he showed the proper deference and contrition to the senate, which agreed to reinstate him.

The forum violence in January of 62 was directly connected to the forum violence in April of 59.[46] Cato and his allies were convinced by their victory over

Caesar and Pompey's associate Nepos that they possessed the strength to block anyone threatening senatorial authority. Ever certain of the righteousness of his cause, Cato became even less willing to compromise with his adversaries, which helps to explain why he and his faction torpedoed Pompey's agrarian and eastern proposals, spearheaded efforts to deny the equestrian appeal for a reduction in their contracts, and filibustered Caesar's request to declare his candidacy for the consulship *in absentia*.

Cato's intransigence, partly inspired by his successes in 62, would help Caesar recognize the value of advance planning, of forming a strategic alliance, and of securing physical control of the assembly space. Nepos, presumably with Caesar's help, had resorted to violence, but their enemies' ability to quickly regroup and counterattack with superior strength won the day, allowing them to prevent passage of Nepos's proposed legislation and temporarily deprive Caesar of his office. Caesar understood that Nepos's preparations had been insufficient: his men were probably outnumbered, they were unskilled in urban warfare, and they had little if any formal military experience. Nepos and Caesar, even with their military training, probably failed to spend time making plans in advance of the vote or drilling their supporters on how to conduct themselves.

To a man of Caesar's character, being forced by his senatorial enemies, and in particular by Cato, into a humiliating capitulation must have been a serious blow. No doubt three years later, in 59, the disgrace remained fresh in his mind. Although Caesar's opponents had not threatened violence thus far in 59, Caesar was well aware of the possibility, and he therefore knew that on April 4 he must be prepared to strike with overwhelming force. He must not allow his enemies to hold a numerical superiority, nor could he rely on random citizens or slaves or even gladiators to do the fighting. Furthermore, an initial victory would not be enough; he must not permit his opponents to regroup as they had in 62.

In 59 Caesar devised a scheme beyond anything yet seen, a scheme that would set the pattern for even greater violence in the years that followed. Caesar would employ Roman soldiers—Pompey's veterans—who had years of training and combat experience. Large numbers of them would be brought from elsewhere in Italy to the capital to vote for the land law and to deliver for Caesar a devastating demonstration of strength. Officers and centurions may also have been recruited to provide a chain of command and to maintain military discipline. Their general, Pompey, would be present as well. As in 62, the vote in 59 would take place at the Temple of Castor and Pollux, and Caesar now understood the tactics needed to secure that space. The occasion would mark only the second time that soldiers had been brought into the city in this type of political situation, but its implications were much more consequential than the first.[47] Timing, as always, was crucial. Caesar would have been well aware that April 4 marked the beginning of the Megalesian Games, a two-day event (April 4 and April 10) commemorating the original arrival of the Great Goddess in Rome from Anatolia (on April 4, 204) and the dedication of her first temple in the city (April 10, 204).[48] He may have strategized that holding the vote on the holiday provided by the games would help the triumvirs, because sympathetic voters would find it easier to participate than they would on a workday. More importantly, the games could provide cover for the sudden appearance of thousands of Pompey's veterans in the city.

Spring 59 BC/695 AUC

April 4

Before leading the soldiers to the forum in the predawn hours of April 4, Caesar and Pompey must have made clear to the men what was required of them. In the darkness, Pompey's veterans occupied strategic positions throughout the forum, in the area directly in front of the temple, on the two stairs that led to the podium, and on the podium itself. The triumvirate had secured control over the voting area, and when Bibulus attempted to halt the proceedings, Pompey's veterans sprang into action. They threw Bibulus and Cato from the podium and dumped a basket of manure on Bibulus's head. They beat the loyal tribunes and *lictors* and smashed the consular *fasces*. From their elevated positions the veterans hurled projectiles down onto Bibulus's followers, and then with military precision and possibly in battle formation they charged, pummeling their enemies and driving them out of the forum. It was all over very quickly. Caesar had learned from the mistakes of 62: his supporters were more numerous and were ex-soldiers who outfought and overwhelmed Bibulus's men. The junior consul could stop the vote neither by constitutional means nor by violence.

Thorough planning and discipline ensured that the operation was a success. Rocks and other objects had been gathered, and the basket to humiliate Bibulus had been prepared in advance. Bibulus was allowed to progress to the temple so he could be made a figure of ridicule. Pompey's men were clearly under orders not to kill—despite the violence, no one died. The men also managed to carry out what must have been another part of the plan: they destroyed Bibulus's *fasces*, a symbolic act representing an end of his consular power to block the law.

Lastly, they prevented Bibulus's men from regrouping and returning to the forum.

The overwhelming display of force frightened the triumvirate's opponents and allowed the people to pass the *lex Julia Agraria.*[49] Furthermore, as the fear persisted for months thereafter, the triumvirate was able to ratify their legislative agenda. And the events of April 4, 59, would serve as a model for others to emulate in the coming decade.

April 5

After Caesar pushed his legislation through the assembly, Bibulus attempted to have it annulled. He summoned the senate (the only time he is attested doing this) to meet on April 5 and, possibly sporting bruises suffered the day before, demanded that Caesar's actions be condemned and the new law invalidated because it had been passed amid violence that prevented the consul and the tribunes from raising the proper religious and political objections to halt the proceedings.[50] He argued that less significant breaches of the peace and violations of the law had met with censure in the past. He may have even demanded that the senate declare a *senatus consultum ultimum*. Unfortunately for Bibulus, when he asked each senator to express his opinions on the situation, none dared to speak openly against the triumvirate's actions or to vote for an *s.c.u.* The land law was overwhelmingly popular with Rome's citizens and, more critically, with Pompey's veterans, who were at that moment roaming around the forum just to the south of the curia. Senators looking out the front doors of the chamber would have seen the ex-soldiers on the senate steps and beyond. And any senator brave enough to support Bibulus and oppose the land law could have dreaded seeing something else: his name published and posted around the city by nightfall. Caesar had already shown a willingness to use violence to gain his ends and likely would not hesitate to do so again. Despite Bibulus's pleas, the terrified senators declined to act. If they were present, even the three loyal tribunes, having been injured the day before, refused to intervene. The law stood.

When this gambit failed, Bibulus tried an apparently novel approach and retired to his house on the Palatine; he would not reappear in public for eight months, until December 29, the last day of the year.[51] The friendly tribunes promptly joined the consul in self-imposed seclusion. But Bibulus did not give up the fight against Caesar; instead, for the remainder of the year, he spent his time employing *obnuntiatio*, a ceremony designed to determine the will of the gods.[52] At night Bibulus and his friends watched the heavens outside his home. If they spotted an unfavorable sign in the sky, which they always did, Bibulus's attendants recorded it. Whenever Caesar planned on holding any type of assembly or vote, Bibulus sent a subordinate, possibly a *lictor*, with a formal notice declaring that due to the unfavorable omens Bibulus had observed in the previous night's sky, all political gatherings were forbidden under Roman law and by the sacred rituals of the Roman religion. If Caesar or any other official ignored the notice, any law passed or decision ratified on such a day would automatically be null and void.

The rules of *obnuntiatio* were governed by the Aelian-Fufian Law enacted sometime during the mid-second century.[53] According to Cicero *obnuntiatio* could be used as a weapon by conservatives to thwart the efforts of popular champions.[54] The exact nature of the law and the ritual engaged to apply it remain obscure. It is possible the Romans were themselves confused about the procedure.[55] As a result, partisan politics again largely dictated how Bibulus's actions were interpreted. His supporters believed that Caesar had already broken Roman law by using violence on April 4 and that he continued to do so by disregarding the will of the gods expressed through the negative omens witnessed by Bibulus.[56] In their view Bibulus's actions annulled all Caesar's laws passed during the remainder of 59.[57] This could provide a religious basis for legal attacks on Caesar and his legislation once he left office.[58] For their part, Caesar's followers argued that Bibulus had not followed proper procedures for *obnuntiatio* and therefore could not hinder the political process. For the formula to be valid, they said, the magistrate who witnessed the omen had to follow a ritual that included saying specific words while standing at a specific place at a specific time before a political meeting began. Furthermore, Bibulus had not proclaimed the *obnuntiatio* in person, despite a requirement to do so; instead, an assistant delivered and announced his edicts—thus rendering them inoperative.[59]

Because Caesar and his allies ignored Bibulus and his pronouncements, Bibulus's retreat on April 5 (and the continuing threat of Pompey's veterans who were still in the city) left them free to control the political process. Cato and others had spent more than two years frustrating Pompey, Crassus, Caesar, the equestrians, the veterans, and the poor citizens of Rome, and although they had won some temporary victories, their efforts eventually backfired. Their obstruction had produced a coalition that now dominated the city. The triumvirs' enemies had been driven from the political field, generating lampoons that circulated in the city and caused great amusement.[60]

At the same time Romans began jokingly referring to the year 695 AUC not as the year of the consulship of Caesar and Bibulus but as the year of Julius and Caesar.[61]

The Triumvirs in Power

Having used violence to break the gridlock that had plagued Rome's government, Caesar delivered a legislative program that rewarded his partners, friends, constituents, and, ultimately, himself. Laws and decisions were ratified in quick succession in the next two months. First the triumvirs implemented the *lex Julia Agraria*. The law contained a "curse" clause requiring each senator to take an oath, possibly within five days, vowing obedience to the new legislation or else face a fine and exile.[62] Celer, Cato, and Cato's ardent supporter Marcus Favonius held out for a time in protest of the law and Caesar's methods.[63] Cicero persuaded them to relent so they could remain in Rome and continue to oppose the triumvirs; on the last possible day, they finally swore the oath—no doubt to Caesar's great amusement. The triumvirs reaped patronage opportunities by distributing the potentially lucrative supervisory and bureaucratic positions to their supporters, most notably those spots on the two boards created by the law.[64] The law's execution also won the triumvirate the support of those eternally grateful, newly landed citizens, and the equestrian companies, who were about to realize an economic windfall.

On April 24 or 26 the triumvirs passed a law officially recognizing Ptolemy XII as king of Egypt, and friend and ally of Rome.[65] Recognition had not come cheap for Ptolemy, who disbursed an enormous bribe of almost six thousand talents to Caesar and his friends to pass the legislation.[66] Roman bankers loaned much of this money to the king, just one illustration of the colossal wealth possessed by the equestrians.[67] In Rome there were many direct links between domestic programs and foreign policy; in this instance Caesar used some of Ptolemy's bribe to finance the land purchases prescribed by the *lex Julia*. He also made sure to siphon off money for himself, however, and Ptolemy's payoff in this way made Caesar rich in his own right for the first time in his life. Presumably he finally paid off his debts, particularly to Crassus. He also used his newfound wealth to increase his influence with the public by sponsoring shows, games, and animal hunts.[68] And he enjoyed the wealth in personal ways, famously giving a pearl worth six million *sesterces* to his lover Servilia.[69]

At roughly the same time or possibly on the same bill, Caesar or the tribune Publius Vatinius passed legislation sanctioning all of Pompey's arrangements in the east.[70] Thus, after more than two years of effort, Pompey finally saw both of his cherished proposals enacted into law. Crassus's publican allies were also happy now that they were allowed to farm the taxes of the new provinces.[71] Those fortunate enough to own shares in the publican companies, including possibly senators such as Caesar and Vatinius, would realize a giant profit. Crucially for the future of Caesar's legislation, the tax revenues received by the treasury would be used to help finance the *lex Julia*.

In this period Caesar or Vatinius passed a law altering the contract awarded to the *publicani* for the Asian taxes, reducing the amount they owed the treasury by one-third.[72] The measure had been blocked for more than a year by Cato and his allies in the senate. The first tribe to vote on this law in the assembly was the Terentina; the equestrian leader Gnaeus Plancius, who had publicly and bitterly denounced the senate and Cato's obstruction of the measure in 60, belonged to that tribe and appropriately cast the first ballot.[73] The law provided Crassus with a significant financial windfall, as he undoubtedly owned shares in the companies involved. For Caesar and Vatinius the law's passage meant increased support from the equestrian order and possibly a great deal of money. It is conceivable that they had been offered shares in the tax companies as an inducement to pass the necessary legislation, or they may have engaged in "insider trading" in anticipation of the law's success.[74] Either way, passage would have drastically increased the value of the stock they probably now possessed.

In late April Caesar proposed a second agrarian law to divide up the state-owned land on the Stella Plain in Campania.[75] The law would bestow seven acres on poor Roman citizens who had at least three children; its supporters estimated the fertile plain could support twenty thousand Roman families. Cicero, an opponent, argued that the numbers were wildly exaggerated.[76] Even worse, he and others feared, since the land would no longer generate revenue for the state, the law could bankrupt the treasury while simultaneously making Caesar and his friends more popular with the people. Despite objections, the measure passed at the end of May.[77] Caesar had incorporated a consequential "curse" clause in this bill, too: all candidates for office in 58 must swear to uphold the new Julian law or be barred from running. Caesar wanted to ensure that once he left office his successors would not attempt to alter or abolish it.[78]

In Rome, women, although they could not vote or hold office, often exercised considerable influence behind the scenes as advisors, envoys, and mediators.[79] Marriage was often a political tool, used to cement an alliance between senatorial families. Sometime between April 26 and May 3, Pompey wed Caesar's daughter, Julia.[80] According to Cicero, the "sudden marriage" shocked

Roman society because of the great age difference between the two (he was forty-six, she was still in her teens), and because Julia had previously been betrothed to Servilius Caepio.[81] The marriage may have been precipitated by whispers that Pompey disliked the methods Caesar employed to achieve their shared goals.[82] Pompey, who had always been sensitive about his public image, may have worried that his "approval rating" had declined as a result of the April 4 violence. Caesar moved quickly to strengthen the relationship. Gnaeus Pompeius of Picenum, whose family first held the consulship only in 141, had now married into an illustrious patrician house.

Although most marriages in the senatorial class were arranged for purely political reasons, this one proved to be unusual, as Pompey and Julia fell in love. According to Plutarch, Pompey adored his young wife, spending all his time with her while ignoring politics in the forum.[83] This happy marriage ensured close relations between Julia's new husband and her father for the foreseeable future. To signify the closer connection, Caesar began to call on Pompey first in the senate rather than Crassus, a break with tradition, because once the ritual order had been set on January 1 it was usually observed throughout the year. Caesar also designated Pompey as his heir in his will.[84]

At around the same time, Caesar married for the third and last time.[85] Divorced from his previous wife, Pompeia, Caesar now wed Calpurnia, the daughter of Lucius Calpurnius Piso Caesoninus. Piso had already been praetor and intended to run for the office of consul for the year 58. His chances increased dramatically thanks to this marriage alliance with the current consul. The union was vital for Caesar as well, since it would be imperative for him to have a close ally in Rome's highest office once his term expired.

Trial, Transfer, and the *Lex Vatinia*

Although all of these activities were significant, two other incidents in the spring of 59 ultimately shaped the last years of the republic. First, with backing by Caesar, Pompey, and Crassus, Publius Clodius Pulcher became a plebian after nearly two years of effort; he would later be elected tribune. Second, the *lex Vatinia* was enacted, providing Caesar with the proconsulship he had always coveted.

Clodius's transfer happened as the result of a trial that culminated almost immediately after Bibulus retired to his home. Sometime between April 6 and April 11, Cicero rose in court to deliver his closing arguments in the defense of his former consular colleague Gaius Antonius (cos. 63).[86] As proconsul in Macedonia (62–60) Antonius was purported to have committed numerous crimes in his province, and he had been recalled to stand trial.[87] The case was tried at the southeastern end of the forum in a small amphitheater known as the Aurelian Steps. Three rows of curved raised wooden benches accommodated the prosecution, the accused and his defense attorneys, and the jury, which usually consisted of fifty men (two-thirds were equestrians, the rest senators). The steps lay near the Temple of Castor and Pollux, whence, according to Cicero, the gods watched over the venue to ensure that justice was done.[88] The praetor Gnaeus Cornelius Lentulus Clodianus presided over the trial from a low tribunal facing the steps. Crowds of people often made the journey down to the lower forum to participate in one of Rome's most popular spectator sports—observing court cases. People stood around the steps or looked on from the nearby temples or the multistory basilicas that surrounded the court on three sides. This case likely drew a large audience, because it featured a prominent defendant from a famous family. A bigger draw was Cicero. He was Rome's greatest orator and advocate, and many citizens were willing to spend hours listening to his soaring eloquence and piercing wit. This time, despite Cicero's efforts, the jury found Antonius guilty, and he went into exile on the Greek island of Cephallenia.[89]

This trial was in many ways typical of Rome's political game, in which senators frequently used the courts to attack and, they hoped, convict rivals. During the decades of the 60s and 50s, 175 known trials were held involving prominent individuals.[90] Even the most powerful politicians could be dragged into court: during this twenty-year period, twenty-three trials involved thirteen former consuls or consuls-elect. Five resulted in convictions. The stakes were high: a guilty verdict could mean a hefty fine, confiscation of property, and, as it did for Gaius Antonius, exile from Italy. In this vein Cicero had warned his brother Quintus that the weapons of their political enemies "will be lawsuits not swords."[91]

The significance of this episode was not Antonius's exile but his trial, and Cicero's summation in particular, for they began a sequence of events that would help define the violence and bloodshed of the 50s. As Cicero rose to speak between the Aurelian Steps and the praetor's tribunal, in front of the jury and a considerable number of onlooking Romans, he decided not to use his closing argument merely to defend his client. He saw an opportunity to speak directly to a large group of his fellow citizens on a topic of great national importance—specifically, the wickedness of the triumvirate.[92] Previously his rants against Caesar and his allies had apparently been confined to private conversations or correspondence with trusted friends such as Atticus. But he was probably in Rome on April 4 and was possibly an eyewitness to the violence that had occurred in the forum just below his Palatine home. Outraged by this event and by Bibulus's subsequent retirement from the senate on April 5, he considered both to be assaults on the Roman constitution and the majesty of Rome's highest office. At Gaius Antonius's trial, possibly for the first time, Cicero expressed his grievances openly.[93] He attacked Caesar, blaming him for instigating Antonius's trial.[94] As part of a diatribe concerning the current political situation, he denounced the triumvirate and decried the loss of freedom in Rome, especially in the senate, and the concentration of power in the hands of three men.[95] Cicero exclaimed that these "three out of control men" threatened the Roman state.[96]

As usual, Cicero's oratorical abilities were greeted with cheers and applause, but his outburst may have come as a surprise to Caesar (who was present) and Pompey, both of whom ostensibly enjoyed good relationships with Cicero and had tried repeatedly since late 60 to gain his support. Cicero had now injured Caesar and his allies by attacking their power openly before a large gathering in the forum, in the heart of Rome. His words would certainly spread through the city and cast the triumvirate in a malevolent light. Cicero's eloquent expression of deep dissatisfaction combined with similar expressions in the future might turn public opinion against the triumvirate. Caesar did not visibly react to Cicero's speech.[97] But Caesar usually punished his political rivals, moving without warning to minimize the danger to himself by preventing a potential target from preparing a defense.

Caesar had the power to quickly finish off an enemy in Rome, and he already had a weapon: Publius Clodius Pulcher. A member of one of Rome's ancient patrician families, Clodius was notorious for his good looks, wild ways, and popular inclinations that had often put him at odds with the more respectable elements of the conservative senate. As a young legate he helped lead a mutiny in the army of his own brother-in-law, Lucullus, in 68. But he was better known as the central figure in the Bona Dea ("Good Goddess") religious scandal (62–61). Once each year secret ceremonies were held to honor the Bona Dea, in which only women could participate. In 62 Pompeia, as the wife of Caesar the Pontifex Maximus, conducted the rituals in the Domus Publica. Clodius wished to seduce Pompeia (or had already done so) and, knowing that all the men of the household would be absent—including Pompeia's husband—he slipped into the residence of the chief priest dressed as a woman. A servant girl recognized him, however, and he swiftly fled the scene. To many Romans this violation of the goddess's sacred rites threatened to bring divine wrath on the empire. To others it looked like an opportunity, and Clodius's enemies came out in force to bring him to trial on a charge of sacrilege. Crassus intervened. Using a slave as an intermediary, he brought the jurors to his house over the course of two evenings and there enticed them with gifts of money, offers to pay their debts, and the promise of introductions to certain young men and women from families of good standing. Regardless of the evidence, and to the shock of Cicero and others, the jury voted 31 to 25 in favor of acquittal.

Despite the Bona Dea scandal, Caesar had maintained good relations with Clodius. He testified at the trial but refused to accuse Clodius or his wife of adultery; nor did he sue Clodius in a separate trial, although this was his right as an aggrieved husband. He did divorce Pompeia, though, and when asked why he had done so if he believed her to be blameless, Caesar replied that his wife must always be "above suspicion."[98] Whatever the true nature of Clodius and Pompeia's relationship, Caesar made a pragmatic decision to maintain a link to Clodius, whose wealth, oratorical ability, and connections inside and outside the senate made him a valuable political ally. Caesar's ambition outweighed his desire for vengeance over his wife's possible infidelity.[99]

Cicero had been friends with Clodius until, urged on by his wife, Terentia, he had testified against Clodius, thereby undermining Clodius's alibi.[100] Even though Clodius secured an acquittal, Cicero's betrayal marked the beginning of one of Rome's great political feuds, lasting unabated until Clodius's death in 52. Clodius vowed to take revenge on those responsible for bringing him to trial, especially Cicero, whose testimony had been so detrimental to his case. Vengeance, however, required power. Still only thirty years old in 61, Clodius, as a patrician, would not be eligible for the consulship for a decade. Unwilling to wait, he decided to try a different, quicker route, determining that becoming tribune offered him the swiftest path to political influence. As demonstrated by a long line of tribunes dating back to Tiberius Gracchus, appealing to the people in the tribal assembly could bring immense power very quickly to a popular politician. Although Clodius was old enough for the tribunate, there remained one small obstacle: only plebians could be tribunes—as a patrician he was ineligible. After returning to Rome in January of 60 from a brief stint as quaestor in Sicily, Clodius had tried, unsuccessfully, to win a transfer from the patrician to the plebian order.[101]

Then the trial of Gaius Antonius took place. Caesar and Pompey were so incensed with Cicero's speech that they decided to act in their roles as priests to grant Clodius's request for a transfer. Crassus, that ally of Clodius's who had bribed the jury in the Bona Dea trial, may have lent his support as well. Caesar summoned the little-used *comitia curiata* on the same day Antonius's trial concluded (between April 6 and April 11).[102] Cicero finished speaking at the trial in the sixth hour of the day (roughly between 12:08 and 1:13 in the afternoon); the procedure to transfer Clodius took place in the *comitia curiata* in the ninth hour (roughly between 3:23 and 4:28 p.m.).[103] Individual *lictors* represented each of the thirty *curiae,* so the whole population did not have to be informed or participate—this mattered in a case where speed was of the essence. Either in the *comitium* or on the Capitoline Hill, Caesar in his capacity as Pontifex Maximus sanctioned the ceremony and officiated while Pompey assisted as *augur*, confirming that no evil omens had been sighted. They then carried out the religious ceremonies necessary to convey Clodius to the plebian order, and the thirty *lictors* authorized the transfer. Publius Fonteius, a plebian two years younger than Clodius, officially adopted him and then promptly had him emancipated. Caesar and Pompey later carried a *lex curiata* in the senate confirming the transfer.[104] A plebian at last, Clodius announced shortly before April 19 that in the July elections he would run for the office of tribune for the year 58.[105]

Cicero had left Rome immediately after the pronouncement of Antonius's verdict and learned of these events only while on vacation. On April 19, on his way to Formiae, Cicero encountered the younger Gaius Scribonius Curio (tr. 50) at Tres Tabernae. No friend, Curio happily became the first to inform Cicero that Clodius was now a plebian and would run for the office of tribune.[106] Cicero, naturally, did not welcome the news. His letters from this point on have one common thread, an almost pathological fear of Clodius ("tell me what P. Clodius is doing").[107] Atticus, as Cicero's representative, met privately with Clodius three times in Rome to discover his plans and work to repair the relationship.[108] Atticus also enlisted Clodia, one of Clodius's three sisters, to act as a liaison to her brother.[109] Cicero makes it clear that he had other friends in Rome working along similar lines. Nothing worked; Clodius quickly disabused Cicero of any notion of reconciliation and spent the rest of the year issuing threats against the orator.[110]

Caesar had no doubt that as tribune Clodius would use his power at least in part to seek revenge against Cicero. Facilitating the transfer was a fitting way for Caesar and Pompey to punish Cicero for speaking out against the triumvirate and for spurning their earlier offers to join their alliance. It also provided a salient warning to others that opposing the triumvirate came at a price. Moreover, Clodius would likely prove to be one of the strong backers the triumvirs needed to have in place for the following year. Although Clodius was unpredictable, his transfer had been accomplished by Caesar and Pompey and, presumably, Crassus.[111] If the triumvirs' acts were declared invalid at some point in the future, Clodius's transition to the plebian order would be nullified, so even if Clodius could not be controlled or trusted, at the very least as tribune he would be a powerful defender of the legislation of 59—if only to safeguard his own position.

More significant to the fate of the republic than Clodius's transfer to the plebian order was the passage of the *lex Vatinia* by early June.[112] Its sponsor, the tribune Publius Vatinius, had already passed legislation favorable to the triumvirate and to the people.[113] Now that all opposition had been routed, he won the approval of the tribal assembly for a measure providing Caesar with an extraordinary command similar to those bestowed on Pompey by the *lex Gabinia* and *lex Manilia* in 67 and 66. After his consulship expired Caesar would not survey the paths and forests of Italy, as his enemies had intended. Instead he would become proconsul of the provinces of Illyria and Cisalpine Gaul (northern Italy) for five years, with an army of three legions and the right to name his own legates. A short time after the law passed, Metellus Celer died; according to vicious gossip, he had been poisoned by his wife Clodia while she carried on an affair with the poet Gaius Valerius Catullus. Not only was one of Pompey's most powerful enemies gone, but his province of Transalpine Gaul was now in need of a governor. At the urging of Pompey and Caesar's new father-in-law, Piso, the senate passed a decree granting Caesar that province and an additional legion.[114]

Administering these lands would provide Caesar with almost limitless opportunities to advance his career. A proconsulship offered an avenue to tremendous wealth extorted from Rome's subjects and newly conquered peoples. After having spent most of his adult life deeply in debt, Caesar would have an opportunity to acquire wealth to add to that he had already accumulated as consul. The power to appoint his legates offered Caesar multiple opportunities for patronage, because positions on a general's staff were highly coveted due to the many military and economic opportunities they provided for aspiring politicians.[115] In addition, as Gaius Sallustius Crispus observed, "Caesar wanted a new war to demonstrate his excellence."[116] These particular provinces offered Caesar potential for military glory. To the north of Transalpina and Cisalpina lay Gaul, whose numerous tribal conflicts and migrations created an unpredictable situation that might call for Caesar's intervention. The length of Caesar's term, five years, would provide sufficient time for extended military campaigns. Caesar's future province of Cisalpine Gaul was significant for other reasons.

Cisalpine Gaul contained a large concentration of Roman citizens who could be recruited or drafted into Caesar's army. Inheriting four legions in 58—three (VII, VIII, IX) at Aquileia in Cisalpine Gaul and one (X) in Transalpine Gaul—Caesar would recruit six new legions by 53 (V, VI, XI, XII, XIII, XIV); five consisted of Roman citizens from Cisalpine Gaul.[117] No doubt the publican companies that outfitted Rome's armies would support such an expansion. Cisalpine Gaul also positioned Caesar in close proximity to Rome. He would be able to monitor the political situation in Rome and, through letters and the continuous delivery of Gallic cash, would continue to influence affairs in the capital.

Furthermore, as proconsul Caesar would continue to enjoy immunity from prosecution. While consul in 59 Caesar could not be brought to trial on any charge relating to his time in office or for transgressions he may have committed before he took office. The constitutionality of Caesar's laws was debated at the time and was generally a matter of partisan interpretation. Caesar's enemies maintained that as consul Caesar had broken the law on numerous occasions, first by employing violence against his political opponents during the vote on the original land law and then by ignoring Bibulus's religious objections while passing subsequent legislation.[118] Consequently, they maintained, not one of Caesar's laws was valid. Once Caesar's term ended, he would ordinarily lose his immunity, and his adversaries believed his transgressions would provide a fruitful line of attack in the courts.[119] But the *lex Vatinia* altered these calculations. Moving from the consulship at the end of 59 to the proconsulship at the beginning of 58, Caesar would retain his legal immunity; he could not be prosecuted while absent on the business of the republic.[120] Foes such as Cato would spend the rest of the decade trying to relieve him of his command.

Summer 59 BC/695 AUC

The Reaction

Beginning with a letter from April 16 or 17, 59, Cicero paints a depressing picture of Romans deprived of their rights and terrorized into silence by Caesar and his allies. He constantly refers to the "tyranny" of the "three" who now ruled Rome.[121] He protested that the republic was dead, freedom had been suppressed, the city was silent, and resistance was futile.[122] According to Cicero, not just Rome but all of Italy hated the triumvirs.[123]

It may not be true that power always corrupts, but it is often true "that power reveals."[124] Historians frequently portray Caesar as the epitome of the charming, cultured nobleman, but as he had demonstrated on April 4, he could be ruthless. In 59, for the first time in his life in possession of great power, he demonstrated a willingness to use that power. In the senate he openly promised to crush anyone who stood in his way.[125] When Lucius Licinius Lucullus spoke out against Caesar in the house, a sharp exchange ensued.[126] Caesar threatened to haul Lucullus into court, whereupon Lucullus dropped to his knees and begged forgiveness. This may have been a piece of political theater designed by Lucullus to highlight the dictatorial nature of Caesar and his consulship, but afterward Lucullus retired to his villa and gardens outside the city on the Pincian Hill and never participated again in Roman politics.[127] Other senators began avoiding meetings as well.[128] Some did so as a form of protest against the triumvirate, others due to fear of renewed violence. When Caesar questioned an elderly senator named Considius about the sparse attendance, Considius blamed the fear of violence. Why then, Caesar asked, did Considius appear in the curia? Because, he replied, "I am too old to fear death."[129] Cicero noted sadly that many frightened *optimates* had given up the struggle and retired from political battle.[130] He bemoaned the fact that they would rather train their fish than fight for the conservative cause in the senate. He began referring to these shirkers pejoratively as the "Tritons of the Fishponds."[131]

Cicero was out of the city for much of April and May, however, so the situation may not have been as bleak as he imagined. It becomes clear from other sources and even from Cicero himself that growing dissatisfaction with the triumvirate began to manifest itself in increasingly public ways. Criticism of the triumvirate at private dinner parties and social gatherings eventually moved into the open at the theater and the gladiatorial shows staged in and around the forum that provided venues for expression of political sentiment.[132] There were no polls or other means to gauge the feelings of the people, but behavior at these festivities sometimes offered a glimpse into prevailing public opinion.

Gaius Scribonius Curio became one of the first individuals to speak out openly against the triumvirate, presumably at a *contio* by invitation of a city magistrate.[133] Curio, the son of the consul of 76, was the leader of a group of younger nobles who had not yet entered the senate and, although not allied with the *boni*, were nevertheless opposed to the triumvirate.[134] People cheered Curio's defiance.[135] During the Games of Apollo (July 7–14), the crowd greeted Caesar with cold silence when he entered the theater, whereas shortly afterward Curio arrived to thunderous applause, even from the equestrians in the front row.[136] In contrast, allies of the triumvirate, such as Aulus Gabinius, an adherent of Pompey who sponsored a gladiatorial event in the forum in anticipation of his run for the consulship later in the year, were booed.[137]

People generally considered Pompey to be the senior partner of the triumvirate, in part because his soldiers executed the coalition's violent policies; as a result he took the brunt of the abuse. Senators, including many notable *consulares* who had supported him during the 60s, now turned against him. Many alleged that he aimed to establish a monarchy or dictatorship. At one theatrical performance in the forum, the actor Diphilus pointed at Pompey in the audience and quoted a line from an unknown tragedy: "To our misery you are Great"—a direct and mocking reference to Pompey's cognomen, "Magnus."[138] He followed with other anti-Pompeian lines, prompting the entire audience to respond with prolonged applause and demands for encores. Some of the attacks occurred while Pompey was absent at Capua, most likely supervising the distribution of land under the second land law, but Caesar and presumably others sent him letters apprising him of the situation.

Caesar too became the object of public criticism and ridicule. Enemies mocked his receding hairline and his penchant for fancy clothing.[139] One early incident in Caesar's career always provided their main target, however.[140] In 81, at the age of 19, Caesar had served as legate in the army of the governor of Asia, Marcus Minucius Thermus (pr. 81). Thermus ordered Caesar to proceed to Bithynia and meet with King Nicomedes IV to arrange for a fleet to aid in the Roman attack on the Greek city of Mytilene. Caesar received such a warm welcome from the king and spent such a long time at his court that a rumor soon began circulating about the true nature of their relationship and Caesar's sexual preferences. Although Caesar vigorously denied the rumor and later slept with as many women as possible to disprove it, his political enemies used the episode against him both in person and in print.[141] Many senators published explicit verses about Caesar in the king's bed.[142] The public attacks became even more pointed during Caesar's consulship, demonstrating that, despite Cicero's complaints, free speech still lived in Rome.

Maybe the most eloquent and spiteful attacks came from Bibulus. While still in his house watching for omens, Bibulus issued a constant stream of edicts, pamphlets, and printed speeches that were published or posted in the city, around Italy, and all over the Roman world.[143] His edicts reminded Caesar and the people that during a sacred period, while Bibulus surveyed the skies, no political business could be transacted.[144] His published speeches denounced Caesar and Pompey. People stopped to read his humorous, scathing, and profane lampoons posted around Rome, and wrote them down to peruse and share later.[145] The large crowds who paused to study the statements created traffic jams in the very narrow Roman streets.[146] Like many of Caesar's enemies since 81, Bibulus used Nicomedes as a line of attack. Bibulus described Caesar as "the Queen of Bithynia . . . who previously wanted to be with a king, but now wants to be a king."[147] Many commended Bibulus, and his standing in public opinion rose accordingly. So clever was the invective that Cicero labeled these attacks "Archilochian," after the seventh-century Greek Archilochus of Paros who was renowned for skewering his enemies in his poetry.[148]

Caesar and Pompey became less popular for a number of reasons after April 59. Many poorer citizens had hoped to benefit from Caesar's land laws. The number of grants made by the first law is unknown; the second provided Campanian land for 20,000 male Roman citizens with three or more children. Although the numbers may seem large, it is doubtful that they provided for all the disadvantaged citizens of the capital. In 45 Caesar found that 320,000 Roman citizens qualified for the free food distributed by the state.[149] After reforms, the number dropped to 150,000. The number of veterans and other citizens who received land in 59 can only be guessed at, but probably was not more than 50,000.[150] The two land laws, then, did not aid a majority of Rome's poorest citizens. Cicero predicted that Caesar and Pompey would lose the backing of those left behind.[151] For citizens who had voted for Caesar and for the tribunes such as Vatinius, disillusion may have led to bitterness and eventually to open hostility in the forum, at the games, and in the theater. Middle-class Romans may never have been enthusiastic supporters of Caesar and his allies. They would have been opposed to government programs that, as they saw it, drained Rome's treasury to help the idle and lazy poor. Caesar's use of violence and questionable constitutional tactics, as well as his disregard of religious laws that risked the wrath of the gods, may have solidified their opposition. As for the *publicani*, Caesar did assist with the Asian tax contracts, but this helped only the companies involved; publican firms that had been outbid for those contracts may have been outraged that the terms of the winning tender had been reduced and that the winning companies had still been allowed to keep the contract. The only penalty imposed was a verbal reprimand from the senior consul.[152] Finally, as the year progressed, more and more people were settled on land throughout Italy, which meant the triumvirs' most zealous supporters were no longer in Rome to offer their support and their vote. In particular, thousands of Pompey's veterans had received their land and left Rome, taking with them their votes and the physical power needed for the triumvirs to control the voting area. Although there were no similar outbursts of violence, the mere presence of these veterans roaming the streets of the capital had previously been enough to intimidate the triumvirs' enemies and dampen public criticism of their tactics and policies.

Curiously, during this period Crassus disappeared from view. Although Pompey and Caesar were attacked repeatedly in the forum, in the senate, and in print, Crassus appeared to have emerged unscathed.[153] Confirming his reputation as a consummate politician, he benefited tremendously from the alliance: the publican contracts had been altered, Pompey's arrangements in the east had been approved (meaning four new provinces were open for taxation and for business for him and his equestrian friends), he had assumed a place on the agrarian board (bringing additional lucrative business opportunities), and his ally Clodius had won his transfer to the plebian order. Yet even as his power and wealth increased, he seems to have managed to keep out of the headlines and avoid the taunts endured by his colleagues. Behind the scenes his extensive network of financial relationships may have helped ensure that people remained loyal and silent. His fearsome reputation may have discouraged outright attack. Events may in fact have played out as well as Crassus could have hoped. Having profited from the alliance, he did not now wish to see Pompey, or even Caesar, grow too powerful. When Pompey's "approval rating" dropped, Cicero noted that Crassus was happy.[154]

Bibulus and his allies saw an opportunity in their enemy's sinking poll numbers. Bibulus sent a herald to the forum to read a proclamation postponing the curule elections (meaning elections for the consulship, praetorship, and curule aedileship only) until October 18.[155] Normally the vote took place in mid-July, after the Games of Apollo. The justification for the delay is unknown but there did not appear to be any protest over the maneuver or any doubt about its legality. Ever the pessimist, Cicero believed Bibulus's ploy to be lawful but pointless. Nevertheless, because the opposition to Caesar and his allies that began in late April had increased by July, Bibulus and his counselors may have concluded that three more months might enhance their unpopularity and increase the odds for *optimate* candidates. In addition, since Roman political alliances were rarely long-lasting, they may have hoped that the delay would lead to dissension in the triumvirate's ranks.

Pompey was furious. Sensing that he and his allies still had the votes in July, he did not wish for a postponement. Pompey condemned Bibulus's lampoons and delaying tactics at a *contio* on July 25; the crowd responded with little enthusiasm.[156] An eyewitness to the assembly, Cicero commented on the remarkable decline in Pompey's popularity since his return from the east in 62 as

Rome's greatest military hero.[157] Always sensitive to criticism, Pompey later confided to Cicero how deeply this had affected him.[158] Caesar, too, spoke, but his efforts to incite the crowd to move against Bibulus's house failed.

Though the curule elections had been postponed, Bibulus did not have control over the plebian elections, so voting for the next year's tribunes, quaestors, and plebian aediles presumably proceeded as scheduled during the summer.[159] As expected, the people elected the new plebian Publius Clodius Pulcher as one of the ten tribunes for 58.

The Vettius "Conspiracy"

Shortly thereafter, the most mysterious event of 59 transpired, involving a man named Lucius Vettius.[160] Vettius had become friends with the younger Gaius Scribonius Curio, the vocal opponent of the triumvirs, and proposed that they should assassinate Pompey. Curio took this information to his father, Gaius, who informed Pompey and the senate. Vettius testified before the house and, after first denying even knowing the younger Curio, eventually volunteered to reveal the details of a supposed conspiracy that threatened Pompey and Rome itself. He claimed that the ringleader was Lucius Aemilius Lepidus Paullus (cos. 50). Paullus certainly had a motive. His father, Marcus Aemilius Lepidus (cos. 78), had rebelled against Rome before finally being defeated by Pompey at Cosa in Etruria; he fled to Sardinia, where he died in 77.[161] Vettius also implicated Marcus Junius Brutus, the future assassin of Caesar. Brutus, too, had motives. His father had served as legate for Lepidus and after surrendering to Pompey at Mutina had been executed.[162] He may also have been Julia's first fiancé before the engagement was broken so she could marry Pompey. Bibulus was linked to the plot, as well; Vettius claimed that Gaius Septimius, Bibulus's chief secretary, was to provide him with the knife to carry out the attack.

The next day Caesar held hearings at a *contio*. Vettius ascended the rostra and once again testified about the plot, although his story and the list of conspirators had changed.[163] Brutus's name no longer appeared; gossip suggested that a late-night visit by Brutus's mother, Servilia, to her long-time lover, Caesar, saved her son. New names were added, including Lucullus who had hated Pompey for almost a decade, and the praetorian candidate Lucius Domitius Ahenobarbus, who had a motive, since Pompey had killed his brother.[164] Vettius claimed Domitius's house was to serve as the embarkation point for the attack. Vettius did not specifically name Cicero, but he declared that an "eloquent former consul now the neighbor of the current consul" encouraged the plot.[165] Cicero's house on the northern slope of the Palatine Hill could be seen from the forum and rose just above Caesar's residence in the Domus Publica. After Caesar dismissed this meeting, the tribune Vatinius called another *contio* and brought Vettius back to the rostra. Vettius now asserted that Curio had informed him that Cicero's son-in-law and Marcus Laterensis, who had refused to swear the oath to Caesar's second land law and had therefore been denied the opportunity to run for the tribunate, had been involved in the plot as well.

Vettius's story had changed so many times that few took him seriously. Nevertheless, Vettius would be brought to trial by Publius Licinius Crassus Dives (pr. 57), a relative and possibly the nephew of the triumvir. Vatinius then proposed a law that if Vettius were convicted, he would be granted immunity and a cash reward in return for testifying against the others involved in the plot; the law would also create a special court to prosecute those he implicated.[166] Vettius was hauled off to the *carcer* to await trial. A formal hearing ultimately proved unnecessary, however, when Vettius was found murdered in his cell the next morning.

Though the episode was shrouded in mystery, Cicero's theory that Caesar hatched the plan is the most likely scenario for a number of reasons. One, the plot may have been part of an effort to frighten Pompey and convince him that despite recent problems his continued membership in the triumvirate was necessary for his safety.[167] Two, it was directed at the younger Curio, the most vociferous of the triumvirate's opponents.[168] Lastly, the scheme could have been conceived as an attack on the triumvirate's other political rivals, especially those running for office for 58. Vatinius's proposal for a special court to try those denounced by Vettius would provide Caesar legal cover to eliminate a number of troublesome critics. Enemies such as Paullus, the consular candidate Lucius Cornelius Lentulus, the praetorian candidate Lucius Domitius Ahenobarbus, and Cato's ally Brutus all conveniently materialized in Vettius's catalog of conspirators. Indeed, Caesar or Pompey's enemies comprised most of the men on Vettius' lists. Cicero feared that the supposed "Vettius conspiracy" potentially could be used by the triumvirs to strengthen their grip on the state or even provide a pretext for employing violence to save a "threatened" republic.[169] Because most of Caesar's political and military maneuvers worked so effectively, it may have seemed surprising when one failed. Vettius's inability to tell a convincing and consistent story in the senate or on the rostra sunk the plan; Caesar cut his losses by seeing to Vettius's elimination.[170]

Fall 59 BC/695 AUC

The Curule Elections

Ultimately, Bibulus's postponement extended the campaigning season for the curule offices by roughly three months. Despite the delay, when the consular elections were finally held on October 18, two close allies of the triumvirate emerged victorious. Aulus Gabinius was an effective politician; as tribune in 67 Gabinius established his popular credentials by passing the law that gave Pompey extraordinary powers to fight the pirates in the east. He served as a legate on Pompey's staff (66–63) before becoming praetor by 61. With the help of Pompey and his allies, Gabinius became the first in his family to reach the top of the political ladder. His colleague would be Lucius Calpurnius Piso Caesonius. Piso's daughter Calpurnia had married Caesar earlier in 59, an alliance that paid off handsomely as Caesar no doubt used his influence on behalf of his new father-in-law. The noble Piso had connections in other senatorial circles as well, and at least in 59 enjoyed the support of Cicero.[171]

In spite of the opposition to Caesar and his allies during the summer of 59, their candidates did well in the most significant elections. Although the ancient sources do not provide an explanation for this apparent turn of events, there were a number of reasons why the hissing at public venues and humorous lampoons posted around the city did not translate into a major rejection at the polls. No doubt in the spring and early summer a reaction against the power and tactics of the triumvirs had begun, but a majority of voters did not necessarily turn against them. If the triumvirate had truly been as detested as Cicero contends, there would have been no need for Bibulus to postpone the elections in July. Instead, the elections would have been held immediately, to capitalize on the ill will felt for Rome's preeminent men. It is possible Cicero had too much faith in his own opinion and those of his close friends and relations with whom he spent much of his time. Their views may have been in part the product of wishful thinking, leading to an exaggeration of the triumvirate's unpopularity. Hopes that the triumvirate might break apart also proved illusory.

In addition, Caesar and Pompey undoubtedly employed massive bribery to help their candidates. Both had bought votes in the past, and now, thanks in part to Ptolemy XII's immense bribe, they would have plenty of cash on hand. The citizens assisted by the two land laws may have returned to Rome in large numbers to vote. Caesar and his allies had plenty of time to organize and pay for thousands of their most vocal supporters to come to the capital on the eighteenth of October. Later, when he was proconsul in Gaul, Caesar annually sent soldiers to Rome to influence elections; there is no reason a similar "get out the vote" operation could not have been arranged in 59 from regions in Italy closer to the capital than Gaul.[172] Having acquired plunder (in the case of the veterans) and land, these citizens would have risen to a higher century. Their votes would now carry more weight and would thus be even more valuable in an election. Even if many in the city were opposed to the triumvirs—and certainly many in the city were—the arrival of the land laws' beneficiaries may have turned the tide, while the mere presence of the veterans in Rome may have reminded people of the violence just six months before. Although the triumvirs issued no overt threats, intimidation may have played a role in the elections and convinced some citizens to stay away from the ballot box. Bibulus never emerged from his house to conduct the elections; Caesar presided, a sure advantage to his allies.

The triumvirate remained the most influential faction in Rome and, despite the booing at the games or the cold silence in the theater, could still mobilize enough support across the social spectrum to put key allies in key positions. One incident involving Gaius Porcius Cato (tr. 56) plainly exhibited the triumvirs' continued power and their willingness to use it.[173] According to Cicero, sometime after October 18 and before December 10, Cato attempted to bring Gabinius up on charges of electoral bribery during the latter's successful campaign for the consulship. Caesar and Pompey could not allow their ally to stand trial; they needed him as consul in 58 to protect their interests. Since a trial could not take place in the standing courts without the approval of a praetor, they put pressure on these magistrates, who in turn refused to give Cato an official opportunity to file his petition. Refusing to let the matter drop, Cato next brought his case to a *contio* to rally popular support for a prosecution. He delivered a passionate speech denouncing Caesar and labeling Pompey a dictator. Caesar and his allies resorted to force. The triumvirate's angry supporters, possibly Pompey's veterans still present in the city for the recently completed elections, assaulted Cato in the forum. The triumvirate resorted to violence only twice in 59; the first time was on April 4. But the assault on Cato clearly revealed that Caesar in particular "was still ready unflinchingly to unleash as much of horror and of force as his circumstances required."[174]

-III-

Clodius

58 BC/696 AUC

Publius Clodius was a noble, eloquent and audacious, who knew no limits in speech or in action.

Velleius Paterculus

THE FOLLOWING POLITICAL YEAR officially began three weeks before the calendar year with the inauguration of the ten new tribunes. Publius Clodius Pulcher, who achieved his transfer to the plebian order through the efforts of Pompey, Caesar, and Crassus, took office along with his nine colleagues on December 10, 59. Having planned for this moment for months, taking advice from friends, confidants, and legal experts, he immediately proposed laws signaling that this would be no ordinary tribunate. Clodius may have promulgated three of his laws the very day he took office. If so, after the necessary *trinundinum*, he could have called for a vote on January 4, 58, the first *comitial* day after the third *nundinae*.

Clodius's first bill was the *lex Clodia Frumentaria*, which sought to solve the long-standing problem of grain shortages in the capital—periodic shortages that drove up food prices, starved some of Rome's poorest citizens, and often led to violent political protests.[1] Clodius's law would provide free grain each month for any Roman citizen who wished to apply.[2] The money to pay for this program would come from imperial tribute. *Optimate* opponents argued that welfare schemes like the *lex Clodia Frumentaria* were wicked for three reasons: they made poor people less willing to work, they would bankrupt the state and force wealthy people to pay exorbitant taxes to keep the program afloat, and they allowed the state to interfere in the working of the free market.[3]

Clodius's second law dealt with the *collegia*, organizations based on occupation, religion, or residence which had purportedly first been organized by King Numa Pompilius (reign c. 715–673) and had long been an integral part of life for many Romans.[4] A *collegium* might have a few dozen members or a few thousand. Each club held regular meetings, elected leaders, hosted dinners, celebrated religious festivals, and ensured their members received proper funeral rites. Since many senators believed these organizations to be centers of "violent and subversive activity," some *collegia* and their festivals had been outlawed by the house in 64.[5] Clodius's law proposed to restore the banned *collegia*, permit the founding of new *collegia*, and create a census to record all the *collegia* and their members in the city.

Prompted by the events of 59, Clodius's third proposal concerned religion and political procedure, specifically *obnuntiatio*.[6] Having a magistrate sit in his house safe from public pressure while he issued edicts to halt the political process was nothing less than a threat to popular sovereignty and an invitation to gridlock. Conservatives such as Cicero loved the law for that very reason—because it provided city officials with a weapon to frustrate popular leaders.[7] Although the nature of Clodius's proposition is obscure, it appears that it would require magistrates who observed the overnight omens to present their findings in person before an assembly began.

On December 29, 59, the last day of the year, Marcus Calpurnius Bibulus finally emerged from his home after 262 days in seclusion. He intended to deliver the consul's traditional year-end speech, describing his deeds while in office and the state of the republic in general—but Clodius vetoed the proceedings. His refusal to allow Bibulus to address the people, only the second time this had happened in the history of the republic, represented a favor to the triumvirs and Caesar in particular, as well as to the people whose legislation Bibulus had spent his entire year in office trying to obstruct.[8]

Caesar, however, did speak. No text of his oration survives, but he surely used his farewell address to expound on the many benefits he had bestowed on the people and Rome during his tenure. Standing on the rostra looking out across the forum at the *togate* citizens on that winter day, Caesar may have reminded the crowd of the political deadlock that had plagued the republic in previous years. Although he probably neglected to mention the forum violence of April 4, he likely noted that through his actions the gridlock that had obstructed the will of the people had finally been broken and an avalanche of impressive bills had followed. Two land laws had been passed and implemented and four new provinces had officially joined the Roman Empire—provinces whose revenues now flowed into the treasury. He had supported equestrian interests by reducing the publican contracts, and by opening new lands in the east for business. Also, the long-standing problem of the Egyptian monarchy had (seemingly) been settled. He had done all this despite the opposition of the *optimate* senators who used political tricks and religious technicalities to block his legislation. Thanks to him and his allies the republic and the empire were far stronger on December 29 than they had been when he entered office twelve months earlier on January 1. In addition, he might have reassured the people about the future, as he reminded them of his law that transferred Clodius to the plebian order and allowed him to secure the tribunate. Clodius had already proposed an extensive program beneficial to the people and would also defend legislation passed in 59, because he could not allow the triumvirate's laws to be declared invalid. Caesar may have pointed out that he had helped Aulus Gabinius and Lucius Calpurnius Piso ascend to the consulship; both would carry on his work. As he stepped down from the rostra amid the cheers of his supporters, Caesar could look back on a successful consulship and look forward to the incredible military and economic opportunities that awaited him in the north.

On the Kalends of January 58 (January 1), the new consuls took office, along with the rest of the new city magistrates. Sometime early in January (January 4 was the earliest possible day), the tribal assembly met and the people passed Clodius's proposals over the strenuous opposition of the *optimates*. Clodius then spent considerable time on the massive task of implementing his new laws. From the Temple of Castor and Pollux, which he established as his headquarters, he began registering the *collegia*, both old ones that were now revived and newly established entities. The list of clubs and their members would provide the framework for the distribution of the free grain to which all Roman citizens were now entitled.

Meanwhile, early in the year, two new praetors, Lucius Domitius Ahenobarbus and Gaius Memmius, directed an attack against Caesar, demanding an official investigation into his conduct as consul. Senatorial debate on the matter dragged on for three days, but out of either loyalty to or fear of the triumvirate, the senate refused to act. Caesar then left the city; by crossing the *pomerium* he was now officially proconsul with the *imperium* and legal immunity. Caesar remained just outside Rome, however, as he continued to watch developments.[9] With Caesar out of reach, the praetors Domitius and Memmius aimed lower, prosecuting one of his allies, an unnamed quaestor from 59 who no longer enjoyed that immunity. The fate of the ex-quaestor is unknown.

Domitius and Memmius then set their sights on Publius Vatinius, one of the tribunes of 59, accusing him of violating the *lex Licinia Junia*. This law prohibited the addition of unrelated riders to legislation and mandated an interval of three market cycles between the proposal and the vote on a specific law. Having been appointed as a legate on Caesar's staff, Vatinius had also acquired legal immunity, so he did not need to return to the city to stand trial. However, he planned to run later in 58 for the following year's aedileship, and he would therefore have to come to the capital at some point and give up his immunity. Rather than wait, he decided to answer the praetors' charges immediately. He entered Rome, publicly claiming he had nothing to hide and that he gladly welcomed the chance to clear his name. Privately, though, he feared conviction and secretly sought aid from the new tribune Clodius.[10]

Thanks to the passage of his laws, Clodius had the power to help. Registering the *collegia* gave him access to their leaders, many of whom would already have been close associates.[11] Clodius met with them in his home to discuss Vatinius's problem; afterward they fanned out to all the areas of the city where their constituents lived and worked. Each association's subordinate officers passed the directive down rapidly through the ranks, a relatively easy process due to the small size of the city and the clubs' elaborate organizations. Clodius had issued the order "to close the shops" so his supporters could leave their place of business or employment to join him in the forum to help Vatinius.[12] For small business owners and itinerant workers, missing work even for a day could mean financial hardship, but memories of the man who had given them "dignity and bread" may have overcome financial concerns.[13] And, too, this case may have been of special interest to the average Roman. Defending a citizen threatened with exile by the oppressive power of an overbearing city magistrate represented a principle many cherished and were willing to fight for. It helped that as tribune Vatinius had passed popular legislation—so he must have enjoyed support among the people in his own right.

Drawn by loyalty and principle, a large group of Clodius's followers accompanied him to the forum to observe Vatinius's trial. At some point Vatinius exercised one of the fundamental rights enjoyed by a Roman and officially applied for the aid of a city tribune, an office created in part to protect citizens against the arbitrary legal power of the other city magistrates. He called on the tribune Publius Clodius Pulcher to defend him against the praetor Memmius's unacceptable violation of his civil rights.[14] Clodius granted Vatinius's request.

At his command, or through a prearranged signal, Clodius's supporters stormed the court, destroying the praetor's bench and the official urns used to collect the jury's votes. This timely use of violence brought the trial to a sudden and dramatic halt; Vatinius walked free. The brutality coincidentally served to frighten anyone who might have contemplated a retrial.

The grain law, and to a lesser extent the *obnuntiatio* law, brought Clodius lasting popularity with a large segment of Rome's population. The *collegia* provided him with an instrument to quickly mobilize large numbers of his supporters for political and physical support in the assemblies, *contiones*, and courts. Clodius's power and his willingness to resort to force offered clear warning to those who might think of opposing him in the future. Vatinius's trial was merely a preview of the violence to come.

Departures: Cicero

Thanks to the abrupt end of his trial, Vatinius would not be forced to leave Rome. Three important senators who played crucial roles in the events of 59, however, would soon be departing the city and Italy. The first was Cicero. He had always worried about what Clodius might do as tribune, but recent developments had allayed his fears. Through various envoys Clodius had managed to convince Cicero that he would spend his time in office passing laws rather than attacking the orator. Privately Pompey assured Cicero that he had nothing to fear from Clodius.[15] Atticus, after repeated meetings with Clodius's sister Clodia, made similar assurances. The two newly elected consuls for 58 were friendly to Cicero, especially Piso, to whom he was related by marriage. Four of the new praetors (Domitius, Nigidius, Memmius, and Lentulus) were his allies. Some of the incoming tribunes, in particular Lucius Ninnius Quadratus, would support him as well. Even Caesar still acted friendly. Cicero boasted that even if Clodius attacked, "all Italy" would defend me.[16]

Cicero's mood changed dramatically when it became apparent that Clodius had orchestrated a carefully coordinated deception.[17] Clodius's well-placed assurances had allowed him to avoid opposition from Cicero and his allies, and in particular permitted him to dodge vetoes from Ninnius. Armed with the power provided by passage of his initial laws, Clodius reneged on the guarantees given to Atticus and others and moved quickly against Cicero. His line of attack involved the Catilinarian conspiracy. As consul in 63, Cicero had executed five ringleaders without trial even though Roman law clearly stated that no Roman citizen could be put to death unless convicted in a court of law. On a later occasion, while discussing a different matter, Cicero claimed that trial by jury and the right of appeal were essential rights possessed by Roman citizens and the mark of a free man. Clodius realized that prosecuting Cicero would be a political boon, because Cicero's acts as consul made him very unpopular with large segments of the population. Many citizens would agree that Cicero must be punished for his actions, if only to serve as a warning to future officials against violating a citizen's sacred rights. Personally, Clodius was still smarting from Cicero's betrayal during the Bona Dea scandal. And he was irritated by the constant abuse Cicero directed at him in the senate and forum, especially Cicero's relentless and public reminders of the rumors concerning Clodius and his incestuous relationship with his sister.[18]

The year 58 had an intercalary period of twenty-seven days between February and March.[19] At some point during the last seven days of this "month," Clodius promulgated a law exiling any magistrate found guilty of executing a Roman citizen without trial or appeal.[20] Although the proposal did not mention anyone by name, it was clearly aimed at Cicero.

In this moment of crisis few senators stood by Cicero. A man who often used his cutting wit to ridicule colleagues, he was not universally loved.[21] His constant boasting that he had saved the state during the Catilinarian crisis caused further annoyance. With consummate skill Clodius had isolated Cicero from the consuls and tribunes. The consul Gabinius, as a former tribune (67) and popular politician, may already have been sympathetic to Clodius's legislation. More pragmatically, he was in a vulnerable position. He was deeply in debt after spending enormous amounts of money on his campaign for the consulship, in particular on splendid but costly gladiatorial shows in the forum. Gabinius desperately needed a lucrative province to govern. In close consultation with both consuls, Clodius let it be known that in return for their acquiescence in the passage of his laws and for their help against Cicero he would provide them with valuable governorships. Wisely, he did not award the consuls their provinces first. Knowing that once they received their recompense his hold on them would diminish, Clodius promulgated the bill aimed at Cicero on the same day he proposed a law assigning Piso the province of Macedonia and Gabinius the province of Cilicia, each for five years. The bitter Cicero called this a "provincial bribe"—but it proved effective: the consuls would continue to support Clodius in his move against Cicero so he would not derail their legislation. They waited patiently (and loyally) for their law to pass in the assembly.[22] The nature of Clodius's law precluded the intercession of the other nine tribunes on Cicero's behalf. As champions of the people they could not veto a law designed to safeguard fundamental rights of a Roman citizen. The triumvirs abandoned Cicero as well. They may have worried that if Cicero remained in Rome he might employ his considerable eloquence to help invalidate Caesar's entire program by highlighting its religious or legal imperfections. To spare Cicero from a trial, and to remove him from the capital, Caesar did offer him an ambassadorship, a place on one of the land commissions, or a position on his staff in Gaul. Any of the three posts would have saved Cicero from Clodius by providing him with legal immunity. It was also a brilliant political maneuver by Caesar: whether Cicero became an ambassador, a commissioner, or a legate he would not be prosecuted but he would be out of Rome and therefore unable to damage the triumvirate in the near future. Pompey, despite repeated assurances to Cicero, refused assistance, going so far as to hide in his house when Cicero tried to visit. Pompey may have grown tired of Cicero's public attacks and private criticisms, or he may have learned of Cicero's propensity to use derogatory nicknames when referring to Pompey.[23]

The *trinundinum* for the two new Clodian laws lasted through the first weeks of March.[24] Between promulgation and vote, the tide turned dramatically against Cicero. Lucullus and Cato advised Cicero to stay and fight the charges in court, but, perhaps influenced by the hostile and potentially violent crowds at Clodius's *contiones,* most friends advocated his departure from the city.[25] On March 18 Clodius's laws regarding Cicero and the consular provinces finally passed in the tribal assembly. Cicero, unwilling to wait in Rome for a trial in which he lacked allies, chose voluntary exile. Later that night, escorted only by a few friends, he took a statue of the goddess Minerva which had long stood in his Palatine home and moved down the hill into the dark and empty forum. Climbing up to the Capitoline Hill, he dedicated the statue with the inscription "To Minerva, Guard of Rome."[26] Then, after taking one last look at the statue and his beloved Rome from the height of the hill, he sneaked out of the city, heading south for Lucania. The next day the people plundered his Palatine home and nearby country villas. Clodius then proposed another bill, this one accusing Cicero by name of murdering Roman citizens without trial. If passed, this bill would officially banish him until the Catilinarians "returned to life."[27] Subsequently, Clodius added the traditional Roman formula making it illegal for Cicero to receive "fire and water" for four hundred miles in all directions from the city of Rome.[28] Clodius proposed the law to the people sometime around March 20, 58, and, after the *trinundinum*, it passed on or shortly after April 24. By the terms of the new law the state confiscated and auctioned off Cicero's property. Cicero later bitterly reproached Clodius and Gabinius among others for profiting from his misfortune—both bought some of his belongings at reduced prices.[29] Cicero's Palatine house was to be razed to the ground and a new shrine to the goddess Libertas was to be built in its place. Because a senator's *domus* was part of his identity, the symbolism of his loss could not be missed. It was "the worst punishment that could be imposed on unholy and criminal citizens."[30] In addition, because Cicero's home was clearly visible to the people in the forum, the new shrine would be visible as well, a monument to the people's rights and a reminder of Cicero's just punishment at the hands of the citizens he had wronged. It would also serve as a testament to the power Clodius now enjoyed, and a warning to his enemies.

Cicero disappeared along with his house. After traveling quickly to southern Italy, he left Brundisium on April 29 for Greece, ending up in Thessalonica, where he would spend more than a year in exile. The rapidity of his fall stunned Cicero and even led him to contemplate suicide. The political game in Rome was indeed dangerous, and the stakes were high. Cicero had been one of Rome's most influential politicians, standing at the pinnacle in December of 63; now, barely four years later, he had been forced into exile by his foes. Cicero's enemies, including Clodius and the triumvirs who had transferred him to the plebian order, had conspired to eliminate him from Roman politics.

Departures: Caesar and Cato

Caesar was the next to exit. Having watched political events in the capital culminate satisfactorily with the failure of his enemies' attacks and Cicero's exile, Caesar left the city's environs as well.[31] He had received word that the Helvetii were preparing to gather on the bank of the Rhone River on March 28, 58, before entering Roman territory and his province of Transalpine Gaul. Caesar moved more than five hundred miles from the vicinity of Rome to Geneva in only seven days, beating the Helvetii to the Rhone, so he must have left Rome by March 20, no more than a day and a half after Cicero did.[32] Caesar would not see Rome again until nine years had passed.

Cato was the last to leave. Clodius passed new legislation that annexed the kingdom of Cyprus to the Roman Empire.[33] Clodius picked Cyprus in part because its king, Ptolemy, had failed to build support in the senate through bribery, as his brother, Ptolemy XII of Egypt, had done. As always with Clodius, personal vengeance also played a role. Ptolemy had insulted Clodius in 67 when the future tribune had been kidnapped in the east by pirates, and the king had provided only meager funds toward his ransom; Clodius had not forgotten.[34]

Cato was chosen for the mission to seize and administer the new Roman province. Clodius's law had thus removed from Rome one of his and the triumvirs' most powerful enemies.[35] At a *contio*, Clodius read out a letter Caesar had sent to him from Gaul offering praise for this political ploy.[36] In addition, this law made Cato complicit in Clodius's legislation and by extension Caesar's. If the laws of Caesar's consulship were to be annulled, Clodius's tribunate would be illegal and the laws he passed void, including the one granting Cato the commission in the east. Clodius's moves put Cato in the position of having to defend his enemies' acts. He had also been given an extraordinary command, similar to those Pompey received in 67 and 66; he would therefore no longer be able to criticize the appointment of a private citizen to this type of assignment. Clodius may have appointed Cato because he was renowned for his financial integrity and therefore would not embezzle most of Cyprus's wealth like so many other Roman senators might have done. It was critical that the money make it from the Cyprian treasury to the Roman treasury to fund Clodius's grain law so the "*optimate* Cassandras" who claimed the *leges Clodiae* would bankrupt the state would be proven wrong.[37] On the other hand, Clodius may have given Cato this job in the hopes that he might surrender to temptation and siphon off some of Cyprus's cash for himself. This would provide Cato's enemies the chance to haul him into court on embezzlement charges. If convicted, he would be removed from Rome permanently.[38]

Cato left Rome sometime in the spring of 58, but before he arrived in Cyprus, King Ptolemy committed suicide. It would take Cato two years to liquidate the king's patrimony. His absence left a large void in *optimate* leadership.[39]

EPILOGUE

Transformation

57–31 BC/697–723 AUC

This is what [my enemies] wanted. After all the great things I had done they would have condemned me, Gaius Caesar [in the courts], if I had not sought help from my army.

Caesar, while staring at the Roman dead after winning the civil war battle of Pharsalus, 48

THE YEAR 59 TRIGGERED TWIN chains of events that unfolded separately through the 50s before ultimately converging in civil war and the republic's collapse. The first concerned Clodius, Pompey, and affairs in Rome; the second, Caesar and his campaigns in Gaul.

The triumvirs' transfer of Clodius to the plebian order in April of 59 led directly to his election to the tribunate in July and his assumption of that office in December. The Clodian laws proposed in late 59 and passed in early 58 helped create a political machine that brought their creator great power. Such was Clodius's popularity and the cohesion of his machine that, unlike past holders of the tribunate, he retained enormous influence long after he left office, largely due to his ability to produce a large and rehearsed crowd of chanting and taunting supporters ready at a sign from their leader to intimidate opponents at *contiones*, elections, legislative assemblies, and trials.[1] And he was willing to use this crowd to employ violence to achieve his ends—Vatinius's case was merely the beginning. Clodius's actions spawned imitators, as his enemies began to adopt similar tactics. In 57 the tribune Titus Annius Milo (pr. 55) began hiring gladiators to attack Clodius's group, initiating an arms race in the city. By the mid-50s most prominent Romans employed armed bands in the streets for protection or to attack rivals. Rome had no police force, and gang warfare became endemic.

The triumvirs took advantage. Convening the Conference of Luca in Cisalpine Gaul in April of 56, the three men reaffirmed their alliance.[2] They agreed that, with Caesar's economic and electoral support, Pompey and Crassus would run for the consulships for 55. Continuing violence in Rome, instigated by Clodius and the triumvirs' allies, led to the postponement of those elections—a delay that allowed Caesar time to send thousands of his soldiers to Rome under the command of Crassus's son Publius to vote and if necessary to fight. One rival consular candidate, Domitius, had vowed to strip Caesar of his provinces and immunity before prosecuting him for his misdeeds. When election day finally arrived, Pompey and Crassus's supporters attacked Domitius and his entourage as they went down into the forum before dawn. Domitius's torchbearer was killed, and many others, including Cato, were wounded.[3] The violence served its purpose: due largely to the physical and electoral assistance of Caesar's soldiers—soldiers who had been granted to him by the *lex Vatinia* in 59—Crassus and Pompey were elected consuls for 55, each for the second time. Once in office they passed a law extending Caesar's proconsulship for five more years while stipulating that a discussion of a potential successor in Gaul could not begin until March 1, 50. Other laws followed, giving Crassus the governorship of Syria while Pompey became proconsul of the two provinces in Spain, both for five years.

The violence in Rome persisted; assemblies, elections, and trials were disrupted in 55 and 54.[4] The fighting became so extreme in 53 that elections could not be held, so the year 52 opened without curule magistrates. Throughout the period Clodius had played a leading role in the troubles before meeting his death on January 18, 52. Returning to Rome along the Via Appia, he encountered Milo, who had left the capital that morning. In the brawl that ensued, Milo's more numerous followers overwhelmed Clodius's supporters and killed Clodius. His body was dumped by the side of the road next to a shrine to the Bona Dea, inspiring many Romans to believe that the Good Goddess had finally taken revenge on the man who had defiled her sacred rites back in 62.

Clodius's death touched off a new wave of violence in the city. His adherents, incited by his widow, Fulvia, and other allies, rioted in the forum and burned Clodius's body inside the curia, destroying Rome's senate house.[5] For fifty-eight days, through January and February and into the intercalary month inserted after February 23, the violence raged on.[6] The idea was floated to appoint Pompey dictator to quell the disturbances, but vivid memories of the atrocities committed by Lucius Cornelius Sulla Felix during his dictatorship thirty years earlier scuttled the idea.[7] So Bibulus and Cato came up with a unique—and unconstitutional—solution. Deciding that working with the hated Pompey was preferable to the continued rioting in the city and the threat of revolution, but afraid to give Pompey the unlimited power of the dictatorship, they concluded that Pompey should instead be appointed consul without a colleague.[8]

As happened often in the late republic, crisis had produced a willingness to break constitutional rules. A sole consulship established a precedent by which one man was entrusted with immense power, a further sign in the disintegration of the republic and another step closer to the advent of monarchy. Ironically, even conservative senators backed this resolution, despite the fact that it had no precedent in republican history. Because of the magnitude of the emergency, the proposition gained widespread support; many citizens had confidence in Pompey's ability to end the crisis and were reassured that as consul—and not dictator—his power would to some extent be limited. While in office he would be subject to the tribunes' veto, and after his term ended he would be liable to prosecution for his acts.

On the twenty-fourth day of the intercalary month Pompey became sole consul. He moved quickly to restore order, bringing soldiers into Rome (including some of his veterans who had received land in 59) to clamp down on the violence. Milo was brought to trial for his role in Clodius's death and, despite the efforts of Cicero (his defense attorney, who had returned from exile in 57), was found guilty on April 7 and banished to Massilia (Marseilles).[9]

The consequences of the triumvirs' success in transferring Clodius to the plebian order in 59 proved to be far greater than Clodius's death or Milo's exile. Clodius's tribunate in 58 dramatically escalated the level of violence in the Roman political process far beyond anything seen in previous decades. Ultimately it was that violence that provided an opportunity for Pompey. At a crucial moment, amid bloodshed and anarchy in the forum, and with the state threatened, he had intervened and seemingly alone had restored peace and order to the city; many believed he had saved the republic. His great success and the high regard in which he was held by his fellow citizens convinced Pompey that he had become Rome's indispensable man.

The violence had forced the *optimates*, for so long Pompey's enemies, to turn to him for help. Increasingly close relations between Pompey and the *boni*, and

Pompey's eventual acceptance into Rome's highest senatorial circles, represented a crucial step in the process by which Pompey would eventually be separated from Caesar—an outcome that Cato and the others no doubt hoped for when they offered him the sole consulship. The reconciliation with Pompey may have come about because the *optimates* already believed that Caesar, thanks to his successes in Gaul, posed a greater threat to the republic than either Pompey or a sole consulship.

Meanwhile, in the north, the other chain of events launched by the year 59 was under way. In March of 58, without sanction from either senate or people, Caesar moved out of his provinces and into Gaul, chasing after the Helvetii. Once in Gaul he had no intention of leaving. Thanks to the meeting at Luca and thanks to his allies, Caesar's original term as proconsul was extended; he would spend the rest of the decade campaigning in Gaul and beyond. His force, eventually swollen to ten legions, would be the first Roman army to cross the Rhine into Germany, in 55. Later in 55 and again in 54 his army was the first to cross the channel to Britain. To the Romans back home, Britain seemed literally to be at the ends of the earth.[10] The climactic battle for Gaul came at Alesia in September of 52, when, after a mammoth struggle, Caesar's army overcame two separate Gallic forces to end the last major resistance to Roman rule. Gaul would be part of the Roman Empire for the next five hundred years.

In response to the violence employed by the triumvirs in 59, Bibulus and his loyal tribunes had retired to their homes and allowed the triumvirate to pass laws without opposition, the most important of which would prove to be the *lex Vatinia*, providing Caesar time and resources that he skillfully used to add a vast new territory to the empire. The unauthorized conquest of Gaul earned him great military glory, incredible wealth, and, most significantly, a large, experienced, and loyal army.

Rome, Gaul, and the Rubicon

The Conference of Luca in 56, the consulships of Pompey and Crassus in 55, and Pompey, Crassus, and Caesar's extraordinary proconsulships in the Spains, Syria, and the Gauls surely made it seem that the alliance's power had only increased by mid-decade. After 55, however, fissures began to appear. In 54 Julia, Caesar's only child and Pompey's wife, died during labor (the baby died as well). Pompey and Julia, married in 59 to cement the alliance between Pompey and Caesar, had enjoyed a loving relationship that strengthened the relationship between her husband and her father. Instead, her death removed this important link. Had she lived, and had the baby or future babies survived, they would have been the children of Pompey and the grandchildren of Caesar, and they might have provided a possibly permanent bond.

Another perhaps greater blow to the triumvirate came in 53. Crassus, trying to win his first triumph and rival the military exploits of his allies, marched east and invaded Parthia, the last great empire still beyond Roman control. At the Battle of Carrhae in 53 he suffered a massive defeat and was eventually captured and killed. The Parthians cut off his head and supposedly used it as a prop in a play.[11] No longer would Crassus's wealth and power provide a counterweight to Pompey and Caesar's ambitions.

Thus by 52, when Pompey had imposed peace on Rome and Caesar had imposed peace on Gaul, the triumvirate had been replaced by a duumvirate whose two members were no longer linked by a marriage tie. To protect what was left of the alliance Caesar had offered Pompey his great-niece Octavia's hand in marriage, but Pompey refused. After his rapprochement with the *optimates* he aimed for a wife from a more illustrious family. In 52 he married Cornelia, the daughter of Quintus Caecilius Metellus Pius Scipio Nasica (cos. 52), by birth a descendent of the Cornelii Scipiones and by adoption a member of the Caecilius Metellus family. This marriage represented another step by Pompey away from Caesar.

Sensing an opportunity, Caesar's foes spent the next two years (52–50) pressing continuously for his supersession as governor of the Gauls. Pompey played an ambiguous game, declaring that he could not allow any discussion of those provinces before March 1, 50. When that date finally arrived, a meeting of the senate was held and the consul Gaius Claudius Marcellus proposed to replace Caesar. The wealth of Gaul, however, stymied the effort. For eight years Caesar had used Gallic plunder to acquire greater influence in Rome. His emissaries were constantly making the trip over the Alps to the capital bringing gold, silver, and the other spoils of war (especially slaves).[12] He provided low-interest loans and distributed bribes to help the city magistrates pay their expenses. Significantly, since it was necessary to keep up appearances in Roman society, money also flowed to the magistrates' wives to help support their lavish lifestyles; in return they influenced their husbands on Caesar's behalf.[13] Caesar sent presents and monetary aid to the slaves and freedmen of prominent citizens as an inducement to gain valuable inside information.[14] Caesar dispatched fifteen hundred talents to Marcellus's colleague, Lucius Aemilius Lepidus Paullus, to help him restore the Basilica Aemilia in the forum.[15] A former enemy, Paullus now worked to defend Caesar's interests and prevent his removal from the Gallic command.

One of the tribunes, Gaius Scribonius Curio, had long been an opponent of Caesar and had been notably outspoken against the triumvirate in the spring and summer of 59 when others had remained silent. However, like so many senators, Curio was deeply in debt—until surreptitious deliveries of cash from Gaul remedied his precarious financial situation.[16] To the great shock of many observers, he suddenly became an outspoken supporter of Caesar and used his veto to block the efforts of Gaius Marcellus and anyone else who moved for Caesar's dismissal.

During the remainder of 50, positions hardened. Pompey still saw himself as Rome's leading military and political figure, reveling in his great victories, stretching back to the 80s, and his labors in the capital during the 50s to restore order. He was clearly unwilling to treat Caesar as an equal, considering that to do so would be an affront to his *dignitas,* his status as the first man in Rome. Fatefully, his feelings were reinforced when at Naples in the summer of 50 he fell seriously ill and appeared to be near death. People all over Italy prayed for his recovery, and when his health improved spontaneous celebrations broke out everywhere on the peninsula.[17] This outpouring of affection only confirmed what Pompey had previously believed about his ranking in Rome's senatorial hierarchy and convinced him more than ever that he need brook no rival. He also came to believe that he need not fear Caesar's army. When Clodius's nephew, Appius Claudius Pulcher (cos. 38), arrived in Rome after having served with Caesar in Gaul, he "belittled" Caesar's accomplishments and told derogatory tales about Caesar himself.[18] Claudius assured Pompey and anyone who would listen that after so many years of difficult service Caesar's soldiers loathed their commander and were on the verge of mutiny. Therefore, while Caesar commanded only one (apparently mutinous) army in Gaul, Pompey as proconsul controlled two armies, one in Spain and another in Italy, and his allies led the two armies of the east. The confident Pompey, possibly referring to his veterans who had been settled back in 59, boasted that if he needed more soldiers "I only have to stamp my foot anywhere in Italy and armies will rise out of the ground."[19]

After Alesia, Caesar had continued with the pacification of Gaul but kept an eye on events in Rome. Despite his great successes he knew that his enemies awaited the termination of his command; once he was again a private citizen he would lose his legal immunity and could be tried for crimes committed as consul in 59 and transgressions perpetrated while in Gaul. Caesar believed that if he laid down his command while Pompey still had his army, his enemies would prosecute him in a reprise of Milo's trial: a court surrounded by Pompey's soldiers packed with Pompey's jurors. Conviction meant exile and political eclipse. Caesar decided that he could not allow his proconsulship in Gaul to expire before he could assume another office that would continue to provide legal immunity. As he had tried to do in 60, he must win the right to stand for the office of consul *in absentia* so he could step right from the proconsulship to a new consulship without the loss of *imperium* that would leave him vulnerable to criminal charges. Initially Pompey appeared to be willing to grant this concession, but by 50 he had changed his mind. He was now loath to indulge Caesar in any way and, along with Cato and Caesar's most determined opponents, had begun demanding that Caesar lay down his command unconditionally.

On January 1, 49, two new tribunes, Quintus Cassius Longinus and Marcus Antonius, whose debts had been satisfied with Caesar's Gallic gold, read out a letter from Caesar to the senate. In it Caesar listed his many accomplishments on behalf of Rome and proposed that he and Pompey both lay down their commands to end the crisis. However, if Pompey was unwilling to make concessions, then he, Caesar, would have no alternative but to resort to force of arms to protect his *dignitas* and his rights. In response, the senate approved an ultimatum proposed by Pompey's father-in-law, Metellus Scipio, that Caesar must lay down his command by a certain date or he would be declared an enemy of the state. Frantic last-minute negotiations ensued, largely orchestrated by Cicero. Caesar offered to give up the Gauls and hold only Illyria with one legion, thus retaining his legal immunity while no longer posing a military threat. The efforts of Cato and the new consuls of 49, Gaius Claudius Marcellus (first cousin of the consul of 50) and Lucius Cornelius Lentulus Crus, thwarted the attempt.[20] Amid (false) reports that Caesar had already invaded Italy, the senate passed an *s.c.u.* on January 7, 49, declaring a state of emergency and authorizing Pompey to raise soldiers and money to safeguard the republic against the invading proconsul from the north. On January 10, 49, Caesar led legion XIII across the Rubicon River, thereby leaving his own province and entering Italy proper. Officially this was an act of treason, which precipitated Rome's sixth civil war. Because the *lex Vatinia* had provided Caesar with the loyal army that he now used against the state, this conflict has been called a "logical continuation of 59."[21]

Civil Wars and the Fall of the Republic

The fighting would drag on for four years (49–45) before Caesar finally defeated his enemies and conquered the empire. Many prominent senators died during the war, including Bibulus, the younger Curio, Milo, Clodius's brother Appius, Domitius (all in 48), Gabinius (47), and Afranius (46). After fleeing his defeat at the Battle of Pharsalus in 48, Pompey fell in Egypt, murdered upon his arrival in that country by agents of King Ptolemy XIII, the son of Pompey's old friend Ptolemy XII. Cato and Metellus Scipio both committed suicide in Utica after their defeat at the Battle of Thapsus (46). Pompey's eldest son, Gnaeus, who had ridden alongside his father's triumphal chariot in 61, was killed after the Battle of Munda (45). The death toll would have been much higher if not for Caesar's *clementia*; he spared many defeated enemies, including his former running mate Lucceius, Cicero, Cicero's brother Quintus and, fatefully, Marcus Junius Brutus and Gaius Cassius Longinus.

The victorious Caesar returned to Rome in 45 and proclaimed himself dictator for ten years. Then, in February 44, he declared himself dictator for life, making it clear that he had no intention of relinquishing power or restoring the republic. Rumors circulated in the city about something worse: that Caesar wished to make himself *rex*, divorce his Roman wife, Calpurnia marry his mistress Queen Cleopatra VII of Egypt (who, thanks to Caesar, had replaced her brother Ptolemy XIII on the throne, but who was now living in Rome), and leave the entire world to their son Ptolemy XV Caesarion. Many senators were unwilling to accept the advent of a new Roman monarchy. To save the republic, a group of them, led by Brutus and Cassius, assassinated Caesar on the Ides of March, March 15, 44, in the Theater of Pompey in the Campus Martius.[22]

Nevertheless, efforts to restore the republic ultimately failed. Marcus Antonius had been an officer in Caesar's army during the Gallic and civil wars and had been named by Caesar as his consular colleague for the year 44. Caesar's assassination removed both a dictator and a consul, making Antonius the chief executive of the Roman government. He used his consular power and his popularity with Caesar's troops, many of whom had served with him in the past, to secure control of a large army. Marcus Aemilius Lepidus (cos. 46) was another Caesarian general, and the dictator's master of horse (46–44). On March 15 Lepidus commanded one legion on the Tiber Island across from Rome, the only army in Italy at the time. As Caesar had intended, Lepidus soon took over the governorship of Nearer Spain and Transalpine Gaul along with even larger forces. Gaius Octavius, only eighteen years old at the time of Caesar's murder, had no political and little military experience, but he was Caesar's great-nephew and thus his closest male Roman relative. Caesar must have seen something in this young man to convince him that Octavius was destined for great things, for Caesar's will named Octavius as his principal heir. He thereby inherited most of Caesar's vast wealth and, more significantly, by the terms of the will was officially adopted as Caesar's son; he would now be known as Gaius Julius Caesar Octavianus, or Octavian.[23] He vowed to avenge his adoptive father by hunting down and killing Caesar's assassins. This pledge, along with Caesar's money and Caesar's name, made the young Octavian very popular with Caesar's soldiers, the one group that now mattered in the empire. Octavian quickly secured control of a large army.

In 43, after a dizzying series of events, Marcus Antonius, Marcus Aemilius Lepidus, and Gaius Octavian joined together and seized control of Rome. On November 27, the three men forced the *lex Titia* through the tribal assembly, legally constituting the *Triumviri Rei Publicae Constituendae*, or Second Triumvirate. The law granted the new triumvirs extraordinary powers to rule and reorganize the Roman state. Each would command armies to be used in the war against Caesar's assassins, who had fled to the east, and each would govern provinces in the west. The triumvirate would be authorized to appoint the city's magistrates and would remain in office for five years. Within a short time after Caesar's death each member of the triumvirate had become extremely powerful, their power based on their relationship to the dead dictator and his army, and therefore ultimately a result of the events of 59.

Once in charge the triumvirs massacred their enemies. Cicero was hunted down and killed in 43; his head and his hand were nailed to the rostra from which he had delivered so many famous speeches. The triumvirs then defeated the armies of Caesar's assassins at the Battle of Philippi in 42; Brutus and Cassius committed suicide. Eventually, after Lepidus's elimination (36), Octavian and Antonius ruled the empire jointly, Octavian in the west and Antonius in the east. Having married Cleopatra, Antonius desired to leave Roman territory in the east to their three children—a desire that helped spark the last civil war of the republic. At the Battle of Actium in 31 Octavian's navy defeated that of Antonius and Cleopatra; both committed suicide the next year. The battle gave Octavian control over the entire empire, now including Egypt, and officially marked the end of the Roman Republic. Octavian, later known as Augustus, was Rome's first emperor in all but name. There would be no going back.

A few moments of violence in front of the Temple of Castor and Pollux in the forum on April 4, 59, ultimately helped transform Rome from a republic into a monarchy. There of course had been political violence before, but without the violence on that day the First Triumvirate would not have taken temporary control of the state and, unopposed, passed many noteworthy laws. Without those laws, Clodius might have waited ten years or more to climb the political ladder to the consulship. Without them, Caesar's enemies would have blocked his acquisition of three provinces and ten loyal legions. Rather than conquer Gaul, he would have spent the year 58 surveying the tracks and forests of Italy.

Certainly the republic was already ailing, due in large part to its poisoned and partisan political atmosphere. Senators had become willing to use any means necessary to triumph over their enemies and to ignore almost any crime committed by allies as long as it furthered their political cause. The republican constitution was hopelessly ill equipped to control the senators' ambitions or to solve the many other major problems the state now faced. It is possible the republic would have died even if the events of 59 had never occurred. There is no doubt, however, that events of this year played an enormous role in hastening the republic's demise, setting in motion the twin chains of events that eventually led to conflict between Caesar and Pompey and to Caesar's crossing of the Rubicon in 49. Caesar's victory and dictatorship would enable the rise of the Second Triumvirate, and especially Octavian. The dire predictions of Cicero, Cato, and many others concerning the First Triumvirate and its potential impact on the republic, although seemingly overstated in early 59, had proved prophetic.[24]

Thus the story does not end happily. The year of Julius and Caesar marked the beginning of the end of the free state, as the republic succumbed to violence and civil war. The monarchy established by Augustus would degenerate into despotism, and political freedom vanished from the western world for more than a thousand years.

APPENDIX A

The Roman Republican Government

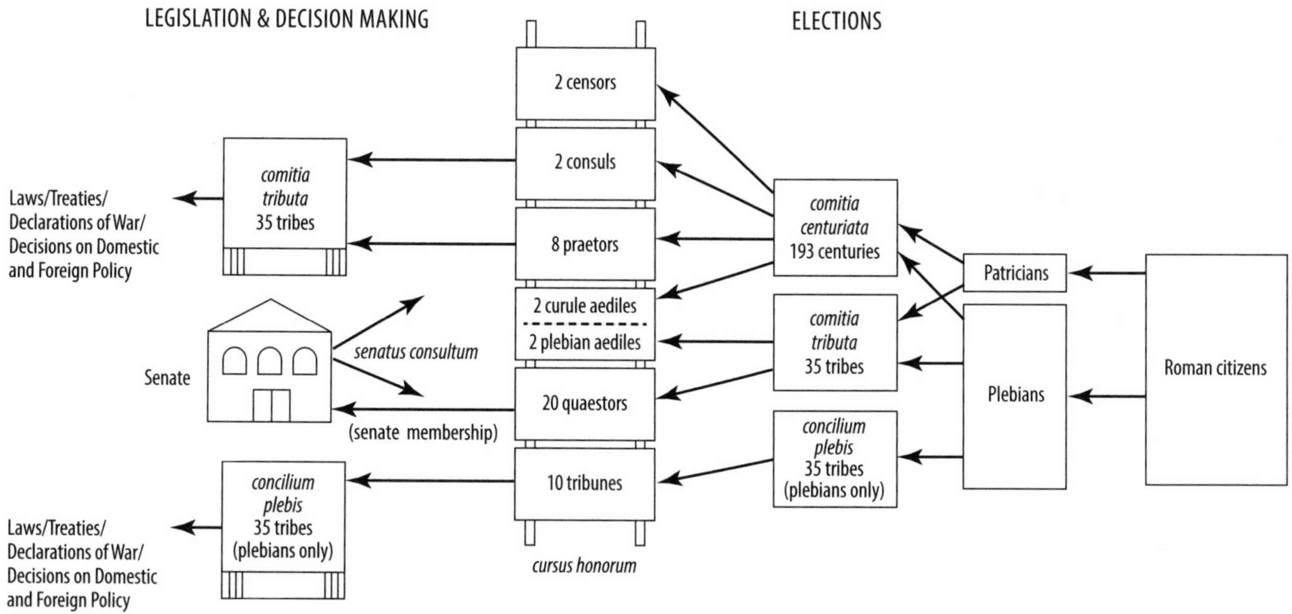

The Roman Republican Government. Diagram by the author

APPENDIX B

Cast of Characters

Note: The name (or names) by which a person is best known appears in CAPITAL LETTERS.

Lucius AFRANIUS
Possibly proconsul in Cisalpine Gaul in 59, Afranius, a *novus homo*, won a triumph for campaigns in Spain. He was an ally and legate of Pompey in the east (66–61); with Pompey's help he was elected consul for 60 but proved to be ineffective in passing Pompey's legislation due to the opposition of his colleague, Metellus Celer.

Quintus ANCHARIUS
A tribune in 59 and an opponent of the triumvirs, Ancharius was in the forum with his ally Bibulus on April 4, 59. Like the consul, he retired to his home on April 5 to observe the heavens for the rest of his term. He rose to be praetor in 56.

Gaius ANTONIUS Hybrida
An ally of Sulla's, Antonius had once been expelled from the senate for, among other things, excessive debt. He became Cicero's consular colleague in 63; when he was proconsul in 62 his army defeated and killed Catiline, ending Rome's fifth civil war. His poor management as governor of Macedonia from 62 to 60 led to a prosecution in 59 after he returned to Rome. Despite the efforts of his defense attorney, Cicero, he was convicted and exiled. More significantly, as a result of the trial Clodius would eventually become tribune.

Marcus ANTONIUS (83–30)
A Caesarian officer during the Gallic and sixth civil wars, Antonius became Caesar's consular colleague before Caesar's assassination. During the next two years he contrived to obtain a position of power and eventually formed the Second Triumvirate with Octavian and Lepidus at the end of 43, marrying Octavian's sister Octavia to cement the alliance. After the defeat of Brutus and Cassius at Philippi (42), he ruled the eastern half of the Roman Empire. The forced retirement of Lepidus (36) and Antonius's divorce of Octavia and subsequent marriage to Cleopatra led to the republic's twelfth and last civil war, during which Antonius and his wife were defeated at Actium. They both committed suicide the next year.

Titus Pomponius ATTICUS
A wealthy equestrian who never held office but was politically influential behind the scenes, Atticus was close friends with many important senators across the political spectrum, especially Cicero. In 59, his correspondence kept Cicero informed of events in Rome during the spring while Cicero was away on vacation.

Lucius Cornelius BALBUS
A wealthy banker from Gades in Spain, Balbus became friends with Pompey and through him gained Roman citizenship. He became an important surrogate of Caesar's, most notably in his attempts to win allies after his election as consul; these efforts may have helped bring about the triumvirate. Balbus was defended by both Pompey and Crassus when his citizenship was challenged in court in 56. In 40 he became Rome's first consul from outside Italy.

Marcus Atius BALBUS
On the Board of Twenty created by Caesar's first land law, Balbus, from Aricia, was praetor by 60 and married to Caesar's sister Julia. Their daughter Atia married Octavius (pr. 61), and they became the parents of the future emperor Augustus.

Marcus Calpurnius BIBULUS (100–48)
Consul in 59, *optimate* politician, and close ally and son-in-law of Cato, Bibulus worked his way up the political ladder alongside Caesar before being elected his consular colleague. In office he attempted to block the triumvirs' popular legislation before the violence of April 4 forced him to retire to his house for the rest of the year, allowing Caesar and his allies to pass numerous laws. He remained an *optimate* stalwart throughout the 50s before dying during the sixth civil war.

Marcus Junius BRUTUS
Son of Servilia, Brutus was possibly Julia's first fiancé. He became a son-in-law and close ally of Cato and the *optimates*. He was implicated in the Vettius conspiracy due in part to his father's death at Pompey's hands, but was later absolved. He fought against Caesar in the civil war and, despite being spared, led the group of senators who assassinated the dictator (44). He committed suicide after the defeat at Philippi (42).

Marcus CAELIUS Rufus
Lead prosecutor in the trial of Gaius Antonius and adherent of Crassus and later Caesar, Caelius began an affair with Clodia before the end of 59.

Gaius Julius CAESAR (100–44)
Consul in 59, Caesar was from an ancient patrician family descended from the gods—a brilliant and ruthless politician, willing to do almost anything to acquire power. He worked his way to the top of the political ladder before forming the First Triumvirate with Pompey and Crassus. He later conquered Gaul (58–49), won Rome's sixth civil war (49–45), and assumed the dictatorship before being assassinated on the Ides of March in 44.

Ptolemy XV CAESARION (47–30)
Son of Cleopatra and Caesar, Caesarion was killed by Octavian after the Battle of Actium.

CALPURNIA
Daughter of Lucius Calpurnius Piso Caesoninus, Calpurnia became Caesar's third and last wife in 59. The resulting alliance helped Piso get elected in 59 for the consulship of 58. Although Caesar was on campaign for most of the next fifteen years, they remained married until his assassination on March 15, 44, when her efforts to convince him to stay home from the senate failed.

Gnaeus Domitius CALVINUS
A tribune in 59 and an opponent of the triumvirs, Calvinus was in the Forum with his ally Bibulus on April 4, 59. Like the consul, he retired to his home on April 5 to observe the heavens for the rest of his term. He rose to be consul in 53.

Lucius CANINIUS Gallus
One of the three lawyers prosecuting Gaius Antonius, Caninius became tribune in 56.

Gaius CASSIUS Longinus
Cassius escaped Crassus's disaster at Carrhae (53) and later served with Pompey during the civil war. Along with Brutus he led the conspiracy against Caesar (44) and committed suicide after Philippi (42).

Lucius Sergius CATILINE
Catiline was a patrician who, when defeated in elections for the consulship of 63 and 62, formed a conspiracy to overthrow the Roman state. When the plot was discovered by the consul Cicero, Catiline left Rome to take command of his army, sparking Rome's fifth civil war (63–62). Catiline was defeated and killed.

Gaius Porcius CATO
In late 59 Cato attempted to prosecute the triumvirs' ally Aulus Gabinius for electoral misconduct but was prevented from doing so when the presiding praetor refused to allow the case to proceed. At a subsequent *contio* he attacked the triumvirs and called Pompey a dictator; as a result he was physically beaten by their followers. After becoming tribune in 56, he reconciled with the triumvirs.

Marcus Porcius CATO Uticensis (95–46)
Cato "the Younger" announced his arrival on the political scene with a fiery speech in the senate demanding the execution of the Catilinarian conspirators without trial (63). He became an *optimate* leader by 59, despite having held only the offices of quaestor (64) and tribune (62). His uncompromising conservatism had made enemies of the people and the equestrians, and drove Caesar, Crassus, and Pompey to form the triumvirate. During the decade of the 50s he continued to fight the triumvirs before finally reconciling with Pompey in opposition to Caesar. He committed suicide in Utica in North Africa during the civil war rather than live under Caesar's dictatorship.

Marcus Tullius CICERO (106–43)
Rome's foremost orator, author, and lawyer, Cicero was (usually) an advocate for *optimate* causes. A *novus homo* from Arpinum, he became consul in 63 and used his year in office to rally Rome against the Catilinarians; his execution of the ringleaders without trial would later help bring about his banishment. His letters provide key contemporary information and a chronological framework for the events of 59. His criticism of the triumvirate eventually led to Clodius's election to the tribunate (58) and his own exile (58–57). After his diplomatic efforts failed to avoid civil war, he sided with Pompey before becoming reconciled to Caesar. He was killed by soldiers of the Second Triumvirate in 43.

Quintus Tullius CICERO
Proconsul in Asia (61–58), Cicero was the younger brother of Marcus Cicero, and perhaps the author of the *Commentariolum Petitionis,* purportedly written to guide his brother's campaign for the consulship of 63. He was praetor in 62.

CLEOPATRA VII (69–30)
Queen of Egypt (51–49, 47–30) and daughter of Ptolemy XII, Cleopatra ruled Egypt jointly with her brother and husband Ptolemy XIII before being forced out in 49. With Caesar's help she returned and reclaimed the throne in 47, and her brother disappeared shortly thereafter. With Caesar she had a son, Ptolemy XV Caesarion; both were in Rome when Caesar was assassinated. She later married Marcus Antonius, with whom she had three children. Defeated by Octavian at Actium (31), the couple returned to Egypt and eventually committed suicide (30). Octavian killed Caesarion but spared her three children by Antonius.

CLODIA
One of Clodius's three notorious and beautiful sisters, Clodia played a large behind-the-scenes role in her brother's political career. Although married to Quintus Caecilius Metellus Celer, she was carrying on an affair with the famous poet Gaius Valerius Catullus; it is generally believed that she inspired the "Lesbia" of his poems. Vicious gossip blamed her for Celer's sudden death in the spring of 59. Later that year she ended her affair with Catullus and began one with Caelius.

Publius CLODIUS Pulcher (92–52)
Although he was a member of a noble patrician family, the handsome and impulsive Clodius became a popular leader willing to use unprecedented methods and even violence to further his political career. Thanks to the triumvirs, he was transferred to the plebian order in 59 and was elected tribune for 58 shortly thereafter. He used his office to build up a base of support among the urban population, which he was able to control even after his term. He was murdered in 52 during a clash with the supporters of Milo outside of Rome.

CONSIDIUS
An elderly senator, Considius still attended senate meetings even after the violence of April 4.

CORNELIA METELLA
Daughter of Quintus Caecilius Metellus Pius Scipio Nasica, Cornelia Metella was married to Crassus's son Publius (55–53) before becoming Pompey's fifth and last wife. Their marriage in 52 represented an important step in the improving relationship between Pompey and the *optimates* and an important step in Pompey's move away from Caesar. During the civil war Cornelia went with him to Egypt where she witnessed his murder in 48.

Gaius COSCONIUS
On the Board of Five created by Caesar's first land law, Cosconius was also praetor in 63.

Marcus Licinius CRASSUS (112–53)
From a noble plebian family, Crassus was probably Rome's richest man; he used that wealth and his own formidable political skills to become one of Rome's most powerful and feared senators, consul twice (70, 55), censor (65), and a member of the First Triumvirate. He was killed in Parthia after the Battle of Carrhae.

Gaius Scribonius CURIO
Sullan adherent and consul in 76, Curio wrote pamphlets and delivered orations that ridiculed Caesar, most notably regarding his relationship with King Nicomedes IV of Bithynia. He publicly mocked Pompey for marrying Caesar's daughter Julia, claiming that Pompey's previous wife Mucia had been having an affair with Caesar. After his son came to him with information about the Vettius conspiracy, however, he informed both Pompey and the senate.

Gaius Scribonius CURIO
Son of the above, Curio was the leader of a young group of nobles that included Clodius, Caelius, and Marcus Antonius. Perhaps the first to speak out critically and publicly against the triumvirate after the violence of April 4, he became a hero to many in Rome. He was implicated but cleared in the Vettius conspiracy later that summer. He shocked Rome when as tribune in 50 he suddenly became a supporter of Caesar, thanks to bribes secretly arriving from Gaul. When his efforts to help Rome avoid civil war failed, he became an officer in Caesar's army before being killed in 49.

Lucius DOMITIUS Ahenobarbus
An *optimate* politician, Domitius was married to Cato's sister Porcia and was a bitter enemy of Pompey, who had killed his brother in the 80s. Colleague and ally of Memmius in the praetorship in 58, he spent most of that year and the following decade opposing the triumvirate. He became consul (54) before siding with Pompey in the civil war. Despite being spared by Caesar in 49, he continued to fight against him and died after Pharsalus in 48.

Quintus FABIUS Maximus
One of three men who prosecuted Gaius Antonius, Fabius became consul in 45.

Gaius FANNIUS
A tribune in 59 and an opponent of the triumvirs, Fannius was in the forum with his ally Bibulus on April 4, 59. Like the consul, he retired to his home on April 5 to observe the heavens for the rest of his term as tribune. He rose to be praetor.

Marcus FAVONIUS
Quaestor in 59 and staunch *optimate* and ally of Cato, whom he consciously imitated, Favonius rose to the office of praetor in 49. He fought against Caesar in the civil war but was spared. He was executed by the victorious Second Triumvirate after the Battle of Philippi in 42.

Lucius FLAVIUS
A popular politician, as tribune in 60 Flavius attempted to pass a land law to benefit the veterans of his ally Pompey. Thanks to the opposition of the consul Metellus Celer the proposal was never voted on. With help from the triumvirs, Flavius won election in 59 for the praetorship of 58.

Gaius Alfius FLAVUS
A tribune in 59, Flavus was an ally of the triumvirs.

Aulus GABINIUS
A popular politician, as tribune in 67 Gabinius passed the *lex Gabinia* giving Pompey an extraordinary command to fight the pirates in the east; he later served as a legate in Pompey's army (66–63). With the support of the triumvirs he won election to the consulship during the year 59, and while in office in 58 he and his colleague Piso allied with Clodius against Cicero, leading to his appointment as proconsul of Syria (57–54) as a reward. Convicted in court and exiled in 54, in part because of the hostility of the *publicani*, he sided with Caesar during the civil war, dying in 47.

TIBERIUS Sempronius GRACCHUS (163–133)
Tiberius Gracchus's year as tribune in 133 began the Roman Revolution. He demonstrated the potential power of his office and of the people voting in the tribal assembly in defiance of the senate. His attempt later in the year to run for reelection led to his assassination by a group of senators and their followers who were unwilling to accept a diminution of senatorial authority. This assassination marked the first use of violence in Roman politics.

Quintus HORTENSIUS Hortalus
Optimate politician, ally of Sulla, and one of Rome's foremost orators and lawyers, Hortensius held the consulship in 69. He was a close friend of Cato, who divorced his wife Marcia so she could marry Hortensius.

JULIA
Daughter of Caesar and his first wife Cornelia, Julia was Caesar's only child in 59. She married Pompey in the spring of that year—shocking Roman society. Although the marriage was a political arrangement, their loving relationship served to cement the alliance between her father and her husband. Her death in childbirth in 54,

and the death of the baby as well, represented the first major blow to the triumvirate.

Gnaeus Cornelius LENTULUS CLODIANUS
As praetor in 59, Lentulus Clodianus presided over the trial of Gaius Antonius in the forum that ended in early April with the defendant's conviction.

Marcus Aemilius LEPIDUS
An ally of Caesar and consul in 46, Lepidus became Pontifex Maximus after Caesar's death in 44 and joined the Second Triumvirate in 43. His misguided effort in 36 to defy Octavian and capture Sicily led to a mutiny of his army and his forced retirement. He retained the title of Pontifex Maximus until his death in 12.

Lucius LUCCEIUS
Wealthy friend of Pompey, and praetor in 67, Lucceius ran for the consulship on the ticket with Caesar in 60. Despite massive bribery, Lucceius lost to the *optimate* candidate Bibulus. He sided with Pompey during the civil war but was spared by Caesar.

Lucius Licinius LUCULLUS (116–56)
Leading *optimate*, ally of Sulla, and brother-in-law of Cato, Lucullus was a bitter enemy of both Clodius, who had participated in a mutiny in his army in the east (68), and Pompey, who he believed had stolen the glory for his victory over Mithridates VI. He helped block approval of Pompey's eastern arrangements and opposed the triumvirate in 59. After the violence of April 4 and the threats issued by Caesar against him in the senate, he retired from politics. His love of luxury became proverbial.

Gaius MARIUS (157–86)
A *novus homo* from Arpinum who held the office of consul seven times (107, 104–100, 86) and won two major wars over King Jugurtha in North Africa (107–105) and against the German tribes (104–101), in 107 Marius eliminated the property requirement for military service, which meant that from that point on most Roman soldiers would be poor citizen volunteers who were sometimes more loyal to their generals than to the state. Ambitious senators would later use those soldiers against Rome. The first example came when Marius attempted to procure the command against Mithridates VI in 88, prompting Sulla's march on Rome. Forced to flee, Marius returned with his own army after Sulla's departure for the east (87), defeating Sulla's adherents in Rome's first civil war and seizing control of the city. After massacring his enemies he became consul for the seventh time in 86 before dying early in the year. His allies, the "Marians," continued to control Rome until Sulla's return.

Gaius MEMMIUS
Hostile to the triumvirs in 59, while praetor in 58 Memmius and his colleague Domitius attempted to launch a senatorial investigation into Caesar's conduct as consul. When this failed they attacked Caesar's allies, first an unnamed quaestor from 59 and then Vatinius. The fate of the quaestor is unknown; Vatinius's trial ended without a verdict thanks to the violence employed by the tribune Clodius.

Marcus Valerius MESSALLA Niger
On the Board of Five created by Caesar's first land law, Messalla was consul in 61 and censor in 55.

Quintus Caecilius METELLUS CELER
Metellus Celer was proconsul of Transalpine Gaul in 59. Like his brother Metellus Nepos, he became a bitter enemy of Pompey's after Pompey divorced their half-sister Mucia Tertia in 62, though he waited until after his election to the consulship in 61 to break openly. As consul in 60 he successfully blocked the efforts of his colleague Afranius and the tribune Lucius Flavius to pass Pompey's legislation. He died suddenly in the spring of 59 before going to his province; gossip blamed his wife Clodia for his death.

Quintus Caecilius METELLUS NEPOS
Brother of Metellus Celer, and a close ally of Pompey's during much of the 60s, Metellus Nepos proposed the law to recall Pompey that was blocked thanks to the violence employed by his fellow tribunes Cato and Thermus. When Pompey divorced Metellus Nepos's half-sister Mucia Tertia in 62, Nepos turned against his former friend. He no doubt aided his brother's resistance to Pompey's legislation during Celer's consulship (60), and was hostile to the triumvirs in 59. He became consul in 57.

Quintus Caecilius METELLUS Pius SCIPIO Nasica
A tribune in 59, Metellus Scipio was born into the Cornelii Scipiones family and adopted into the Caecilii Metelli family—an illustrious lineage unequaled in Rome. He and Cato were bitter enemies, in part because Metellus married Aemilia Lepida, whom Cato had intended to marry. He was prosecuted by Favonius in 60. He also detested Caesar, although he remained friendly with Pompey. He became Pompey's consular colleague in 52 after Pompey married his daughter Cornelia. He committed suicide in North Africa after defeat at the hands of Caesar in the civil war in 46.

Titus Annius MILO
From Lanuvium, Milo became tribune in 57 and praetor in 55. He was an ally of Pompey and chief rival of Clodius. He formed his own band of gladiators and spent much of the 50s battling his enemies in the streets of Rome. The violence culminated in Clodius's death in 52 at the hands of Milo's men and the appointment of Pompey as sole consul. In a courtroom surrounded by Pompey's soldiers, Milo was convicted of Clodius's murder and exiled to Massilia. He was killed in the civil war (48).

MITHRIDATES VI
King of Pontus (120–63), Mithridates fought and lost the three Mithridatic Wars against Rome (89–85, 83–82, 74–63). Finally he was forced to order his own bodyguard to kill him in 63.

MUCIA TERTIA
Mucia Tertia became Pompey's third wife in 79 and was the mother of his three children, but she was unfaithful (possibly with Caesar) while Pompey campaigned in

the east. His divorce of her in 62 would transform her half-brothers Metellus Celer and Metellus Nepos from Pompey's political allies into his enemies.

MUNATIUS Rufus
Munatius was a close friend of Cato's, who was present with him on the podium of the Temple of Castor and Pollux when violence broke out in 62. He was possibly an eyewitness to the events of 59 as well. Later he accompanied Cato to Cyprus (58) before a falling-out between the two led him to pen an unflattering biography of his former friend that was used by later historians.

NICOMEDES IV Philopator
King of Bithynia (94–74), Nicomedes's close relationship with Caesar generated rumors in Rome that followed the latter throughout his political career.

Lucius NINNIUS Quadratus
A tribune in 58 and ally of Cicero, Ninnius failed in his efforts to prevent Cicero's exile at the hands of his fellow tribune Clodius.

Gaius OCTAVIUS
From Velitrae, Octavius held the praetorship in 61 and was proconsul in Macedonia (60–59). He died sometime in 59 and never rose to the consulship. He was married to Atia, Caesar's niece, and was the father of Gaius Octavius, later known as Augustus.

Gaius OCTAVIUS (63 BC–AD 14)
Son of the above and Caesar's great-nephew, Octavius was only eighteen when Caesar was killed in 44. By Caesar's will he was adopted as his son, which meant he inherited Caesar's wealth and Caesar's name and would thenceforth be known as Gaius Julius Caesar Octavianus, or Octavian. He used his wealth and his name to secure the loyalty of many of Caesar's soldiers. Despite his youth, he outmaneuvered his more experienced rivals, and with his victory at Actium in 31 secured control of the Roman world as emperor in all but name. In 27 he took the title Augustus.

Lucius Aemilius Lepidus PAULLUS
Paullus was quaestor in 59. His father, Marcus Aemilius Lepidus (cos. 78), had rebelled against Rome, precipitating the fourth civil war, before being defeated by Pompey and killed while in flight. *Optimate* enemy of the triumvirate, though serving under Gaius Octavius in Macedonia in 59, he was implicated by Vettius in the alleged conspiracy to kill Pompey. While consul in 50, he surprised Rome by becoming a defender of Caesar's interests during the buildup to the civil war, thanks to money sent by Caesar from Gaul.

Marcus PETREIUS
With a long career of military service, Petreius became praetor by 64, and in 59 he protested in the senate against Caesar's autocratic methods. Pompey's legate in Spain (55–49), he committed suicide in Africa during the civil war (46).

Lucius Calpurnius PISO Caesoninus
Roman noble with political ties that spanned the political spectrum, Piso's daughter Calpurnia married Caesar in 59 before his successful campaign for the consulship for 58. After the sudden death of Metellus Celer, the governor of the province of Transalpine Gaul, Piso and Pompey convinced the senate to add that province to Caesar's command. Along with his consular colleague Gabinius, he worked with Clodius against Cicero and in exchange received the proconsulship of the lucrative province of Macedonia (57–55). He remained neutral during the civil war.

Lucius PLANCIUS
A prominent publican leader and managing director of a company that was probably involved in the dispute over the Asian tax contract leased by the censors in 61, Plancius protested vociferously against the ill treatment of his order by Cato and other senators. He happily cast the first vote in the assembly to revise the contract in 59.

POMPEIA
Granddaughter of Sulla, Pompeia was the second of Caesar's three wives. The marriage ended after five years as a result of the Bona Dea scandal (62–61) and rumors of her affair with Clodius. Though Caesar publicly declared her innocent, he nevertheless divorced her.

Gnaeus POMPEY Magnus (106–48)
Nicknamed Magnus ("the Great") due to his early military successes and his youthful resemblance to Alexander, Pompey was from a wealthy family from Picenum. He triumphed over three continents, making him Rome's outstanding general in 59. Military glory translated into political power, and as part of the First Triumvirate he remained preeminent throughout the 50s before being challenged by his former ally and father-in-law, Caesar. After losing the civil war battle at Pharsalus in Greece he fled to Egypt, where he was assassinated by agents of Ptolemy XIII upon his arrival.

PTOLEMY
King of Cyprus (80–58), Ptolemy, the son of King Ptolemy IX of Egypt and younger brother of Ptolemy XII, ruled Cyprus until Clodius's law determined that the island was to be absorbed by Rome. He committed suicide before Cato arrived to organize Rome's new territory and add it to the province of Cilicia.

PTOLEMY XII Auletes
King of Egypt (80–58, 55–51), Ptolemy XII was the son of Ptolemy IX. He gave the triumvirs and other senators enormous amounts of money to win recognition as a friend and ally of Rome. Driven out of Egypt in a rebellion led by his own daughter, Berenice (58), he was eventually restored by Gabinius (55) and ruled until his death in 51. He was the father of Cleopatra and Ptolemy XIII.

PTOLEMY XIII
King of Egypt (51–47), Ptolemy XIII was the son of Ptolemy XII. Younger brother and husband of Cleopatra, he ruled Egypt jointly with her until he drove her out in 49. He

had his agents assassinate the fleeing Pompey after the Battle of Pharsalus in 48 to curry favor with the victorious Caesar, but the plan backfired: Caesar restored Cleopatra to the throne and Ptolemy disappeared; purportedly he drowned in the Nile River.

Publius Servilius RULLUS
A popular politician who consciously affected the look and dress of tribunes from the early republic, as tribune in 63 Rullus promulgated a land law to help the poor and Pompey's veterans that in many ways foreshadowed Caesar's proposal of 59. It was defeated in part due to speeches delivered by Cicero at a series of *contiones*.

SERVILIA
Half-sister of Cato, mother of Brutus, mother-in-law of Cassius, and lover of Caesar, Servilia played an important role in Roman politics throughout the 50s and 40s. Supposedly, when her son was implicated in the Vettius conspiracy, her late-night visit to Caesar led to his removal from the list of plotters.

Lucius Cornelius SULLA Felix (138–78)
Sulla ("the Lucky") became consul in 88 and was given the command in the war against Mithridates VI. When Marius attempted to replace him, he used his army to march on Rome, the first time a Roman general had captured the capital. After killing some of his enemies he left for the east and won the First Mithridatic War. His return to Italy sparked Rome's second civil war (83–82), and his victory allowed him to assume Rome's first individual, extended dictatorship (82–79), during which he murdered thousands of his enemies. Despite his revolutionary actions, he was an *optimate* politician, passing legislation that he hoped would put the collective body of the senate firmly in control of Rome. He retired in 79 and died a year later. Although his reforms failed, his brutal reign would long be remembered.

TERENTIA
Cicero's first wife, Terentia, because of her hatred for Clodia convinced Cicero to testify against Clodius in the Bona Dea trial, with disastrous results.

Quintus Minucius THERMUS
In 62 Thermus allied with his fellow tribune Cato to oppose Nepos, participating in the violence that ultimately blocked the latter's proposed legislation to recall Pompey to Italy to finish the war against the Catilinarians.

Gnaeus TREMELLIUS Scrofa
On the Board of Twenty created by Caesar's first land law, Tremellius was praetor by 58.

Marcus Terentius VARRO
On the Board of Twenty created by Caesar's first land law, praetor, and legate of Pompey in Spain and the east, Varro wrote a pamphlet to instruct his friend on senatorial practices.

Publius VATINIUS
A tribune in 59 and a popular politician and ally of the triumvirs, while in office Vatinius passed the *lex Vatinia* and other important legislation. He became praetor (55) and consul (47), and served as legate on Caesar's staff in Gaul and during the civil war.

Lucius VETTIUS
Involved in the Catilinarian conspiracy (63), Vettius became an informant and helped Cicero foil the plot. In 59 he claimed to be involved in another scheme, this time to assassinate Pompey, and he named numerous senators as co-conspirators including the younger Curio, Paullus, Brutus, Bibulus, Lucullus, Domitius, and Cicero. His claims were doubted, leading to his imprisonment and subsequent murder by unknown parties. The truth behind the Vettius conspiracy has been the subject of debate ever since.

APPENDIX C
Chronology

This chronology for the year 59 in particular is based on the ancient literary sources discussed in appendix D and the reconstruction of the evidence provided in appendix E. Some months and days are conjectural. Events listed with a dash (—) happened sometime between the date above and the next date listed in the timeline. All dates are BC unless otherwise noted.

753–61 BC

753	Romulus founds the city of Rome after killing his twin brother, Remus
753–509	Roman monarchy; seven kings rule the city
509–31	Roman Republic
494–287	Conflict of the patrician and plebian orders
146	Destruction of Carthage renders Rome supreme in the Mediterranean world
133	Tiberius Sempronius Gracchus is tribune; Roman Revolution begins
133–31	Roman Revolution
107	Consul Gaius Marius eliminates property requirement for military service
88	Consul Lucius Cornelius Sulla becomes first Roman general to march on Rome
87	Sulla leaves for the east to fight King Mithridates VI of Pontus
	First Civil War: Marius and his followers, the "Marians," capture Rome
86	Death of Marius; "Marians" continue to control Rome
83–82	Second Civil War: Sulla defeats the Marians
82–79	Sulla's dictatorship; thousands massacred
80–72	Third Civil War: Roman forces in Spain fighting the Roman general Quintus Sertorius
79	Gnaeus Pompey Magnus celebrates his first triumph
	Sulla retires
78	Death of Sulla
78–77	Fourth Civil War: rebellion of the consul Marcus Aemilius Lepidus

74–63	Third Mithridatic War
73–71	Slave revolt of Spartacus
71	Marcus Licinius Crassus celebrates an *ovatio*
	Pompey celebrates his second triumph on December 29
70	Marcus Licinius Crassus and Gnaeus Pompey Magnus are consuls
67	*Lex Gabinia*
67–62	Pompey in the east
66	*Lex Manilia*
64	Senate places restrictions on *collegia* and games
63	Marcus Tullius Cicero and Gaius Antonius Hybrida are consuls
	Catilinarian conspiracy
63–62	Fifth Civil War: Catilinarians defeated in Italy
62–61	Bona Dea scandal
62	Gaius Julius Caesar is praetor and Marcus Porcius Cato is tribune; violence in the forum leads to the passing of the *s.c.u.*
	Pompey returns from the east
61–60	Caesar proconsul in Further Spain
61	Unknown censors grant contract to farm the taxes of Asia to publican companies
	Pompey celebrates his third triumph September 28–29
	New tribune Lucius Flavius proposes land law in December

60 BC	
January	
1	Lucius Afranius and Quintus Caecilius Metellus Celer inaugurated as consuls
—	Cato opposes *publicani*
—	Celer opposes Flavian land law
March	
15	Flavius still pushing land law
June	
3	Caesar returns from Spain
—	Cato blocks Caesar's request to stand for the consulship *in absentia*
—	Caesar skips triumph and stands for election
—	By early June Flavius has dropped his land law thanks to Celer's resistance
26	Last day for the *professio* for the consular candidates for 59
July	
13	Elections after this date; Caesar and Marcus Calpurnius Bibulus elected consuls
December	
10	Ten tribunes for 59 take office

— Caesar working to reconcile Pompey and Crassus; Lucius Cornelius Balbus's visit to Cicero

59 BC

Winter

January

1 Inauguration Day; Caesar assumes the *fasces*

— Caesar proposes land law in the senate

— Law filibustered by Cato

February

1 Bibulus assumes the *fasces*

March

1 Caesar assumes the *fasces*

— At senate meeting Cato's filibuster leads to his arrest by Caesar's *lictors*; Cato is quickly freed

— Caesar takes bill away from senate and brings it to a *contio*

9 Last day to officially promulgate the *lex Julia Agraria*

Spring

April

1 Bibulus assumes the *fasces*

3 *C* day but nundinal; no meeting of the assembly

4 *C* day, first day of Megalesian Games

Violence in the forum; Bibulus and allies forced out

Passage of *lex Julia Agraria*

5 *N* day, Bibulus presides over senate meeting; after senate refuses to authorize *s.c.u.* he retires to his house until the last day of the year

6 Earliest possible day for Cicero's closing arguments and conclusion of Gaius Antonius's trial; Antonius found guilty; later that afternoon Cicero leaves on vacation and Clodius is transferred to the plebian order

10 Second day of the Megalesian Games

11 Last possible day for end of Antonius's trial, Cicero's departure, and Clodius's transfer

18 Last day for Clodius to announce he will run for the tribunate of 58

24 *C* day, the first since April 4

25 Rumors circulating in Rome about a new land law

26 *C* day, last day to pass laws on publican contract, on Pompey's eastern settlements, on Ptolemy XII's confirmation on the Egyptian throne; proposal of a new Campanian land law; latest date for the proposal of the *lex Vatinia*; earliest possible day for Pompey's marriage to Julia; Pompey becomes Caesar's heir and

will now speak first in the senate; at roughly the same time Caesar marries Calpurnia

27 *C* day, nundinal

28 *C* day

29 Last day of April, *C* day

May

3 Last possible day for Pompey's marriage to Julia

25 *C* day, earliest possible day for the passage of the Campanian land law; earliest possible day for the passage of the *lex Vatinia;* shortly thereafter, following the sudden death of Metellus Celer, Transalpine Gaul is added to Caesar's provinces by the senate at the behest of Pompey and Piso

June

1 By this day the Campanian land law has passed

3 *C* day, Curio cheered at the theater, Caesar greeted with silence and his allies booed

4 *C* day, last possible day for the passage of the *lex Vatinia*; the senate decision on Transalpine Gaul follows a short time later

Summer

July

7 Games of Apollo begin

Pompey at Capua distributing land

13 Continuing protests against the triumvirs and their allies

14 Games of Apollo conclude

— Bibulus postpones curule elections to October 18

— Elections for the following year's plebian aediles, quaestors, and tribunes

Clodius elected tribune

25 Pompey speaks out at a *contio* against Bibulus

— Vettius affair

Fall

October

18 Curule elections: Aulus Gabinius and Lucius Calpurnius Piso Caesonius elected consuls

— Gaius Porcius Cato attempts to indict Gabinius on bribery charges, beaten in forum at a *contio* by triumvirs' supporters

December

10 New tribunes take office; Clodius proposes legislative program

29 Last day of the year, Bibulus emerges from his house; is barred from speaking to a *contio*

— Caesar delivers his farewell address

58 BC

January	
1	Inauguration Day
4	*C* day, first on which Clodius's laws could be passed
February	
—	During this month Clodius passes laws on foreign policy
—	The praetors Domitius and Memmius attack legality of Caesar's laws in the senate
—	Domitius and Memmius attack an unnamed quaestor (an ally of Caesar's) from 59
—	Vatinius returns to Rome to stand trial
Intercalaris	
20	Earliest day for Clodius's proposed law mandating exile for magistrates who put citizens to death without trial; Clodius proposes a law making Gabinius proconsul of Cilicia and Piso proconsul of Macedonia, each for five years
27	Last possible day for above events
March	
18	First *C* day to pass Clodius's new proposals; during the night Cicero leaves Rome
20	Clodius proposes new law that specifically names Cicero; Caesar leaves the environs of Rome for his provinces
27	Caesar arrives in the neighborhood of Geneva
28	Helvetii scheduled to assemble on the bank of the Rhone River
April	
—	Cato appointed proquaestor to annex Cyprus
—	Clodian law appoints Gabinius proconsul of Syria for five years
29	Cicero leaves Brundisium heading for Thessalonica in Greece

57–31 BC

57	Cicero returns from exile August 5
	Titus Annius Milo recruits his own followers to battle Clodius
	Violence in Rome
56	Conference of Luca reaffirms triumvirate
	Violence in Rome surrounding elections
55	Crassus and Pompey are consuls
54	Violence in Rome
	Death of Julia
	Gabinius exiled
53	Violence in Rome postpones elections
	Crassus killed in Parthia
52	Violence in Rome
	Year begins without curule magistrates
	Clodius killed; rioting in the city

	Pompey becomes consul without a colleague
	Pompey marries Cornelia Metella
	Caesar's victory at Alesia ends resistance to Roman conquest of Gaul
50	On March 1 the consul Gaius Claudius Marcellus tries to persuade the senate to recall Caesar
	Consul Lucius Aemilius Paullus and tribune Gaius Scribonius Curio block efforts
49	Caesar crosses the Rubicon River
49–45	Sixth Civil War
48	Death of Bibulus; Caesar defeats Pompey's army at the Battle of Pharsalus; Pompey assassinated in Egypt
47	Caesar replaces King Ptolemy XIII with Ptolemy's sister Queen Cleopatra VII; Cleopatra gives birth to Caesar's son Ptolemy XV Caesarion
46	Suicide of Cato at Utica
45	Caesar wins the civil war; returns to Rome and appoints himself dictator for ten years
44	Caesar makes himself dictator for life (February); Caesar assassinated at a meeting of the senate in the Theater of Pompey on the Ides of March (March 15) by a group of senators led by Marcus Junius Brutus and Gaius Cassius Longinus; Caesar's will names his great-nephew Gaius Octavius as his adopted son and heir
44–43	Seventh Civil War: battles in Italy following Caesar's assassination culminate in Battle of Mutina
44–43	Eighth Civil War: Brutus, Cassius, and their allies seize control of the eastern half of the empire
43	After more than a year of violence and civil war Octavian, Marcus Antonius, and Marcus Aemilius Lepidus form the Second Triumvirate, seize control of Rome and the western half of the empire, and proceed to massacre their enemies
42	Ninth Civil War: Campaign and Battle of Philippi; the armies of the Second Triumvirate defeat the army of Brutus and Cassius, and both commit suicide; the Second Triumvirate divides up the empire: Antonius rules the east, Octavius takes Italy, Gaul, and Spain, and Lepidus takes North Africa
41–40	Tenth Civil War: Perusine War in Italy
40–36	Eleventh Civil War: sporadic naval warfare against Sextus Pompey
37	Antonius marries Cleopatra
36	Defeat of Sextus Pompey; Octavian forces Lepidus out of the triumvirate and into retirement; Octavius rules all of the west while Antonius continues to rule the east

34	Donations of Alexandria: Antonius vows to leave Roman lands in the east to his children by Cleopatra
32–30	Twelfth (and last) Civil War of the republic
31	Octavian's navy destroys that of Antonius and Cleopatra at the Battle of Actium (September 2), and Antonius and Cleopatra flee back to Egypt, where they both commit suicide (30); Egypt is absorbed by Rome
31 BC–AD 14	Octavian rules Rome as first "emperor" and receives the title Augustus (27)
31 BC–AD 476	Roman Empire

APPENDIX D
The Ancient Evidence

How the events of 59 are reconstructed of necessity relies on the source material that has survived. Fortunately, more information is extant for this period than almost any other in ancient history. Extensive research by archeologists into the ruins in and around the forum has enhanced understanding of the physical setting of the events of 59. Inscriptions have survived on stone and metal, though unfortunately they are not as plentiful for the republic as they are for the empire. Coinage can also provide insight. By far the most important source of information is literary, however.[1] No contemporary historical narrative survived, but the literature that did survive provides sufficient information. Through the judicious use of this evidence and the careful consideration of the reliability of each source it is possible to reconstruct the events of the year 59.

Marcus Tullius Cicero (106–43 BC; cos. 63), a successful politician, gifted orator, and prolific writer, is an essential source for 59. Twenty-three of his letters from that year survive. Twenty-two of those were written to his friend Titus Pomponius Atticus, a group of fourteen in April and May when Cicero was on vacation, and eight more during the summer when Atticus was out of Rome.[2] Although these letters written to a close friend contain allusions and inside jokes that are often obscure, and although they do not contain a continuous narrative, they are invaluable for a number of reasons. First, they provide the best evidence concerning the year's chronology. Second, they offer behind-the-scenes information and gossip about the mechanics of Roman politics and Rome's political figures. Certainly, Cicero is hardly fair and balanced, especially when discussing political enemies such as Clodius, but he is writing to Atticus, who, though he was not a senator, was extremely knowledgeable about these matters. Cicero could not invent information Atticus would have known from other sources to be false. Corresponding with such a close friend also allowed Cicero to speak freely, permitting him to express his true opinions about partisan politics and partisan politicians. Third, Cicero may have been present at many of the assemblies, elections, and senate meetings of 59, and he may have witnessed the violence of April 4. He certainly beheld the manifestation of the triumviral backlash at the games and in the theater, and he read the lampoons and edicts issued by the triumvirate's enemies. Lastly, the letters are not contaminated by hindsight, because Cicero wrote about these events before the civil war commenced in 49. Thus, Cicero's warnings about the triumvirate's threat to the republic proved to be prescient.

Cicero also wrote numerous speeches that he delivered in trials or at *contiones*, many of which touch directly on the events of 59. The relevant court orations include speeches in defense of Flaccus in 59 and Sestius in 56, as well as those he used to prosecute enemies such as the tribune Vatinius (56) and Piso the consul (55). A number of orations delivered upon his return from exile, including the *Post reditum ad Quirites* ("To the Citizens after his Return"), and the *De domo sua* ("On His House"), also shed light on the events of 59. He composed numerous discourses on various topics, such as his treatises on the *Laws* and the *Republic*, which provide detailed descriptions of Rome's politics and government. Included in the Ciceronian corpus is the handbook on elections that is generally agreed to have been written by his brother Quintus. The *Commentariolum Petitionis* is an invaluable source of information on Roman political campaigns.

Perhaps the most valuable narrative source for the year 59 (though now lost) is the history of Gaius Asinius Pollio (76 BC–AD 4). Pollio was well qualified to write about this period. He was senator, tribune (47), praetor (45), and consul (40). He served in various military capacities, including command, and governed a number of provinces. More importantly, he was an eyewitness to many key events, including the Rubicon crossing (49) and the Battle of Pharsalus (48). He was about seventeen years old during Caesar's consulship; possibly he already frequented the forum and may have watched some of the principal events of that year unfold, perhaps even the violence of April 4.[3] Most significantly for this study, like many others he realized the crucial importance of Caesar's consulship, so his history began with the formation of the First Triumvirate.[4] His work followed events down to the Battle of Philippi (42), covering nineteen years of history in seventeen books. This expanse of writing would have provided him with plenty of space to construct an extremely detailed look at the history of each year, and in particular Caesar's consulship, which he considered to be of such importance. Although a later partisan of Caesar's, Pollio maintained his literary independence, often contradicting Caesar's version of events.[5]

Many later historians relied upon and quoted Pollio, including Appian, Dio, Plutarch, Livy, Suetonius, and Velleius.[6] And, although they disagree on some details, they generally followed a standard version of events for 59. For the first part of the year they touch on the same important highlights: the proposal of the first land law,[7] the opposition's political and religious delaying tactics,[8] Cato's arrest,[9] Caesar's decision to bypass the senate and take his proposition to the people,[10] the resulting *contio* with Bibulus, Crassus, and Pompey delivering memorable speeches to the people concerning the law,[11] and especially the violence in the forum on April 4,[12] and the breaking of the consular *fasces*.[13] Afterward the sources continue to follow the same story line, beginning with the following day's senate meeting[14] and continuing with Bibulus's long retirement,[15] the second land law,[16] the revision of the publican contracts,[17] Caesar's extraordinary command in the Gauls,[18] and the Vettius affair.[19] The ultimate source for this tradition is a matter of conjecture, but Pollio is a likely candidate. It is certain that all relevant later writers consulted his chronicle for their works, and it is very possible that they used him either directly or indirectly for the events of 59 as well. Perhaps thanks to Pollio, Plutarch knew that Bibulus stayed in his home for eight months after the violence of April 4. It is probable that later authors appropriated Pollio's basic framework, which they expanded or condensed to fit their own agenda.

The main extant authors include Cassius Dio (AD 150–235), who wrote a massive work on Rome's history from its origins to his own times and who provides the longest narrative of the events leading up to and including 59. Dio was not as fortunate as Appian or Plutarch. Born during the period of the five good emperors, he had witnessed a steady deterioration in Rome's fortunes. Dio had extensive political and military experience. He was consul suffectus in AD 204, proconsul in Africa, and consul in 229. Dio may have had access to the *acta diurna,* essentially a newsletter published in Rome that recorded important events, senatorial decrees, notable legislation, rituals, court cases, and speeches. This archive may have provided records about the significant proceedings of 59, such as Caesar's first land law and Pompey's speech in favor of that law, which Dio quotes in detail. Pompey's oration contains thorough and seemingly contemporary information, in particular the material on the *lex Plotia*. Dio was undoubtedly "familiar with senatorial and comitial procedure" and both of Caesar's land laws, and he knew about the assembly law and senatorial act that provided Caesar with his three provinces.[20] Dio may also have been familiar with Cicero's work. One example involved the trial of Gaius Antonius. Cicero spoke in Antonius's defense and later published his summation; Dio most likely made use of this work (now lost), since he provides many details about the case.[21] Dio was also certainly acquainted with Pollio.[22] In general, therefore, Dio is a dependable source for the events of 59.[23]

Plutarch of Chaeronea (AD 46–120) wrote a series of biographies comparing famous Romans to famous Greeks. Most importantly for this study, he composed twelve biographies of notable Roman politicians from the late republic, including Crassus, Lucullus, Pompey, Caesar, Cicero, and Cato. Plutarch was not necessarily interested in composing continuous historical narratives and warns his readers that he will summarize many significant events or skip over them altogether.[24] Instead, his focus was the character of his subjects and how their personal traits and their historical achievements reveal their virtues, vices, and "soul."[25] Plutarch sought to provide models for individuals to emulate, along with examples that were to be avoided.[26] Political success and a leader's ability to inspire the respect and loyalty of his fellow citizens are of great interest to Plutarch. Crucially, he discusses his protagonists' youth, family life, their personality traits, appearance, and how these all translated into the accumulation of political power. This biographical detail about men like Crassus and Pompey generally cannot be found in any other source.

Plutarch relied heavily on Pollio's lost history. However, Plutarch discovered Pollio later in his career, and so his earlier biographies (on Lucullus and Cicero) did not provide detailed information about Roman politics in the 60s and 50s.[27] Thanks in part to Pollio, the later lives demonstrate a much greater understanding of the Roman political process. Though Pollio was an important source for political history, his work was deficient in biographical information. To find the vivid evidence he needed, Plutarch therefore turned to other sources, including many now lost. For example, for the details of Pompey's early life and rise to power he made use of Theophanes's biography of his patron.

Comfortably removed in time from the events he was describing, Plutarch did not have a political agenda that colored his presentation; therefore, he did not suppress or embellish to fit a preconceived political picture. Instead he often allowed both friendly and hostile voices to be heard so that the mingling of sources provided more than one viewpoint on his biographical subjects. For instance, Plutarch used two diametrically opposed sources for his biography of Lucullus. The first is the epic poem of Archias, written to celebrate his patron Lucullus.[28] Plutarch's second source is the lost *Histories* of Sallust, which represents a tradition hostile to Lucullus. Because he draws on these contradictory sources, he portrays Lucullus not only as a great general and politician but also as a typically haughty noble unpopular with the people.[29] The *Life of Caesar* includes information from the laudatory Oppius and criticism from Pollio and others. Cato's *Life* is another case in point. Plutarch used the admiring biographies of Brutus and Cicero as well as the "hagiographies" of Lucan and Seneca. The description of Cato's march from the senate to the *carcer* surrounded by "all" of his supportive fellow citizens may derive from one of these sources. Yet Plutarch also included unflattering details from Cato's life derived from negative pamphlets, including one written by Augustus, and the *Anticato,* composed by Caesar immediately following Cato's death. Plutarch relied on another source written by Cato's former friend Munatius Rufus. Munatius was present in the forum during the turmoil concerning the vote on the command against Catiline in 62, and was in fact on the podium with Cato and Caesar when the violence began.[30] Pompey used Munatius to bring an offer of a marriage alliance to Cato.[31] As a close associate of Cato's, he may have been an eyewitness to the key events of 59, before eventually accompanying Cato to Cyprus in 58. After a falling-out between the two men, Munatius published a biography of Cato that included a number of disparaging references to his excessive drinking and his unhappy marriages.[32] Using so many different sources allowed Plutarch to paint a nuanced picture of his subjects, rather than presenting either partisan screed or eulogy. Plutarch admires Cato and provides many examples of his rectitude, but at the same time he criticizes his rigidity and his unwillingness to negotiate or bend on any issue, a trait that led to the formation of the First Triumvirate and, Plutarch believed, ultimately to the fall of the republic.

Another critical but concise source is Gaius Suetonius Tranquillus (AD 70–130). Suetonius wrote biographies of Caesar and Rome's first eleven emperors. Under Trajan (reign AD 98–117) and Hadrian (reign AD 117–138) Suetonius became manager of the imperial libraries and then was made responsible for the emperor's mail. These positions offered him a unique opportunity to make use of the libraries and archives, and allowed him to employ legislative documents, letters, and many other important records in his biographies. He sometimes incorporated verbatim quotes from material he found in the records. Unlike many other authors, he is not attempting to tell a dramatic story or use his history as a morality lesson. Therefore, he provides material that is both favorable and unfavorable to his subjects, usually without editorial comment. This level of impartiality and detachment renders Suetonius a valuable resource. For his biography of Caesar, Suetonius provides detailed information about Caesar's early life and rise to power.[33] He also presents some interesting insight into Caesar's consulship, offering evidence on Caesar's various laws that he may have found in the archives.

Titus Livius, or Livy (59 BC–AD 17), wrote 142 books on Roman history from the founding of the city, of which only thirty-five survive (I–X, XXI–XLV), all from the early or middle republic. Also surviving were the *Periochae*, abstracts of all Livy's books, which spring directly from the originals, representing "a reasonably faithful summary."[34] Livy apparently covered the year 59 in some detail, but unfortunately that part of his history has vanished and only a brief summary remains.[35] However, the original may have been used by many later ancient authors, such as Dio and Plutarch, whose works have survived.[36] In addition, Livy's first ten books, though ostensibly about early Rome, borrow heavily from the history of the late republic to fill the sparse historical tradition. Thus, much of the political history detailed in those books is based on or wholly borrowed from the history of the late republic.

Other ancient authors provide some information for the events of 59. These included the early imperial writers Velleius Paterculus and Appian. Velleius had extensive political and military experience, becoming quaestor (AD 6) and later praetor (AD 15). Velleius technically wrote a historical narrative, but because he attempted to compress all of Roman history into two books, his work is often light on description and detail, although it does provide a brief outline of the year 59 and some important biographical notes on Pompey and Caesar. Appian of Alexandria (AD 95–165) wrote five books on Rome's civil wars and others on Rome's foreign wars (the *Mithridatica*, for example). For the late republic Appian made extensive use of Pollio, among others.[37]

There are a number of authors whose works influence our understanding of Roman politics in the late republic, even though they did not write about the year 59. Polybius (200–118), a native of Megalopolis in Greece, possessed political and military experience in his own city and in the Achaean League, for which he served as *hipparch* (170–169). After being deported to Rome, he decided to write a universal history that would trace and explain Rome's rise to power in the Mediterranean. Rome provided him with the resources he needed to produce an excellent history: public and private archives, and the very people who made the history of his time. Polybius supplemented his own early political and military experience in Greece by accompanying Scipio Aemilianus around Rome, certainly learning about Roman politics in the process. He was therefore well qualified to write a history of Rome. Although Polybius was born a century before Caesar, he is still a very important source for the year 59. Book six of his history provides a study of the Roman political system that is unparalleled in the extant sources. In addition, Polybius died before the civil wars and violence of the late republic. He is the only historian who was not influenced by the history of the Roman Revolution, and one of the few who was not prejudiced by the advent of the empire and later imperial history. His account was therefore not contaminated by hindsight.[38]

Another key author is Gaius Sallustius Crispus (86–35 BC). Sallust was a Roman senator who, with Caesar's help, rose to the praetorship in 46 and became governor of Africa in 46–45. He commanded a legion in Illyria in 49 and served in Caesar's army in the African campaign in 46. He lived through the period in question and knew many of the key players, most notably Caesar. He was twenty-seven in 59 and may have been in the capital in that year. He wrote two monographs that survive, *The Jugurthine War* and *The Catilinarian Conspiracy*. He also composed the *Histories* that covered the years from

Sulla's death in 78 to 67 BC, but most of this work is now lost. While Sallust did not specifically cover the year 59, he provides insight into political life during the first century and offers detailed descriptions of the workings of the political system and partisan politics.

The upper-class background of the authors or the difficult, often anarchic times through which some of them lived generally led to prejudice in favor of the senate. Mostly negative themes, or *topoi*, were employed to describe the behavior of the mass of poor citizens in what was part of the standard rhetorical techniques. For instance, the people were portrayed as irresponsible, weak, and gullible, but, like a calm sea, they were harmless and quiet, posing little threat to those who sail on it. However, when violent winds stir up this sea, the sea takes on the characteristics of that violent wind and become dangerous. Troubles begin only when a demagogue (like Clodius), the "violent wind," begins to instigate unrest among the weak-willed citizens. In those circumstances the people exhibited a mob mentality, becoming bolder the larger their numbers. Yet poor citizens were to some extent also portrayed as gullible children, easily led or misled, in need of a firm hand.[39] They would behave alternately angry and menacing, or cowardly and afraid. One minute they would lash out violently, the next they would repent. Indulging the people led to trouble, so politicians who could keep the people under control, who used ancient, old-fashioned authority to restrain the mob, were usually portrayed in a positive light. As a result, the ancient narratives tend to favor the *optimate* cause and the senators who refused to pander to the people.

Furthermore, although Plutarch, Appian, and others enjoyed the benefits of the *Pax Romana*, there was a certain nostalgia for the lost republic, the free state led by the senate. Therefore, Cato emerges as a tragic hero, fighting (futilely in the long run) to stop the (inevitable) slide toward monarchy. Conversely, while many of the authors may have respected or admired Caesar's political and military abilities, for many reasons he is generally portrayed as the villain of the piece. In 59 it was Caesar who passed numerous laws favorable to the people in the fashion of a "revolutionary" tribune rather than a responsible consul, and of course it was Caesar who used violence to realize his political program, attacking magistrates and senators in the heart of the city. More importantly, later authors knew Caesar was to blame not just for the troubles of 59 but for later actions that would contribute to the republic's fall. Thus, he was a "great actor," concealing his true desires to attain absolute power.[40] Pompey too comes in for criticism. It was his veterans who provided the force necessary for Caesar's actions and according to Plutarch during the course of the year 59 he generally acted "unworthy of his own dignity."[41] Historians writing after the period addressed in this book knew what the ultimate outcomes of the formation of the First Triumvirate and Caesar's first consulship were, and their histories were influenced by hindsight: their narratives assert that from the beginning the republic's fall had been part of a well-designed plan whose perpetrators purposely "plotted to destroy the state."[42]

APPENDIX E

Dating of Events of the Year 59

Determining the chronology of the events of 59 is crucial but often extremely difficult. Historians have long debated the year's precise timeline, particularly the exact date of the forum violence and the final vote on Caesar's first agrarian law. Fortunately, a reexamination of the ancient sources can provide a chronological framework. Specifically, the date for the violence and vote can be fixed, which then allows for a reasonable estimate regarding the dates for the year's other important events.

Critical chronological clues are provided by the vacationing Cicero, who in April 59 wrote seven letters to Atticus in Rome.[1] The seventh letter, penned at four in the afternoon at Tres Tabernae, can be firmly dated to April 19, 59, "Ceres Day."[2] The dating of the others is less precise; the fifth and sixth letters were written around April 16 and 17.[3] The first four were written on separate days earlier in April; the absolute latest they could have been composed if written on consecutive days was April 12 through April 15.[4] Cicero makes clear that by mid-April certain important events had taken place in Rome, most notably that Caesar's first *lex Agraria* had passed.[5] Cicero mentions the law in a letter that was written in Antium on April 14 at the latest.[6] Factoring in the time it would take a messenger to bring the breaking political news to Antium, the last day the first law could have been approved in the capital was April 13.

The historians who have weighed in on this problem agree that Caesar's legislation must have been ratified by the voters before April 13, 59. But the question remains: When exactly did the law pass? The theories range from late January (Lintott, Scullard, Goldsworthy), and specifically January 29 (Taylor), to sometime in March (Gelzer).[7] To find the answer, the role of the *lictors* and their *fasces* in these events must first be examined, something scholars have generally failed to do. Roman consuls held the *fasces* in alternate months during their year in office. The *consul prior* (the consul elected first for a given year) held the *fasces* in January and in each odd-numbered month that followed; the consul elected second held the *fasces* in even-numbered months.[8] When a consul "held" the *fasces* during his month they were in reality carried by his twelve *lictors*, who marched before him in single file. Meanwhile, his colleague was preceded by only one *accensus* (attendant), while his twelve *lictors* followed behind him without the symbols of consular authority.[9] Since Caesar's name comes first in the *fasti* (the official consular list) it is commonly accepted that he was elected first and held the *fasces* in January, March, and the other odd-numbered months of 59.[10] Bibulus possessed the *fasces* in February, April, and the even-numbered months. The timing of the holding of the *fasces* is well known, but the link between that timing and the year 59 has gone unnoticed. The ancient evidence makes clear that on the dramatic day in the forum it was Bibulus's *lictors* who walked in front of him carrying the *fasces*. When violence erupted, Caesar's followers smashed Bibulus's *fasces* to symbolize that his power to obstruct the land law had been broken as well.[11] It is therefore certain that on the day of the forum violence Bibulus held the *fasces*. That day must have been in an even-numbered month, either February or April, before the thirteenth.

Another important piece of evidence can help determine the month. The sources make clear that Bibulus retreated to his house the day after the violence in the forum.[12] He remained there until the last day of the year, December 29, 59. Possibly drawing upon information found in Pollio's history or Munatius Rufus's biography of Cato, Plutarch maintains in his *Life of Pompey* that Bibulus stayed in his house for eight months.[13] Plutarch is the only source to provide a specific length of time.[14] This indicates that April is the only plausible month, since it was necessary for Bibulus both to possess the *fasces* and to leave the political stage for an eight-month period. Some historians who argue for a different date completely ignore Plutarch's evidence. Those who do acknowledge Plutarch's claim contend that the author was confused; unaware of Caesar's first land law, he knew only that the second, Campanian legislation passed around June 1.[15] He then incorrectly reckoned the time of Bibulus's confinement based on the later date. However, Plutarch composed the *Caesar* first, before the *Cato* and the *Pompey*, which were "prepared together."[16] In both the *Caesar* and the *Cato* Plutarch recognized that there were two separate land laws.[17] He mentioned only one law in the *Pompey*, but Plutarch definitely knew from his source that Bibulus withdrew after the first law passed and he knew the correct length of time he stayed home.[18] A January retreat for Bibulus would require eleven months at home; a June departure would require six months—definitely not the greater part of the year that Velleius speaks of. Only April allows for the eight-month retirement Plutarch described.

The Roman calendar can help determine the exact day. The forum violence and the assembly vote happened in April, sometime before the thirteenth. There were only two *comitial* days at the beginning of the month: April 3 and April 4. There was then a long gap before the next *comitial* day of April 24, eleven days after the last possible date for passage of Caesar's first law. April 3, however, was nundinal, a market day, which could not be used for voting assemblies.[19] Therefore the only possible day for the pivotal event of 59 was April 4.

One other piece of evidence corroborates the April 4 date. The violence and vote happened on a *C* day, on which holding an assembly was permitted by the calendar. The next day Bibulus convened and presided over the senate.[20] That day could not be a *C* day, which would preclude a senate meeting. Consequently, there had to be the proper two-day combination for these events to transpire: a *C* day (which was not also a market day) for an assembly, followed by a different type of day for a senate meeting. Between January 1 and April 13 there are thirteen instances of the correct combination. Four (January 4–5, 8–9, 10–11, 12–13) are too early in January; there was not enough time for a bill to be proposed and then, after the mandatory *trinundinum*, to be voted on. Five more (January 29–February 1, March 6–7, 12–13, 21–22, March 31–April 1) can be eliminated because on each of the *C* days Bibulus was not holding the *fasces,* so they therefore could not have been broken by Caesar's supporters. Three are in February (February 20–21, 25–26, February 28–March 1); these are also too early in the year, for if Bibulus retired to his home on any of those days his stay would have been more than ten months, too long according to Plutarch. The only two-day combination that works is April 4–5. In April Bibulus held the *fasces,* and April 4 was indeed a *C* day, allowing the assembly to meet and the *fasces* to be smashed. April 5 was an *N* day, allowing the senate to convene. Bibulus's retirement on that day meant that he would be in his house for eight months until the end of December.

Despite the above evidence, a number of objections have been raised. It has been claimed that April 4 cannot work because it marked the beginning of the Megalesian Games, a two-day event (April 4 and April 10) that commemorated the original arrival of the Great Goddess into Rome from Anatolia (on April 4) and the dedication of her first temple in the city (April 10).[21] It has been argued that such a festival precluded the holding of an assembly. Consequently, this argument goes, since April 3 was nundinal, and April 4 was reserved for the first day of the games, and the next *comitial* day was not until April 24, after the law had definitely been passed, it must have been approved before the month of April.[22] However, although magistrates may have generally avoided holding assemblies on game days, no evidence exists that doing so was unconstitutional or contrary to religious law. There is no evidence that the Megalesian Games or any similar event precluded an assembly vote or other important political business.[23] For example, in 66 the tribune Gaius Manilius held an assembly vote during the *ludi compitalicii.*[24]

Another argument against an April date involves the boards established to divide up the land under the new law. Taylor has maintained that it would be impossible to pass the law and elect commissioners on the same day.[25] Therefore, she argues, there must have been votes on two different days, which would then preclude an April date, since only April 4 was available for an assembly. A number of counterarguments can be made. First, when Caesar took control of the voting area he may have used that control to hold another vote to push through his slate of board candidates. Even if this act was unconstitutional, would Caesar have cared after having driven his colleague out of the forum by force?[26] Or, it is possible that the board members were already named in the original proposal. In that case, when the bill became law the boards would have been automatically created. This scenario would illuminate one reason for *optimate* opposition, since they already knew that Pompey, Crassus, and their friends would get those very important positions. Possibly the law stated that its sponsor was allowed to name the boards' members. This would provide another explanation for *optimate* opposition, since they already knew that Caesar would acquire this very important patronage opportunity. Whatever the case, it is clear that Caesar and his allies controlled the boards' membership, because five members of the Board of Twenty are known and each had a connection to them.[27] In addition, Caesar's later offer to put Cicero on one of the boards is possible only if he controlled the selection process and could ensure Cicero's inclusion.

It has also been argued that because of Caesar's celebrated alacrity, he never would have waited so long to get the bill through.[28] However, it is highly possible that with all the weapons of obstruction at their disposal Caesar's enemies could indeed have stalled the measure for months in the senate and in the forum. If the vote took place in early April, the latest it could have been proposed, due to the *trinundinum*, would have been March 9, meaning sixty-six days since Caesar became consul. This helps explain why Caesar became so enraged when Cato (again) began to filibuster: the delay had lasted not a few days but more than two months. Also, the events of the previous year clearly illustrate how opponents could impede a bill for long periods and even prevent a vote from ever being taken. Six months after Flavius's bill was first proposed, it finally appeared dead.[29] It is not implausible that Caesar's opponents, led by the determined, filibustering Cato, could have stymied his efforts from the time he took office until an early April vote. In fact, if Caesar had not employed violence to break the political impasse his bill might have suffered the same fate as Flavius's.

Ironically, April 4, the pivotal day of 59, is one of the few that can be fixed with some confidence. Other dates are harder to pin down, but thanks to the sources, once the date for the violence and vote has been established, the order of events can be discerned. In particular, Cicero's letters provide chronological "windows" when specific episodes took place. A timeline based on this reconstruction appears in appendix C.

GLOSSARY

aedile Roman magistrate who held office for one year and was responsible for the city of Rome and the public games. Two curule aediles were elected by the centuriate assembly (*comitia centuriata*); two plebian aediles were elected by the *concilium plebis*. *See also* curule aedile and plebian aedile.

atrium Area open to the sky that served as the focal point of a Roman house and usually was kept open to the public.

augur Roman priest designated to observe and interpret the auspices before any public business was conducted in the assemblies or in the senate.

Aurelian Steps Small amphitheater at the eastern end of the forum in which trials were held.

auspices The signs sent by the gods regarding the advisability of conducting political business.

Bona Dea The "Good Goddess." Secret rituals, from which men were excluded, were held annually in her honor.

boni The "good men." Another name for the *optimates*.

carcer Rome's prison.

censor Roman magistrate who held office for eighteen months and, among other duties, awarded contracts to publican companies to collect Rome's provincial taxes. Two censors were elected every five years by the centuriate assembly.

centuriate assembly The *comitia centuriata*. Elected the two consuls, eight praetors, two curule aediles, and two censors. The voting system generally favored the wealthier citizens, who controlled 98 of the 193 centuries.

century A Roman category used for voting purposes. In the centuriate assembly, all male Roman citizens were assigned based on wealth to one of the assembly's 193 centuries.

Circus Maximus The largest Roman stadium, situated between the Palatine and Aventine Hills, used mostly for chariot races. The Circus Maximus also served as part of the triumphal route.

cista Box in which to collect votes at an assembly.

clementia Mercy.

collegium An organization based on occupation, religion, or residence. *Collegia* provided important social amenities for their members. Many were outlawed by the senate in 64 but were then restored by Clodius in 58.

comitia centuriata The centuriate assembly. Elected the two consuls, eight praetors, two curule aediles, and two censors. The voting system generally favored the wealthier citizens, who controlled 98 of the 193 centuries.

comitia curiata The curiate assembly. Rarely used assembly in which citizens were divided into thirty *curiae* based on birth. By the late republic each *curia* could be represented by a *lictor*, so it was not necessary to summon the citizens themselves to participate.

comitia tributa One of two tribal assemblies (the other was the *concilium plebis*). Divided into thirty-five tribes for voting purposes, making voting more democratic. Elected the two curule aediles and twenty quaestors, and therefore indirectly bestowed membership in the senate. It could be summoned by the consuls or the praetors to pass laws and make other important decisions.

comitial *Comitial* days were marked with a *C* on the calendar; 195 of these days were allotted randomly throughout the year. Electoral, legislative, and decision-making assemblies could be held only on *C* days, while the senate could meet on any day except a *C* day.

comitium Circular, stepped well situated between the senate house and the rostra where assemblies had once been held, until the growth of the Roman population rendered the area too small. In the late republic only the rarely convened *comitia curiata* continued to meet in the *comitium*.

Commentariolum Petitionis Manual purportedly written by Quintus Cicero in 64 as a guide for his brother Marcus's campaign for the consulship. Although there is some debate over its authenticity, it appears to provide an important trove of information about late republican elections.

concilium plebis One of two tribal assemblies (the other was the *comitia tributa*). Divided into thirty-five tribes for voting purposes, making voting more democratic. Could be convened only by a tribune, and only plebians could participate—patricians were excluded. After 287, most of Rome's laws and major decisions were ratified here. Also elected the ten tribunes and the two plebian aediles.

Conflict of the Orders Long struggle of the plebians to win political and social concessions from the patricians. Although the conflict lasted off and on for more than two centuries (494–287), it never degenerated into violence and ultimately resulted in significant gains for the plebian order. These gains included the codification of the law, the right to intermarriage, the right to hold office, and eligibility for senate membership.

consul/consuls Two Roman magistrates who held office for one year. Co-presidents of the Roman state, they could summon the senate, *comitia tributa*, and *contiones*. Consuls were elected by the centuriate assembly. Often chosen to command Rome's armies and govern Rome's provinces, usually after taking the title of proconsul.

consularis Person or persons (*consulares*) who had once held the office of consul.

contio Nonvoting assembly or assemblies (*contiones*) summoned by a city magistrate to discuss upcoming elections, votes on legislation, or other important public business.

curatore Official or officials (*curatores*) who ran the headquarters of the tribes in Rome.

curia One of the voting districts (*curiae*) of the city of Rome used for the *comitia curiata*.

Curia Hostilia Rome's senate house; often known simply as the curia.

curiate assembly See *comitia curiata*.

curule aedile Roman magistrate elected by the centuriate assembly.

cursus honorum The political "ladder of honor."

custos Official or officials (*custodes*) in charge of the ballots in legislative and electoral assemblies; also responsible for counting the votes.

decemviri Board of ten men.

dignitas Dignity. The rank or standing of a Roman senator in relation to his senatorial colleagues, determined in large part by his political and military accomplishments and those of his ancestors. It was of major significance to all Roman senators; Caesar famously stated that his *dignitas* was more important to him than his life.

divisores Assistants to the *curatores* (tribal leaders).

domus A Roman house.

Domus Publica Official residence of the Pontifex Maximus, which stood on the south side of the Via Sacra. Caesar's residence from his election as chief priest in 63 until his assassination in 44.

duas partes Two parties. Referred to the *optimates* and the *populares*, the two political factions in Roman politics.

equestrians Roman businessmen engaged in trade, manufacturing, and banking, among other lucrative enterprises.

fasces A bundle of wooden rods about five feet long and held together by red rope, the *fasces* were the symbols of consular authority carried by the twelve *lictors*. When the *lictors* were outside the *pomerium*, an axe was included among the rods; when inside, the axe was removed.

filibuster A method by which senators could talk out senate meetings to block a vote. The Romans had no procedure by which a filibuster could be halted.

First Triumvirate An informal agreement between Caesar, Crassus, and Pompey that was typical of senators' political alliances. Though it would have an enormous impact on Roman history, the First Triumvirate had no standing under Roman law.

Fornix Fabianus The first great triumphal arch built in Rome by Quintus Fabius Maximus (cos. 121) at the southeastern entrance to the forum to commemorate his victories over Gallic tribes.

gratia A favor. Granting a favor was a very important way for a senator to acquire political support.

imagines Wax masks that depicted senators' ancestors. They were kept in the atrium in wooden temples that included a small plaque commemorating the deeds of each ancestor.

imperator Title given to a commander by his soldiers after a military victory.

imperium Power invested in a Roman proconsul or propraetor to command soldiers in war and to govern a province in peace.

in absentia Not present. When running for office in Rome, a candidate was considered *in absentia* when he was not physically present to officially declare himself a candidate at least three market cycles (twenty-four days) before the vote, as was required by law.

insulae Apartment buildings in the city of Rome; most of the population lived in *insulae*.

intercalary Since the Roman calendar had only 355 days it was sometime necessary to insert an extra month of days between February and March. The year 58 had an intercalary month.

intercessio The power of a consul to veto the acts of his colleague.

legates Army officers who were part of a general's staff. Usually senators, they were nominated by a commander and then approved by the senate.

lex Law or laws (*leges*). Titles of laws were always accompanied by the feminine version of the name of the magistrate or magistrates who promulgated the legislation; for instance, *lex Julia Agraria*.

libera legatio Unofficial senatorial embassy sent out by the senate to the provinces or to foreign countries. Represented an easy way for house members to take long vacations that would be paid for by the state.

libertas Freedom.

lictor Magistrate's bodyguards appointed by the state, twelve for each consul and six for each praetor. The lictors carried the *fasces*.

Mare Nostrum "Our Sea." The Mediterranean.

Megalesian Games Held on April 4 and April 10 to celebrate the arrival in Rome of the Great Goddess from Anatolia and the dedication of her first temple in 204.

money Rome had numerous types of coins in circulation, the most important of which were the bronze *as*, the silver *sesterce*, and the silver *denarius*. In the late republic four *asses* equaled one *sesterce*, and four *sesterces* equaled one denarius. Prices were generally referred to in sums of *sesterces*, with the amount usually preceded by the letters *HS* (a symbol analogous to a modern dollar sign). The talent was sometimes used to denote extremely large sums of money. In the late republic one talent was equal to 24,000 *sesterces*.

Converting Roman monetary values into modern dollars is difficult; however, it is known that a Roman soldier in Caesar's army in the late republic earned 900 *sesterces* per year, while his civilian counterpart living and working in Rome typically earned about 1,000. Living in the big city was expensive: renting even a small apartment on an undesirable upper floor in a Roman *insula* might cost half of a worker's yearly salary. At the other end of the spectrum, members of the senate and of the equestrian order were usually worth at least 400,000 *sesterces* (almost 17 talents). But the wealth of the richest Romans was truly staggering. Crassus's net worth of 7,100 talents was roughly equal to that of 426 "poor" equestrians and senators (illustrating why his fortune bought him so much influence), or approximately the annual income of 170,400 of his typical fellow citizens. Pompey paid 3.5 million *sesterces* (almost 146 talents) for his mansion in Rome. The money Caesar owed in 61 (830 talents) could therefore have paid for at least five mansions in the capital. The 6,000-talent bribe (144 million *sesterces*) by King Ptolemy XII was more than adequate to pay off Caesar's debts (even after he had given some of the money to his allies), with plenty left over for him to buy a 6-million-*sesterce* pearl for Servilia.

nobilis Roman noble or nobles (*nobiles*). Most likely referred to someone with at least one ancestor who had held the consulship.

nomenclator A person hired by politicians or candidates for office who remembered people's names and whispered them to their employer. The use of a *nomenclator* during Roman campaigns had been outlawed by 59.

novus homo A "new man." Generally believed to be a Roman who became consul despite having no previous family members in the senate. Gaius Marius and Marcus Tullius Cicero are two famous examples.

nundinae Market days.

nundinum The eight-day market cycle.

obnuntiatio A ceremony performed at a magistrate's home in which he observes the night sky to determine the will of the gods. If he spots an evil omen he must report his finding the next day so that no public business of any kind will be conducted.

optimates The *boni*, the "good men." Conservative politicians who usually attempted to acquire power by defending the authority of the senate and the wealthiest elements of Roman society against the people and their representatives, the *populares*.

order The two social classes in Rome into which a person was born, namely the patrician and plebian. Membership was usually for life but on occasion transfers did occur.

ovatio Lesser version of the triumph awarded for lesser military victories.

patrician One of Rome's two social orders. (The other was composed of the plebians.)

plebian One of Rome's two social orders. (The other was composed of the patricians.)

plebian aedile Roman magistrate elected by the *concilium plebis*.

pomerium The religious boundary enclosing Rome's city limits.

Pontifex Maximus Rome's chief priest, elected by popular vote. Caesar held the office from 63 until his death in 44.

populares Politicians who usually attempted to acquire power by appealing to the people and by defending the people's rights against the encroachment of the *optimate* senators.

praetor Second on the political ladder just below the consuls, the praetors were in charge of Rome's courts and were often sent to govern provinces or command armies, usually with the title of propraetor. The centuriate assembly elected eight praetors for one-year terms.

proconsul When a consul, or in some cases a praetor, was appointed to govern a province or command an army, he received the title of proconsul.

propraetor *See* praetor.

provocatio A Roman citizen's right of appeal against summary judgment by any Roman magistrate.

publicani The most powerful element within the equestrian order. The *publicani* ran Rome's banks, owned various types of companies (complete with boards of directors, stock, and shareholders), and leased contracts from the state to collect provincial taxes, among other important and lucrative endeavors.

quaestor Twenty quaestors were elected each year by the *comitia tributa* to run Rome's treasury and on occasion to serve as the financial officers on the staffs of provincial governors or generals. Election to this office automatically bestowed lifetime membership in the senate.

res publica "Public thing." The republic.

rex King.

rostra Twelve-foot-high podium directly south of the *comitium* and the senate house that provided the stage from which magistrates and those they designated spoke to the people at *contiones* in the open area of the forum.

sacrosanct The inviolability of the tribune, which was guaranteed by the gods. Anyone who harmed a tribune in any way could be killed by any citizen without fear of reprisal by gods or men.

salutatio The morning greeting at a senator's home.

Second Triumvirate Unlike the First Triumvirate, which was an informal agreement between three senators, the Second Triumvirate was instituted by law in 43 granting Marcus Antonius, Gaius Octavian, and Marcus Aemilius Lepidus the power to rule the Roman Empire for five years.

***senatus consultum* (*s.c.*)** A decree formally expressing the opinion of the senate. Although not a law, the *s.c.* was often followed by city magistrates.

***senatus consultum ultimum* (*s.c.u.*)** "Ultimate Decree." Fundamentally a declaration of martial law, which suspended normal legal procedures and protections. Invoked when the senate directed the consuls to use any means necessary, even violence, to resolve a crisis. The constitutionality of the decree was in dispute.

Servian Wall Seven miles of fortifications that surrounded the city of Rome.

sesterce Most common denomination of Roman coinage. *See also* money.

Subura Three-pronged valley located just east of the forum that was home to much of Rome's urban population.

tablinum A room in a home dedicated as a study, a *tablinum* sometimes doubled as a senator's campaign headquarters.

Tabularium Home of Rome's archives, located at the western end of the forum.

talent A unit of weight. The Greek talent was roughly fifty-seven pounds, the Roman talent around seventy-two pounds. The term was also applied to large sums of money.

toga Traditional white attire of the Roman citizen necessary for participating in a formal political function.

toga praetexta White toga with a purple border worn by consuls and former consuls.

togate Wearing a toga.

tribal assemblies Two assemblies in which male citizens were divided into thirty-five tribes for voting purposes to make votes more democratic.

tribune Ten city officials elected each year by the plebians alone in the *concilium plebis*. Each tribune had the power to call the assembly into session, submit legislation and other proposals to a vote, summon *contiones*, and exercise the tribunician veto. The office of tribune was created during the Conflict of the Orders to defend the rights of the plebians.

trinundinum Three eight-day market periods, or twenty-four days.

triumph A parade in Rome to commemorate a military victory.

veto "I forbid." Power granted to each individual tribune by which he alone could block the actions of any governmental body or city magistrate in Rome.

Via Appia Appian Way. Rome's first highway in Italy, begun in 312. The Via Appia connected Rome to Capua and was later extended to Brundisium.

Via Sacra Sacred Way. The city of Rome's earliest and most important thoroughfare. It followed a downhill slope, and many politicians used this route to make a grand entrance into the forum.

NOTES

PROLOGUE: CAESAR AND BIBULUS

1. All dates are BC unless otherwise noted.

2. Unfamiliar terms (such as *pomerium* and Servian Wall) are explained in the glossary.

3. Hor. *Odes* 2.1.1.

4. The ancient sources for the events of April 4, 59: Plu. *Pomp.* 47–48, *Caes.* 14, *Cat. Min.* 31–33; Livy *Per.* 103; Suet. *Div. Jul.* 19–20, 45; V.P. 2.44; Dio 38.1–12; Ap. *B.C.* 2.10–14; Cic. *Att.* 2.4–24, *Fam.* 1.9, 13.4, *Vat.* 22, *Har. Resp.* 48, *Dom.* 39–40, *Planc.* 35. A discussion of the continuing debate over the chronology of the year 59 is provided in appendix E along with the reconstruction upon which the chronology of this book is based.

5. Cicero provides the formula in *Laws* 11–12.

CHAPTER I: CAESAR AND CATO

Epigraph: Sal. *Jug.* 41–42.

1. Rome was freed when a rebellion forced out the tyrannical Etruscan monarch Lucius Tarquinius Superbus (Tarquin the "Proud," reign c. 534–509).

2. Ancient commentators (Polybius 6.3, 18; Cicero *Rep.* 3.23–24) believed this structure helped to explain Rome's longevity and success. Many of America's Founding Fathers agreed (James Madison *Federalist* 51); hence its incorporation in the American constitution.

3. P. Brunt, 1971, *Italian Manpower*, Oxford: 13–14.

4. Occasionally citizens moved from one order to another through adoption. One famous transfer dramatically impacted the republic in 59 and beyond.

5. For example, *provocatio* allowed a Roman citizen to appeal arbitrary rulings by a city official and have his case heard in a legal proceeding. A magistrate who ignored the appeal was liable to criminal prosecution. Another example: it was illegal to flog a Roman citizen.

6. Sal. *Jug.* 31; Cic. *Phil.* 11.3. Romans believed that this was one of the most important rights enjoyed by a Roman citizen, and that free expression was the main characteristic of a free man. In practice, there were few if any restrictions on the exercise of this right by all Roman citizens.

7. This fourth assembly seldom met, although it would play a role in the events of 59.

8. The Villian Law (180) established the age requirements and order of occupation for offices. Consuls had to be at least forty-two years old and praetors thirty-nine, although patricians enjoyed the privilege of holding office one year earlier than plebians. Quaestors were between twenty-seven and thirty, and tribunes usually held office after having first

been a quaestor, which means they were at least thirty years old. (Appendix A includes a chart that illustrates the Roman Republican government.)

9. For examples of *contiones* see Cic. *Att.* 1.19, 4.1, *lex Man.* 51–56, 68, *leg. Ag.* 1.6, 2.23–24, 53, 99, 3.16; Livy 42.34, 45.36, Plu. *Cras.* 12, *T.G.* 21. Modern studies include F. Millar, 1986, "Politics, Persuasion and the People before the Social War (150–90 BC)," *JRS* 76: 1–11; F. Millar, 1998, *The Crowd in Rome in the Late Republic,* Ann Arbor; F. Pina Polo, 1995, "Procedures and Functions of Civil and Military *Contiones* in Rome," *Klio* 77: 203–216; J. Tan, 2008, "*Contiones* in the Age of Cicero," *CA* 27: 163–201; R. Morstein-Marx, 2004, *Mass Oratory and Political Power in the Late Roman Republic*, Cambridge.

10. Senators wore maroon leather shoes and an iron or gold ring to distinguish them from their fellow citizens.

11. Cic. *Att.* 4.2.

12. Cic. *Att.* 1.16, *Q.F.* 2.1; A. W. Lintott, 1999, *The Constitution of the Roman Republic*, Oxford, 69–70.

13. Cic. *Dom.* 1.

14. The fourteen provinces: Nearer Spain, Further Spain, Transalpine Gaul (southern France), Cisalpine Gaul (northern Italy), Macedonia, Cilicia (southern Anatolia), Syria, Africa, Sicily, Asia (western Anatolia), Bithynia-Pontus (northern Anatolia), Cyrenaica (Libya) and Crete, Illyria, and Corsica and Sardinia.

15. The two Spanish provinces each had two legions, Transalpine Gaul one, Cisalpine Gaul three, Macedonia three legions in 60 and two in 59, Cilicia two, and Syria two. The legion was the main unit in the republican army, which (if at full strength) consisted of 4,800 soldiers. However, Rome still did not possess a standing professional army; instead citizens were recruited, usually from the rural areas of Italy, for a specific campaign, after which they received discharge. After 107 all male citizens regardless of wealth were eligible for military service.

16. Gracchus came from a celebrated family. His father, Tiberius, had been consul twice (177, 163) and censor (169). His maternal grandfather was Rome's military hero Publius Cornelius Scipio Africanus, consul twice (205, 194), censor (199), and the conqueror of Rome's greatest enemy, Hannibal Barca of Carthage, in the Second Punic War (218–202).

17. Plu. *T.G.* 20.

18. Sal. *Cat.* 38.

19. Cic. *Sest.* 96.

20. Cic. *Sest.* 98.

21. Cic. *De Off.* 2.73.

22. Cic. *De Off.* 2.78.

23. Cic. *Att.* 1.16.

24. Cic. *Att.* 1.16, *Leg. Ag.* 10.

25. Cic. *De Off.* 2.78, 84.

26. Plu. *Cat. Min.* 16–18.

27. See P. Brunt, 1966, "The Roman Mob," *Past and Present* 15: 5.

28. Cic. *Q.F.* 2.9.

29. Cic. *Sest.* 96, *Pis.* 12.

30. Millar 1986: 7.

31. Plu. *T.G.* 14.

32. R. Morstein-Marx, 2013, "Cultural Hegemony and the Communicative Power of the Roman Elite" in *Community and Communication: Oratory and Politics in the Roman Republic,* edited by C. Steel and H. van der Blom, Oxford: 34–36. Morstein-Marx provides an extensive list of "SAPS" ("successful assertions of popular authority"), bills passed between 133 and 60 "against significant opposition from the senate."

33. Sal. *Jug.* 31–32.

34. Sal. *Jug.* 85.

35. Morstein-Marx 2013: 39; W. J. Tatum, 1999, *The Patrician Tribune—Publius Clodius Pulcher,* Chapel Hill: 7.

36. Sal. *Jug.* 31–32.

37. Sal. *Cat.* 38; Thucy. 3.82.

38. A. W. Lintott, 1968, *Violence in Republican Rome,* Oxford: 209.

39. Popular tribunes such as Tiberius's brother Gaius Sempronius Gracchus (121), Lucius Appuleius Saturninus (100), and Marcus Livius Drusus (91) were all assassinated during this period.

40. The civil wars:

I (87). Fought in Italy, ended in the streets of Rome. It produced the autocratic rule of Marius and after his death (86) that of the "Marians" (his supporters), which lasted until 83.

II (83–82). Fought in Italy, ended outside Rome's Colline Gate. Led to Rome's first individual, unlimited dictatorship as the victorious Sulla ruled for the next three years (82–79); he went on to massacre thousands of his enemies.

III (80–72). Quintus Sertorius (pr. 83), a former supporter of Marius, campaigned in Spain against a number of Roman armies sent against him before he was finally defeated by Quintus Caecilius Metellus Pius (cos. 80) and Pompey.

IV (78–77). The brief rebellion of the consul Marcus Aemilius Lepidus.

V (63–62). The Catilinarian conspiracy. Lucius Sergius Catiline (pr. 68) tried to overthrow the state; his forces were defeated and he died in battle.

41. Plu. *Caes.* 4.

42. Plu. *Caes.* 5; Suet. *Div. Jul.* 10; Cic. *Mur.* 76. Private frugality was respected by the people, whereas public frugality could lose an election; in Cicero's words, the people "hated private luxury, but loved public grandeur." Tatum 1999: 21. In a "society with almost no state safety net financial support could be crucial."

43. Suet. *Div. Jul.* 6

44. M. W. Frederiksen, 1966, "Caesar, Cicero and the Problem of Debt," *JRS* 56: 128–141.

45. Plu. *Caes.* 7; Suet. *Div. Jul.* 13.

46. Plu. *Caes.* 7; Suet. *Div. Jul.* 13.

47. Publius Servilius Vatia Isauricus (cos. 79) and Quintus Lutatius Catulus (cos. 78) were the unlucky candidates.

48. Plu. *Caes.* 11; Suet. *Div. Jul.* 18. Please see glossary ("money") for an explanation of Roman monetary terms, including the value of a talent.

49. Plu. *Caes.* 11.

50. Cic. *Att.* 2.1.

51. Cic. *Att.* 1.17.

52. Ap. *B.C.* 2.8.

53. Cic. *Att.* 2.1; Plu. *Cat. Min.* 1–2, 21.

54. Plu. *Cat. Min.* 6; Sal. *Cat.* 52–55.

55. Cato's faction included his son-in-law Bibulus, the orator Quintus Hortensius Hortalus (cos. 69), his brothers-in-law Lucius Licinius Lucullus (cos. 74) and Lucius Domitius Ahenobarbus (cos. 54), Marcus Favonius (pr. 49), and later his son-in-law Marcus Junius Brutus (pr. 44).

56. Plu. *Cat. Min.* 4, 6.

57. Plu. *Cat. Min.* 16.

58. H. Smith, 1988, *The Power Game: How Washington Works*, New York: 58.

59. Cic. *Att.* 2.1.

60. Plu. *Cat. Min.* 24, *Brut.* 5.

61. Plu. *Cato Min.* 31, *Caes.* 13; Dio 37.54. Although there is no exact Latin equivalent for "filibuster," this label does convey the meaning of what Cato and other senators often did to obstruct the political process, so out of convenience the term will be used. Usually, the sources describe senators "talking out" a session (Cic. *Att.* 4.3).

62. United States Senate Rule XXII.

63. Cic. *Att.* 1.18.

64. Cic. *Leg.* 40–42.

65. Plu. *Caes.* 13; Suet. *Div. Jul.* 18.

66. Cic. *Fam.* 8.2.

67. Cic. *Att.* 1.1. In a letter written to Atticus in July 65, Cicero described his plan to begin his run for the consulship a year before the election in July of 64, and 18 months before he would take office, in January 63.

68. There has been intense debate concerning the authenticity of the document. Although its veracity can never be definitively confirmed, it is generally agreed that the document is indeed genuine or, if a forgery, written by someone who knew a great deal about first century BC elections. R. Morstein-Marx, 1998, "Publicity, Popularity and Patronage in the *Commentariolum Petitionis*," *CA* 17: 259–288, makes an argument in favor of authenticity; R. G. M. Nisbet, 1961, "The *Commentariolum Petitionis*: Some Arguments against Authenticity," *JRS* 51: 84–87, makes one against.

69. Cic. *Fam.* 2.6, *Com. Pet.* 47. Preferably he chose someone like Gaius Aurelius Cotta (cos. 75), who was known as an "electioneering master." Most likely Caesar had already prearranged much of this by mail from Spain in anticipation of his run.

70. Cic. *Att.* 1.2, *Fam.* 1.9; *Com. Pet.* 5, 29, 32, 33; Plu. *Cras.* 7, 14, *Pomp.* 22; Sal. *Jug.* 65, 73. Cicero performed this duty for Titus Annius Milo in 53, contacting numerous senators on his behalf. Writing to Curio (*Fam.* 2.6), Cicero promised that if Curio openly endorsed and campaigned for Milo, Curio would have not only Milo's undying support but also that of Cicero. Even friends not present in Rome could be of help in an election. Marius (Plu. *Mar.* 7), for instance, persuaded soldiers in the army to write to their associates in Rome to convince them to campaign and vote for Marius.

71. A partial list includes: (1) the candidate's family, including blood relatives and in-laws; (2) the candidate's friends; (3) the candidate's clients, freedmen, and slaves; (4) senators, including the *nobiles*, *consulares*, back benchers, sitting magistrates, and the sons of senators; (5) the equestrian order, especially the *publicani*, and the young equestrians; (6) citizens in Rome—the people in the capital were divided into groups, including organizations based on residence (for example, the neighborhoods), profession, religion, and

tribal affiliation; (7) citizens of Italy in the colonies, communities incorporated into the Roman state, tribes, rural districts, and praefectures.

72. Cic. *Att.* 1.20; Plu. *C.G.* 8.

73. *Com. Pet.* 4–5, 18, 29; Plu. *Pomp.* 44, *Cras.* 7; Cic. *Fam.* 2.6; Sal. *Jug.* 73.

74. *Com. Pet.* 3, 29, 33; Cic. *Fam.* 2.6.

75. *Com. Pet.* 50, *Q.Fr.* 2.9.

76. Vit. *De Arch.* 6.5; M. Grant, 1970, *The Roman Forum*, New York: 70. Small remnants of Caesar's dwelling in the Domus Publica, including floor mosaics and paintings, have been uncovered by archeologists.

77. Suet. *Div. Jul.* 2. For military decorations in general see Polyb. 6.39.

78. For a detailed discussion of the importance of ancestor masks see H. I. Flower, 2000, *Ancestor Masks and Aristocratic Culture in Roman Culture*, Oxford.

79. *Com. Pet.* 34–36, Cic. *Att.* 2.1, *Mur.* 69–71; P. J. Aicher, 2004, *Rome Alive: A Source-Guide to the Ancient City*, Wauconda, IL: 124.

80. The period of daylight in Rome was divided by the sundial into twelve equal parts called hours; the length of an hour varied during the year along with the length of time between sunrise and sunset. For those candidates who lived on the Palatine or Carinae, the motorcade was very dramatic as the crowd moved down the Velian slope and then "came down into the forum" (a phrase repeatedly used in the sources) in full view of the people below. Cic. *Att.* 2.1; *Com. Pet.* 34–38.

81. Cic. *lex Man.* 70.

82. Cic. *Mur.* 67–69, 73.

83. *Com. Pet.* 5, 22, 34, 36, 53, Cic. *Planc.* 22, *Mur.* 44. In the late republic, an age of political violence, a large retinue also provided protection against attack, and unscrupulous politicians could use the crowd to intimidate or even physically assault the opposition.

84. R. Laurence, 1994, "Rumour and Communication in Roman Politics," *G&R* 41: 62–74.

85. Plu. *Cras.* 3; Cic. *Off.* 2.32; *Com. Pet.* 41, 44.

86. P. Brunt, 1982, "*Nobilitas* and *Novitas*," *JRS* 72: 1–17. Exactly what criteria bestowed the *nobiles* label has been the subject of debate; it is generally believed that these were citizens descended from someone who had held the consulship, no matter how many years in the past. K. Hopkins, 1984, *Death and Renewal*, Cambridge, UK: 112. Roughly 40 percent of Roman consuls in the late republic had a father or a grandfather who also held that office, and the percentage rose to nearly 90 if more distant ancestors are included.

87. Cic. *Off.* 2.49–52, 65; *Mur.* 24, 29–31.

88. Cic. *Mur.* 20–22, 29–31, 36–38.

89. *Com. Pet.* 42. Although the practice was illegal, candidates with faulty memories sometimes hired a professional *nomenclator* to provide them with the names of the people they met in the forum.

90. Cic. *Mur.* 42–43.

91. *Com. Pet.* 52.

92. *Com. Pet.* 53.

93. *Com. Pet.* 5, 53.

94. *Com. Pet.* 53.

95. *Com. Pet.* 51–53.

96. Cic. *Planc.* 47; Plu. *Cat.* 6, *Cras.* 7.

97. *Com. Pet.* 38.

98. *Com. Pet.* 4, 20, 21, 38.

99. R. Caro, 2002, *The Years of Lyndon Johnson: Master of the Senate*, New York: 506.

100. *Com. Pet.* 47–48.

101. *Com. Pet.* 16.

102. *Com. Pet.* 19, 21, 23–25.

103. *Com. Pet.* 30.

104. Val. Max. 7.5.2.

105. Cic. *Mur.* 46.

106. *Com. Pet.* 28, Cic. *Planc.* 12.

107. Cic. *Planc.* 9.

108. Cic. *Planc.* 12.

109. Plu. *Cat. Min.* 49; Dio 40.58.

110. Plu. *T.G.* 8.

111. *Com. Pet.* 44; Cic. *Mur.* 72.

112. *Com. Pet.* 30–31, Cic. *Q.Fr.* 2.14, *Sest.* 9, *Phil.* 2.102, *Fam.* 13.4, *Caec.* 97, *Scaur.* 27.

113. Cic. *Att.* 1.1, *Com. Pet.* 3, 30–33, *Planc.* 8–9, 19–23, *Mur.* 36–38, 42; Sal. *Jug.* 41; Asc. 31C; Caes. *B.G.* 8.50. Soldiers and their friends often influenced the outcome of an election; unfortunately for Caesar, his soldiers were still in Spain.

114. Polyb. 6.56. For just a few examples of bribery in Roman public life see: Cic. *Att.* 1.16, 20, 4.16, *Q.F.* 1.2, 2.1, 14, 3.4, *Fam.* 1.1, 8.8; Plu. *Cat. Min.* 49, *Cic.* 8, 29, *Pomp.* 51, 58, *Caes.* 29, *Sul.* 6; Suet. *Div. Jul.* 12, 19, 29; Gell. *N.A.* 12.12; Ap. *B.C.* 2.17, 26; Sal. *Cat.* 49, *Jug.* 13–14, 17, 26, 32–35.

115. Cic. *Q.F.* 2.15b.

116. Cic. *Q.F.* 2.2; Sal. *Jug.* 13, 28–29, 31–34. The North African king Jugurtha (reign 118–105) observed that Rome was "a city for sale." He took advantage, famously suborning a Roman general and his officers to grant him a lenient peace in 111. Brought to Rome to provide information into the corruption, he bribed a tribune, who, much to the outrage of the people in the forum, interposed his veto to halt the proceedings.

117. Plu. *Cat. Min.* 30, 42, *Mar.* 5, 28, *Pomp.* 44, *Caes.* 7, 21, *Sul.* 6; Suet. *Div. Jul.* 13, 19; Cic. *Planc.* 55, *Mur.* 54, *De Off.* 2.22, *Q.F.* 2.14; Asc. 33C; Ap. *B.C.* 2.19.

118. Suet. *Div. Jul.* 19.

119. Cic. *Att.* 1.16; Plu. *Cat. Min.* 30, *Pomp.* 44, *Cic.* 29.

120. Cic. *Att.* 1.16, 18, *Verr.* 1.22–23, 25.

121. Cic. *Planc.* 37, 47, *Q.F.* 3.1; Plu. *Cat.* 48.

122. Plin. *N.H.* 35.162; Cic. *De. Or.* 2.274.

123. Plu. *Cras.* 12; Cic. *Off.* 2.55, 58, 72; Dio 37.51; N. Purcell, 1994, "The City of Rome and the *plebs urbana* in the Late Republic," In *Cambridge Ancient History volume IX*: 685.

124. Cic. *Sest.* 104.

125. Suet. *Div. Jul.* 19.

126. For what is still perhaps the best description of this process see L. R. Taylor, 1966, *Roman Voting Assemblies*, Ann Arbor: 47–58.

127. E. Best, 1974, "Literacy and Roman Voting," *Historia* 23: 430.

128. Like every custom surrounding the political process, omens were sometimes manipulated for political advantage. One archaic ritual reported by Dio (37.27–28) dictated that sentries were stationed across the Tiber River on the Janiculum Hill to watch for enemy armies. If they believed a foe approached they would hoist a red flag and voting would cease so citizens could don their armor and defend the city.

129. Cic. *Mur.* 38.

130. Cic. *Sest.* 113–114, *Att.* 2.6, 24, *Vat.* 5, 13, 16, 38; Suet. *Div. Jul.* 20; Plu. *Pomp.* 48, *Caes.* 14, *Cat. Min.* 32–33; Ap. *B.C.* 2.11–12; Dio 38.1–7. Around the same time the centuriate assembly elected the praetors and the curule aediles, and the tribal assembly elected the ten tribunes. Of the praetors, both Titus Ampius Balbus and Gnaeus Cornelius Lentulus Clodianus were potential supporters of Caesar. Another praetor-elect, Quintus Fufius Calenus, was Caesar's associate, and later served with him in Gaul. Of the aediles, Marcus Favonius was a staunch supporter of Cato and therefore of Bibulus. Three tribunes would prove to be allies of Bibulus: Quintus Ancharius (pr. 56), Gnaeus Domitius Calvinus (cos. 53), and Gaius Fannius (pr. 55). Two would back Caesar: Gaius Alfius Flavus and Publius Vatinius (cos. 47).

131. Suet. *Div. Jul.* 19.

132. Cic. *Att.* 2.3. For generations, prominent senators owned villas in Tusculum, which was located about fifteen miles down the Via Latina from Rome, in the country but still relatively close to the city. With many senators living in the neighborhood, Balbus had an opportunity to see others besides Cicero.

133. Cic. *Top.* 1.

134. Cic. *Att.* 2.3.

135. Hom. *Il.* 12.243.

136. Ap. *Mith.* 116–117; Plu. *Pomp.* 45.

137. First Mithridatic War 89–85; Second Mithridatic War 83–82; Third Mithridatic War 74–63.

138. Plu. *Pomp.* 2.

139. He fought in Sicily (82), in Italy against the rebellious consul Marcus Aemilius Lepidus (78–77), and in Spain versus the renegade Roman general Quintus Sertorius (77–71). He then returned to Italy to fight the slave army of Spartacus (71).

140. Val. Max. 6.2.8.

141. Cic. *Att.* 1.18.

142. M. Crawford, 1976, "Review Article: Hamlet without the Prince," *JRS* 66: 216. His success "marked a further stage in the disintegration of collective rule."

143. Cic. *Att.* 1.12, 16, 18–19, *Piso* 58; Plu. *Sert.* 19, *Pomp.* 34, 42, 44, 46, *Cat. Min.* 20, 27–31; Dio 37.5, 43, 49.

144. The Metelli had held eighteen consulships since 284, including an unprecedented run of six between 123 and 109, and another four between 69 and 57.

145. Suet. *Div. Jul.* 50. According to gossip spread by the senior Curio, Caesar was one of her lovers.

146. Dio 37.49.

147. Cic. *Pro Mur.* 31. Cato had constantly denigrated Pompey's military achievements, calling them "victories over women." Pompey's efforts to win over Cato with a marriage alliance failed (Plu. *Pomp.* 44).

148. Plu., *Luc.* 38, 42–43. A retirement that apparently included experimentation with hallucinogenic drugs brought from Anatolia.

149. Cic. *Att.* 1.18–19.

150. Dio 37.49.

151. Cic. *Leg. Ag.* 2.11–13, 79, 3.4; *Sul.* 65, *Pis.* 5, *Fam.* 5.2, 5; Plu. *Cic.* 12; Dio 37.25; G. V. Sumner, 1966, "Cicero, Pompeius, and Rullus," *TAPA* 97: 569–582. Flavius's law was also

similar to an earlier *lex Plotia Agraria* (70) passed in the assembly by the tribune Plotius. The Plotian Law provided public funds to buy land in Italy to distribute to the soldiers of Pompey and Quintus Caecilius Metellus Pius (cos. 80), who had fought in Spain against Sertorius. However, the soldiers never received their land. Blaming an empty treasury, senatorial opponents ensured that the law was never implemented. Cic. *Att.* 1.18; Dio 38.5; Plu. *Luc.* 34; Ap. *Mith.* 95; Flor. 1.41.9; R. E. Smith, 1957, "The *Lex Plotia Agraria* and Pompey's Spanish Veterans," *CQ* 51: 82–85.

152. Cic. *Leg. Ag.* 2.32.

153. Cic. *Leg. Ag.* 2.12, 20.

154. T. Rice Holmes, 1923, *The Roman Republic volume I*, Oxford: 249.

155. Cic. *Pis.* 4. Cicero's performance in the forum in 63 clearly illustrated why Caesar wanted him as an ally during his consulship in 59.

156. Cic. *Att.* 1.19. Particularly, the law could not be allowed to authorize the expropriation of land, as unwilling owners should never be forced to sell. Those veterans who had received land during Sulla's distributions should be allowed to keep their property. Also, the money to buy the land must come only from revenues derived from Pompey's new provinces so as not to overburden the treasury and force good citizens to pay higher taxes. Cicero told Atticus that if these criteria were met the law might be good for Rome, "clearing out the dregs of the urban population" who would then repopulate barren Italian lands. Although he did not state this in his letters, he may also have come to understand that "clearing out" thousands of poor citizens from Rome meant that poor citizens, who normally voted against the *optimates* and in favor of popular candidates and causes, would no longer be in the city.

157. Cic. *Att.* 1.19; Dio 37.50.

158. Cic. *Att.* 1.18, 19, 2.1.

159. Plu. *Cras.* 11, *Marc.* 22. Roman generals who were not entitled to a full triumph celebrated an *ovatio* because their victory had been unimpressive or indecisive or because, as in Crassus's case, the victory had been won not over free men but over escaped slaves. Pompey would celebrate his second triumph a few days later, on December 29, 71.

160. Plu. *Cras.* 2–3, 6–7, 12; Cic. *De Off.* 1.25; Plin. *N.H.* 33.47. Crassus is quoted as saying that "no man is rich unless he can afford to pay for a legion."

161. It is unsurprising that some of the most influential politicians during the last two decades of the republic were men like Crassus, sufficiently solvent to avoid debt while at the same time able and willing to provide loans to their fellow senators.

162. Plu. *Cras.* 7.

163. Sal. *Cat.* 48.

164. Dio 37.56.

165. T. J. Cadoux, 1956, "Marcus Crassus: A Revaluation," *G&R* 3: 158.

166. Plu. *Cras.* 7; *Pomp.* 22.

167. Cic. *De Fin.* 2.57, *Att.* 1.16. Cicero did mock Crassus by calling him "Baldy" but only in private correspondence.

168. Sal. *Cat.* 48. Later Roman historians concurred: V.P. 2.30, Dio 37.35.

169. Members wore a thin purple stripe on their toga to distinguish themselves from the senators and the rest of the population.

170. D. H. Berry, 2003, "*Eqvester Ordo Tvvs Est*: Did Cicero Win His Cases Because of His Support for the *Eqvites*?" *CQ* 53: 223. The rest of the jury consisted of senators.

171. Cic. *Planc.* 23.

172. E. Badian, 1972, *Publicans and Sinners*, Ithaca: 103. Each company had a headquarters in Rome, a president, a board of directors, regular board meetings, treasurers, accountants, clerks that kept extensive and detailed records, and representatives to deal and negotiate with the government. They also had branch offices in the provinces run by former officers. Apparently these companies had shares with specific market values which could be bought by citizens from the company itself or from a shareholder. The companies owned buildings and ships all over the empire to carry on their business, and employed, in some cases, hundreds of workers, including slaves and private security guards. Their numbers, organization, and wealth meant they wielded a significant block of voters come election time, especially in the centuriate assembly.

173. Cic. *lex Man.* 4, *Q. Fr.* 2.16, 3.1; Badian 1972: 77.

174. Polyb. 6.17; Cic. *lex Man.* 16; J. Roth, 1999, *The Logistics of the Roman Army at War*, Leiden: 230–231. As part of the "military-industrial complex" they supplied the Roman army. In addition they collected customs dues, harbor fees, river dues, export duties, temple dues, and pasture and grazing taxes on public lands. Their companies worked mines, built roads and aqueducts, took care of the sacred chickens on the Capitoline Hill, and maintained Rome's walls, among other important public tasks.

175. Cic. *lex Man.* 4. One example: in 66 letters poured in from businessmen in Asia to their counterparts in Rome warning of the imminent threat to the province (and their investments) from the kings Mithridates VI of Pontus and Tigranes of Armenia. The equestrians in Rome then had private meetings with Cicero and other senators urging them to speak publicly in favor of the *lex Manilia* to give Pompey command in the east. Bribery may have been employed as well. Cicero and others went before the people at *contiones* and expressed their support for the law, which eventually passed.

176. Cic. *Q.F.* 1.1; Badian 1972: 98, 111; P. Brunt, 1988, *The Fall of the Roman Republic and Related Essays*, Oxford: 164. Cicero repeatedly warned his brother Quintus that while governor of Asia (61–58) he must never antagonize the equestrians in the province and thus jeopardize both men's political futures. His fears were justified. After Publius Rutilius Rufus (cos. 105) thwarted the mistreatment of the provincials by the *publicani* while serving as a legate (97) in Asia province they had hauled him into court in 92 and charged him with misconduct in his province. Despite being innocent, and an ex-consul, an equestrian jury convicted him of extortion and forced him into exile; ironically, he chose to live among the very provincials he had supposedly oppressed. This episode set a precedent by clearly demonstrating that the equestrian order had arrived as a "major force in the state." For details of the events surrounding the trial and exile of Rutilius Rufus see R. Kallett-Marx, 1990, "The Trial of Rutilius Rufus," *Phoenix* 44: 122–139.

177. Livy 21.63; Plu. *Cat. Mai.* 21. Cato the Censor, for example, expertly concealed his many investments in trade behind front men, slaves, and dummy companies.

178. Dio 37.46; Cic. *Att.* 1.17; Badian 1972: 103–105, 111.

179. Polyb. 6.17; Livy 39.44.

180. Cic. *Att.* 1.17, 2.1.

181. Cic. *Att.* 1.17, 18.

182. Cic. *Att.* 1.17, 18, 19, 2.1; Val. Max. 2.10.7.

183. Cic. *Att.* 1.18.

184. Cic. *Att.* 2.1. Cato's measure was spawned in part by the massive corruption that produced Publius Clodius Pulcher's acquittal in the Bona Dea trial of 61. Equestrian jurors possessed immunity and could not be prosecuted for accepting bribes or for any misconduct during jury service; only senators could be charged in such circumstances. The senate approved a decree criminalizing equestrian wrongdoing while on jury service and sent the bill forward to the assembly. The equestrians did not wish to surrender the lucrative perks of jury service; thanks to their considerable opposition (and generous bribery), the measure died in the assembly.

185. Cic. *Planc.* 24, 34.

186. Cic. *Att.* 2.1.

187. Suet. *Div. Jul.* 19.

188. Cic. *Att.* 2.1.

189. Plu. *Cras.* 11–12, 14, *Pomp.* 21; Dio 37.54; Suet. *Div. Jul.* 19.

190. Plu. *Pomp.* 43, *Cras.* 7; Sal. *Cat.* 18.

191. Cic. *Att.* 1.14.

192. Ap. *B.C.* 2.9.

193. Dio 37.44; Plu. *Cat. Min.* 27–28.

194. Cic. *Att.* 2.3.

195. Plu. *Cras.* 7.

196. Cic. *Att.* 2.3; Plu. *Caes.* 13, *Pomp.* 47, *Cras.* 14, *Cat. Min.* 31; Ap. *B.C.* 2.9; Dio 37.54–57. According to the historian Gaius Asinius Pollio, the First Triumvirate was established "in the consulship of Metellus" or 60 BC (Hor. *Odes* 2.1.).

197. Ap. *B.C.* 2.9. Although "First Triumvirate" and "triumvirs" are not technically accurate constitutional or legal titles for the alliance or for its members, out of convenience these familiar labels will be used. However, this was and would remain an unofficial alliance that had no standing under Roman law, unlike the "Second Triumvirate," whose legitimacy was codified by legislation in 43.

198. Hor. *Odes* 2.1.

199. Plu. *Pomp.* 47. Cato famously stated Pompey and Caesar's friendship, not their later enmity, ruined the state.

200. Cic. *Att.* 2.1.

CHAPTER II: Caesar, Pompey, and Crassus

Epigraph: V.P. 2.44.

1. For a recent study of the geography in and around the forum, see J. Patterson, 2010, "The City of Rome Revisited: From Mid-Republic to Mid-Empire," *JRS* 100: 210–232; J. Patterson, 2010, "The City of Rome," in *A Companion to the Roman Republic*, edited by N. Rosenstein and R. Morstein-Marx, Chichester.

2. Z. Yavetz, 1958, "The Living Conditions of the Plebs in Republican Rome," *Latomus* 17: 503. According to a much later census by the emperor Constantine I (reign AD 306–337), there were 1,782 houses in the entire city of Rome, representing only 4 percent of residential structures. Most of Rome's population lived in apartment buildings. The palaces of Rome's emperors were later located on the Palatine.

3. Morstein-Marx 2004: 52.

4. Construction of the forty-thousand-square-foot temple began during Sulla's dictatorship (82–79) and was completed and dedicated in 69 by Quintus Lutatius Catulus

(cos. 78). The back part of the temple housed statues of Jupiter, Juno, and Minerva, while the front half could accommodate a meeting of all the senators, although the eighteen massive columns supporting the roof might interfere with sightlines.

5. Suet. *Div. Jul.* 20.

6. Cic. *Att.* 1.13.

7. Ap. *B.C.* 2.10.

8. Dio 38.1; Ap. *B.C.* 2.10; Suet. *Div. Jul.* 20; Plu. *Caes.* 14, *Pomp.* 47.

9. Dio 38.1–2.

10. For example, Rullus's law of 63 covered at least forty chapters.

11. Dio 38.2; Suet. *Div. Jul.* 20; Plu. *Pomp.* 47.

12. Dio 38.3. Ironically the senatorial defenders of Roman tradition had either intentionally or inadvertently forgotten their early Roman history. Caesar's law was not innovative; instead, Rome had a long history of establishing colonies in Italy dating back to the beginning of the republic. In most cases colonists were poor Roman citizens who volunteered to move in return for an allotment of land. These colonies were of immense importance to Rome's ultimately successful efforts to conquer the peninsula. For early colonization, see T. J. Cornell, 1995, *The Beginnings of Rome,* London: 301–304.

13. Cic. *Pis.* 4.

14. Dio 38.2.

15. Dio 38.2.

16. Dio 38.3.

17. Cic. *Q.F.* 2.2.

18. Cic. *Fam.* 1.4.

19. Dio 38.2.

20. March 3, 4, 5, and 6 were all *C* days.

21. Dio 38.3.

22. Suet. *Div. Jul.* 20; Plu. *Cat. Min.* 33; Val. Max. 2.10.7.

23. Plu. *Cat. Min.* 33.

24. Dio 38.3.

25. Plu. *Cat. Min.* 33.

26. Plu. *Caes.* 14; Dio 38.3–4; Ap. *B.C.* 2.10.

27. Morstein-Marx 2004: 54.

28. Statues of famous Roman heroes stood here, including those of Marcus Furius Camillus (dictator in 390), "Rome's Second Founder," who had saved the city from invading Gauls, and Lucius Cornelius Sulla (dictator 82–79).

29. Dio 38.4.

30. Plu. *Caes.* 14.

31. Dio 38.4.

32. Dio 38.4.

33. Dio 38.4–5; Plu. *Caes.* 14, *Pomp.* 47; Ap. *B.C.* 2.10.

34. Dio 38.5.

35. Cic. *Att.* 1.18; Smith 1957: 82–85.

36. Dio 38.5; Plu. *Caes.* 14, *Pomp.* 47.

37. Dio 38.6.

38. Cic. *Vat.* 30, *Att.* 2.7.

39. This lull provided plenty of time for people, if so inclined, to travel to Rome to participate. It also served another purpose, as Cicero and others often pointed out. In a Greek city-state, a law could be proposed and passed at the same assembly meeting. This provided little opportunity for the citizens to reflect on how a measure might affect the city. In the heat of the moment, with thousands of people clamoring to vote, mistakes could easily be made. The Romans avoided hasty decisions by providing the necessary time to consider the ramifications of their vote. The *trinundinum* also allowed both proponents and opponents of the measure to make their case and attempt to sway the voting public.

40. See appendix E for the arguments supporting a reconstruction of events placing the vote on April 4 rather than earlier in the year.

41. Lintott 1999: 209–213.

42. Plu. *Cat. Min.* 26–29; Cic. *Sest.* 62, *Cael.* 70; Dio 37.43; Suet. *Div. Jul.* 16.

43. Plu. *Cat. Min.* 27.

44. Plu. *Cat. Min.* 27. Munatius Rufus later wrote a biography of Cato that provided Plutarch with an eyewitness account of the violence of 62 from someone actually on the podium when the fighting began. It is possible Rufus provided accounts of similar events in the early 50s.

45. Caes. *B.C.* 1.5. The legality of this device engendered intense debate, and often came down to partisan interpretation. Many *optimates* argued for its constitutionality. Their opponents disagreed, contending that the senate overstepped its statutory bounds because the fundamental right enjoyed by even the lowliest Roman citizen was the right to a trial as protection against arbitrary abuses by the senate and city magistrates.

46. T. P. Wiseman, 1994, "The Senate and the *populares*, 69–60 BC," in *The Cambridge Ancient History volume IX*, Cambridge: 359–360; A. Goldsworthy, 2006, *Caesar: Life of a Colossus*, New Haven: 143–145; Millar 1998: 113–114; Lintott 1999: 70. Many historians have overlooked the importance of these events to the course of republican history in general and to the events of 59 in particular. Sandwiched between two more famous incidents, the Catilinarian conspiracy and the Bona Dea scandal, this affair has been treated as a dramatic but isolated episode, "a passing squall" (H. H. Scullard, 1982, *From the Gracchi to Nero*, London: 111) with no lasting impact.

47. Ap. *B.C.* 1.29–30. In 100 the tribune Lucius Appuleius Saturninus brought Marius's former soldiers into the city to vote for his new land law. After initially being driven out of the forum by citizens from Rome, they regrouped and counterattacked; the law passed.

48. Cic. *Cael.* 1; Livy 29.10–11, 14, 36.36; Ovid *Fast.* 4.179–182, 389–392; G. D. Hadzsits, 1930, "The Dates of Megalesia," *TAPA* 61: 165–174; L. R. Taylor, 1950, "The Date and Meaning of the Vettius Affair," *Historia* 1: 45–51, 1951, "On the Chronology of Caesar's First Consulship," *AJP* 72: 254–268, 1968, "The Dating of Major Legislation and Elections in Caesar's First Consulship," *Historia* 17: 173–193; A. K. Michels, 1967, *The Calendar of the Roman Republic*, Princeton: 41.

49. Plu. *Caes.* 14, *Pomp.* 47.

50. Dio 38.6; Suet. *Div. Jul.* 20; F. X. Ryan, 1996, "Bibulus as President of the Senate," *Latomus* 1996: 384–388.

51. Plu. *Pomp.* 48.

52. Dio 38.6; Suet. *Div. Jul.* 20; Plu. *Caes.* 14, *Pomp.* 48; Cic. *Dom.* 40.

53. Cic. *Har. Resp.* 27, 58.

54. Cic. *Post Red.* 11.

55. Tatum 1999: 130.

56. Cic. *Dom.* 53.

57. Cic. *Dom.* 39–40.

58. R. E. Smith, 1964, "The Significance of Caesar's Consulship in 59 BC," *Phoenix* 18: 305; T. N. Mitchell, 1986, "The *Leges Clodiae* and *obnuntiatio*," *CQ* 36: 173–174. Both agree that there was "no doubt" Caesar's later laws were indeed "invalid."

59. Modern scholars generally follow the argument that Bibulus's use of the procedure for eight months was "unprecedented" and represented an "abuse of auspices." See J. Linderski, 1965, "Constitutional Aspects of the Consular Elections in 59 BC," *Historia* 14: 423–442; Lintott 1968: 144–145; Taylor 1968: 179.

60. Suet. *Div. Jul.* 20.

61. Dio 38.8; Suet. *Div. Jul.* 20.

62. Ap. *B.C.* 1.29–32; *C.I.L.* 1.2.582; Plu. *Mar.* 29; E. Gruen, 1965, "The Exile of Metellus Numidicus," *Latomus* 24: 571–580. Although there may have been earlier instances, the first definitive example of a "curse" clause dates to 100, when the tribune Lucius Appuleius Saturninus (tr. 103, 100) attached such a clause to an agrarian law; the senators had five days to take the oath. Quintus Caecilius Metellus Numidicus (cos. 109) refused to swear the oath and went into exile. Other examples followed; for a *lex Bantina* passed around the same time, magistrates had to swear within five days, senators in ten.

63. Ap. *B.C.* 2.12; Plu. *Cat. Min.* 32.

64. Suet. *Aug.* 4; Cic. *Att.* 2.12, 19; Dio 38.1; Plin. *N.H.* 7.176; Varro *RR* 1.2.10, 2.4.1. Some members of the Board of Twenty can be safely identified. Pompey and almost certainly Crassus received appointments. The other three known members were each connected to the triumvirs: Marcus Atius Balbus (pr. by 60), Marcus Terentius Varro, and Gnaeus Tremellius Scrofa. The known members of the Board of Five included Gaius Cosconius (pr. 63) and Marcus Valerius Messalla Niger (cos. 61).

65. Cic. *Att.* 2.5, 9, 16.

66. Suet. *Div. Jul.* 54. The exorbitant sums Ptolemy XII funneled to Roman politicians would prove to be money well spent. Led by his eldest daughter, Berenice, Ptolemy's subjects revolted in 58 and he was forced to flee to Rome. In 55 the Romans restored him to the throne by force and executed Berenice. It is unknown if Ptolemy's middle daughter, the famous Cleopatra, accompanied him into exile.

67. One lender, Gaius Rabirius Postumus, would later become Ptolemy's finance minister in Alexandria to ensure the loan's repayment.

68. Cic. *Att.* 2.17; Ap. *B.C.* 2.13.

69. Suet. *Div. Jul.* 50. Please see glossary ("money") for an explanation of Roman monetary terms, including the value of a *sesterce*.

70. Dio 38.7; Ap. *B.C.* 2.13; Plu. *Pomp.* 48. Later complaints by the triumvirate's enemies about "tacking," illegally combining unrelated items into the same law in violation of the *lex Caecilia-Didia*, might refer to this aspect of the legislation.

71. Badian 1972: 99–100.

72. Suet. *Div. Jul.* 20; Ap. *B.C.* 2.13; Cic. *Att.* 2.16, *Planc.* 35; Dio 38.7.

73. Cic. *Planc.* 35.

74. Cic. *Vat.* 29.

75. Dio 38.7; Plu. *Cic.* 26, *Cat. Min.* 33; Suet. *Div. Jul.* 20; Cic. *Att.* 2.15–16.

76. Cic. *Att.* 2.16.

77. Cic. *Att.* 2.18.

78. Cic. *Att.* 2.18. One candidate for the tribunate, Marcus Juventius Laterensis (pr. 51), refused to swear and dropped out of the campaign.

79. Cic. *Att.* 2.17, *Fam.* 5.2, 6; Plu. *Pomp.* 47, *Sul.* 6, *Luc.* 6; Suet. *Div. Jul.* 21.

80. Dio 38.9; Cic. *Att.* 2.17; Plu. *Cat. Min.* 31, 33, *Pomp.* 47–48, *Caes.* 14; Suet. *Div. Jul.* 21; Ap. *B.C.* 2.14. One vocal critic, Cato, protested that Rome's government was being "prostituted" by marriages that exploited women for political advancement. He had not shied away, however, from making similar arrangements for the women of his own family to cement political ties.

81. Suet. *Div. Jul.* 21; Plu. *Caes.* 14, *Pomp.* 47. This was perhaps the man who would lead the plot to assassinate Caesar, known better by his birth name, Marcus Junius Brutus. Brutus was adopted by an uncle, Quintus Servilius Caepio, sometime before 59 and was occasionally called by his adoptive father's name. Unfortunately, the truth of the matter cannot be recovered.

82. Cic. *Att.* 2.16.

83. Plu. *Pomp.* 48.

84. Suet. *Div. Jul.* 83.

85. Suet. *Div. Jul.* 21; Plu. *Caes.* 14, *Pomp.* 48, *Cat. Min.* 33; Dio 38.9; Ap. *B.C.* 2.14.

86. Dio 38.10, Suet. *Div. Jul.* 20; E. Gruen, 1973, "The Trial of C. Antonius," *Latomus* 32: 301–310, 1974, *The Last Generation of the Roman Republic,* Berkeley: 309–310; M. C. Alexander, 1990, *Trials in the Late Roman Republic, 149–50 BC,* Toronto: 241–242; R. J. Rowland, 1966, "Crassus, Clodius, and Curio in the Year 59 BC," *Historia* 15: 220; Michel 1967: 50–51. Trials could take place on calendar "days of every type." Since Cicero mentions the harsh methods employed by the triumvirate in his speech, the trial must have occurred after the forum violence but before he left for Antium on vacation (*Att.* 2.7–9, 11–12). Cicero, although no fan, served as Gaius Antonius's defense attorney in part due to his admiration for Antonius's father, Marcus (cos. 99), a famous orator, and because Antonius had helped him crush the Catilinarian conspiracy in 63–62. Cicero believed any attack on Antonius also represented an attack on his consulship and his handling of that crisis. Lastly, Antonius had spent his time in Macedonia extorting considerable amounts of money from the provincials; through intermediaries some of that cash found its way to Cicero in Rome (*Fam.* 5.5). Gaius Antonius was the uncle of Marcus Antonius (Marc Antony).

87. Livy *Per.* 103; Cic. *Att.* 1.12, 2.2, *Cael.* 9, *In Vat.* 27–28, *Fam.* 1.2, 4, 7, 5.2, *Q. Fr.* 2.2, 4; Plu. *Cic.* 12, *Pomp.* 49; Sal. *Cat.* 25; Dio 37.40, 38.10; Quint. *Instit. Grat.* 4.2; Asc. 84.C. Antonius had powerful enemies: since 61 Pompey had tried to bring him to trial, and back in the 70s Caesar had sued him as well. The three prosecutors in 59 were connected to the triumvirate: Marcus Caelius Rufus (pr. 48), Lucius Caninius Gallus (tr. 56), and Quintus Fabius Maximus (cos. 45). All three were looking to make names for themselves, and prosecuting a case in the forum was a traditional way to do this; at the same time, they would be doing a service for Rome's most powerful men.

88. Cic. *Verr.* 2.5.186.

89. Cic. *Vat.* 27. A recent law passed by the triumvirs' ally Vatinius had altered the procedure for challenging the selection of jurors in a way that apparently favored defendants. However, the law would not benefit Antonius since it specifically stipulated that it would not take effect until after his trial.

90. Alexander 1990: 87–169. For a detailed discussion of these trials see Gruen 1974: 260–357.

91. Cic. *Q.F.* 1.4.

92. Suet. *Div. Jul.* 20.

93. Cic. *Att.* 2.6–7, 9, 13–14. Although Cicero's speech does not survive it is possible to reconstruct the essence of his tirade based on sentiments expressed in his letters sent later in April.

94. Dio 38.10.

95. Suet. *Div. Jul.* 20.

96. Cic. *Att.* 2.9.

97. Dio 38.11. Cicero, like so many politicians in history, later insisted his words were largely taken out of context; his defense ignores the fact that Caesar had been in the forum at the time.

98. Plu. *Caes.* 10.

99. Dio 38.12.

100. Plu. *Cic.* 29.

101. Cic. *Att.* 1.18, 2.1. A Gaius Herennius (tr. 60) proposed such a bill on Clodius's behalf, but his fellow tribunes and the consul Celer vetoed the effort.

102. Michel 1967: 46–47. There is "no evidence" that the curiate assembly was restricted by the calendar.

103. Suet. *Div. Jul.* 20; Cic. *Dom.* 34–38 Ap. *B.C.* 2.14; Dio 38.12. In early April daylight in Rome averages thirteen hours, so each hour lasted about one hour and five minutes.

104. Suet. *Div. Jul.* 20.

105. Cic. *Att.* 2.1, 12, *Dom.* 37; R. Seager, 1965, "Clodius, Pompeius and the Exile of Cicero," *Latomus* 24: 520–521, 1979, *Pompey: A Political Biography,* Berkeley 1979: 92. Seager has argued that although the triumvirs made Clodius a plebian, they had no intention of allowing him to stand for the tribunate for 58. If this is true, it is extremely difficult to understand the purpose of the transfer, since the only real change it produced was Clodius's eligibility for the tribunate. As Cicero made clear, Clodius had wanted to be a plebian since June of 60 so that he could become tribune.

106. Cic. *Att.* 2.12.

107. Cic. *Att.* 2.5. See also Cic. *Att.* 2.7, 9, 12, 15.

108. Cic. *Att.* 2.9.

109. Cic. *Att.* 2.9. It is surprising that Cicero would look to Clodia for help, as he had often publicly repeated the rumors that she had engaged in an incestuous relationship with her brother (*Att.* 2.1). His nickname for her, "Ox-eyes," is a reference to a Homeric description of the goddess Hera, who was the wife of her brother Zeus.

110. Cic. *Att.* 2.19, 20, 22, 23, 24.

111. Cic. *Att.* 2.22.

112. Suet. *Div. Jul.* 22; Cic. *Att.* 2.16, 18, *Vat.* 36; Livy *Per.* 103; V.P. 2.44; Plu. *Caes.* 14, *Pomp.* 48, *Cras.* 14, *Cat. Min.* 33; Ap. *B.C.* 2.13; Dio 38.8. The dates of the Vatinian law's promulgation and passage cannot be known for certain. Many possibilities have been postulated. M. Gelzer, 1968, *Caesar: Politician and Statesman,* Cambridge: 86, puts the law's passage in late May or early June. Tatum 1999: 108, proposed April; Taylor 1968: 82, 187, suggested the law was proposed in early March and passed later that month. See also D. R. Shackleton Bailey,

1965, *Cicero's Letters to Atticus, Volume III,* Cambridge: 408; Millar 1998: 132. Since Cicero refers to the pending legislation in a letter from late April (*Att.* 2.16), and again to the law having been passed in June (*Att.* 2.18), the latest it could have been proposed was April 27, allowing for passage in late May or early June.

113. Suet. *Div. Jul.* 28.

114. Suet. *Div. Jul.* 22.

115. Legates such as Aulus Hirtius (cos. 43), Lucius Munatius Plancus (cos. 42), Quintus Fufius Calenus (cos. 47), and Marcus Antonius (cos. 44) would rank among his closest and most valuable adherents in Gaul and afterward.

116. Sal. *Cat.* 54.

117. Caes. *B.G.* 1.10, 2.2, 5.24–37, 6.1, 7.51; S. G. Chrissanthos, 2001, "Caesar and the Mutiny of 47 BC," *JRS* 91: 66–67. Each Roman legion was assigned a Roman numeral.

118. Cic. *Att.* 2.9. Cicero argued that the triumvirs and their allies had broken at least three major laws, the *lex Aelia, lex Licinia Junia,* and the *lex Caecilia-Didia.*

119. Cic. *Att.* 2.16.

120. Val. Max. 3.7.9.

121. Cic. *Att.* 2.9, 12, 19, 21.

122. Cic. *Att.* 2.13, 20, 21. Cicero had even begun to write his letters in code in case they were intercepted. Even Cato declined outright protest, although he later refused to use the official names of Caesar's laws because they contained the word *Julia* (Dio 38.7).

123. Cic. *Att.* 2.13.

124. Caro 2012: xiv.

125. Suet. *Div. Jul.* 22.

126. Suet. *Div. Jul.* 20.

127. Plu. *Pomp.* 48, *Luc.* 38–39.

128. Plu. *Caes.* 14.

129. Plu. *Caes.* 14; Cic. *Att.* 2.24.

130. Cic. *Att.* 2.5.

131. Cic. *Att.* 2.9.

132. Cic. *Sest.* 105–106.

133. Cic. *Att.* 2.8, 18.

134. Cic. *Att.* 2.8, 12, 16. Cicero called them "The Youths with the Weak Beards." The faction included Clodius, Gaius Memmius (pr. 58), and the young Marcus Antonius (cos. 44).

135. Cic. *Att.* 2.19.

136. Cic. *Att.* 2.19.

137. Cic. *Att.* 2.19.

138. Cic. *Att.* 2.19; Val Max. 6.2.9.

139. Suet. *Div. Jul.* 45.

140. Suet. *Div. Jul.* 2, 49; Dio 43.20; Ap. *Mith.* 66.

141. Suet. *Div. Jul.* 22, 50.

142. Suet. *Div. Jul.* 49.

143. Cic. *Att.* 2.19. Atticus received copies while in Epirus.

144. Dio 38.6.

145. Cic. *Att.* 2.20.

146. Cic. *Att.* 2.21.

147. Suet. *Div. Jul.* 49.

148. Cic. *Att.* 2.21.

149. Suet. *Div. Jul.* 41; Plu. *Caes.* 55.

150. Brunt 1971: 313–319, 342–343.

151. Cic. *Att.* 2.16.

152. Suet. *Div. Jul.* 20.

153. Dio 37.56.

154. Cic. *Att.* 2.21; Rowland 1966: 217–223. Despite Rowland's arguments to the contrary, Cicero's letter to Atticus (2.22), written sometime in August 59, makes clear that there was still a triumvirate and Crassus was still a member.

155. Cic. *Att.* 2.21; W. C. Grummel, 1954, "The Consular Elections of 59 BC," *CJ* 49: 351–354.

156. Cic. *Att.* 2.19, 21.

157. Cic. *Att.* 2.21.

158. Cic. *Att.* 2.23.

159. Taylor 1968: 193. Five of the other successful tribunician candidates are known: Aelius Ligus, Lucius Antistius, Lucius Ninnius Quadratus, Lucius Novius, and Quintus Terentius Culleo.

160. Cic. *Att.* 2.20–24, *Sest.* 132, *Vat.* 24–26; Dio 38.9; Plu. *Luc.* 42; Suet. *Div. Jul.* 17, 20; Ap. *B.C.* 2.12; A. M. Ward, 1977, *Marcus Crassus and the Late Roman Republic*, Columbia, MO: 238; P. Greenhalgh, 1980, *Pompey: The Roman Alexander*, London: 224; Seager 1965: 524–525, 1979: 99–100; Taylor 1950: 45–51; C. Meier, 1961, "*Zur Chronologie und Politik in Caesars ersten Konsulat*," *Historia* 10: 93; W. Allen, 1950, "The 'Vettius Affair' Once More," *TAPA* 81: 153–163. Even the date of the episode is unclear: Taylor 1950: 45–51 (mid-July); Meier 1961: 93 (August); Seager 1965: 525 (early October).

161. Plu. *Pomp.* 16.

162. Plu. *Pomp.* 16, *Brut.* 4; Val. Max. 6.2.8.

163. Cic. *Att.* 2.24. Cicero bitterly noted that while Vettius could speak to the people from the rostra, Bibulus the consul was still trapped in his house.

164. Val. Max. 6.2.8.

165. Cic. *Att.* 2.24.

166. Cic. *Att.* 2.24, *Vat.* 26, *Sest.* 132.

167. Cic. *Att.* 2.23.

168. Cic. *Vat.* 24, *Phil.* 2.4, *Fam.* 2.6, *Com. Pet.* 6, 33.

169. Cic. *Att.* 2.24. According to Cicero his relationship with Pompey still suffered as a result of Vettius's charges.

170. Suet. *Div. Jul.* 20. Suetonius agreed with Cicero's hypothesis.

171. Cic. *Pis.* 11. Cicero even cast the first century's first vote for Piso at the elections. Of the new praetors, six are known: Lucius Cornelius Lentulus Crus (cos. 49), Lucius Domitius Ahenobarbus (cos. 54), Gaius Fabius Hadrianus, Lucius Flavius, Gaius Memmius, and Publius Nigidius Figulus. Lentulus Crus and Memmius had once been allies of Pompey, but they, along with Domitius, would later prove hostile.

172. Plu. *Cras.* 14, *Pomp.* 51; Cic. *Q.F.* 3.1.

173. Cic. *Q. Fr.* 1.2.

174. Smith 1964: 313.

CHAPTER III: CLODIUS

Epigraph: V.P. 2.45.

1. Livy 10.11; Plu. *C.G.* 5–6, *Cat. Min.* 26; Cic. *Verr.* 2.3.163, 173, 5.52; Sal. *Hist.* 3.48.19.

2. Suet. *Div. Jul.* 41; Tatum 1999: 122. By 44, the number of citizens receiving grain reached 320,000.

3. Cic. *Sest.* 103.

4. Cic. *Mur.* 71, *Pis.* 8; *Com. Pet.* 16, 17, 19, 30, 32.

5. Tatum 1999: 117.

6. Cic. *Vat.* 18; Dio 38.13; Mitchell 1986: 172–176.

7. Cic. *Post Red.* 11.

8. Dio 38.12; Cic. *Pis.* 6, *Fam.* 5.2. Cicero had been prevented from speaking at the end of his consulship in 63.

9. Suet. *Div. Jul.* 23; Caes. *B.G.* 1.7–10; Smith 1964: 309. It has been asserted (Allen 1950: 154; Brunt 1966: 23) that Caesar spent this time recruiting soldiers for his Gallic provinces, soldiers who could also be used to intimidate enemies inside Rome. Cicero claimed that Caesar remained nearby with a large army. However, the origins of his legions and the years of their recruitment are known; none were enlisted while Caesar remained in central Italy in 58. See Chrissanthos 2001: 66–67.

10. For a discussion of the attack on Vatinius and Clodius's role in his defense see Tatum 1999: 140–142, 147–149.

11. For a discussion of Clodius's supporters (the "*Clodiani*") see Tatum 1999: 142–147.

12. Cic. *Dom.* 54, 89.

13. Tatum 1999: 142.

14. Cic. *Vat.* 33; *Schol. Bob.* 97, 149–150.

15. Cic. *Q. Fr.* 1.2.

16. Cic. *Q. Fr.* 1.2.

17. Plu. *Cic.* 30.

18. Cic. *Att.* 2.1.

19. Michel 1967; A. W. Lintott, 1968, "*Nundinae* and the Chronology of the Late Republic," *CQ* 18: 192. Since the Roman calendar had only 355 days, the Roman year was ten and a quarter days short of a solar year, making it necessary every few years to insert what the Romans called an intercalary period, a number of days added into the calendar between February and March to keep the year in sync with the seasons. As dictator (45–44), Caesar would institute a solar calendar, the "Julian" calendar, based on the calendar he had observed during his brief sojourn in Egypt during the civil war (48–47). The new Julian calendar had 365 days with one extra day added in February every fourth year. Pope Gregory XIII would later introduce minor reforms in AD 1582, but this is essentially the calendar still in use today.

20. Dio 37.42; Cic. *Sest.* 25–26, *Att.* 2.7; V.P. 2.45; Plu. *Cic.* 15, 22, 30; Sal. *Cat.* 28.

21. Dio 38.12; Plu. *Cic.* 24–28; Cic. *Att.* 1.16.

22. Cic. *Pis.* 12, *Dom.* 55.

23. Cic. *Att.* 2.14, 16. For example, Cicero often insultingly referred to Pompey as "Sampsiceramus," an insignificant king from Emesa in Syria.

24. Plu. *Cic.* 30, *Caes.* 14; Dio 38.16; Cic. *Dom.* 55, *Post Red.* 12, *Red. Sen.* 12–13, *Sest.* 25–28, 32–33, *Pis.* 11–14, 18, 22, *Dom.* 54–55.

25. Plu. *Cic.* 31; Cic. *Pis.* 77, *Pis.* 12–13, 72–79; *Sest.* 39–41, *Post Red.* 6, 17.

26. Plu. *Cic.* 31; R. A. Kaster, 2006, *Cicero: The Speech on Behalf of Publius Sestius*, Oxford: 406. Minerva's festival was scheduled for the following day, March 19.

27. Plu. *Cic.* 31–33; Cic. *Att.* 3.1, *Dom.* 62, 70, 116, *Pis.* 26, *Red. Sen.* 4, 18.

28. Cic. *Att.* 3.4.

29. Cic. *Dom.* 62, 116, *Pis.* 26, *Red. Sen.* 18.

30. For the importance of a noble's house in general and Cicero's in particular see S. Hales, 2000, "At Home with Cicero," *G&R* 47: 44–55.

31. Plu. *Caes.* 14.

32. Caes. *B.G.* 1.6–10; Plu. *Caes.* 17. Clearly Caesar's speed was possible because he had no army slowing him down; his soldiers awaited him on the Rhone.

33. Vel. Pat. 2.45; Livy *Per.* 104; Cic. *Dom.* 20–21, 52–53, 64, *Sest.* 56–57, 59–61; Plu. *Cat. Min.* 34–40; Ap. *B.C.* 2.23. For Cato's title and mission see E. Badian, 1965, "M. Porcius Cato and the Annexation and Early Administration of Cyprus," *JRS* 55: 110–121; S. I. Oost, 1955, "Cato Uticensis and the Annexation of Cyprus," *CP* 50: 98–112.

34. Dio 36.17, 30; Ap. *B.C.* 2.23; Cic. *Dom.* 20, 25, 52, *Pis.* 11, 23, *Sest.* 34 56–59, *Har. Resp.* 42; Plu. *Caes.* 2.

35. Cic. *Sest.* 57–59. Cicero asserted that the purpose of the law was to banish Cato.

36. Cic. *Dom.* 22, 65, *Sest.* 60.

37. Badian 1965: 117.

38. Cic. *Dom.* 25; Plu. *Cat. Min.* 36, 38–39; Plin. *N.H.* 29.96, 8.196.

39. To compensate Gabinius, who as governor of Cilicia would originally have been given this lucrative assignment, Clodius arranged for an even more lucrative assignment. He passed another law appointing Gabinius proconsul of the much richer province of Syria for five years. This region represented a potential jumping off point for attacks against Parthia or Arabia and, since Ptolemy XII had just been driven out of Egypt by his subjects and needed Roman help, his restoration might bring incredible rewards to the new Syrian governor.

EPILOGUE: TRANSFORMATION

Epigraph: Suet. *Div. Jul.* 30; Plu. *Caes.* 46.

1. Cic. *Q.F.* 2.3.

2. Plu. *Pomp.* 51, *Caes.* 21. According to Plutarch two hundred senators also made the trek to Luca to meet with and ask favors of the triumvirs, an indication of the power the alliance still exercised.

3. Plu. *Crass.* 15, *Pomp.* 52.

4. Dio 39.32, 34, 65, 40.45; Plu. *Cat. Min.* 42, 43, 44, *Pomp.* 53–54; Asc. 20C; Ap. *B.C.* 2.19; Cic. *Att.* 4.15, 16.

5. Dio 40.49; Cic. *Mil.* 13, 61, 67–70; Asc. 30–34. Cremation was common in Rome, and sometimes, as in this case, it also served as a form of protest. (After Caesar's death a similar cremation-riot occurred.)

6. Michel 1967: 160.

7. Dio 40.50; Ap. *B.C.* 2.23.

8. Dio 40.50; Ap. *B.C.* 2.23; Plu. *Pomp.* 54, *Caes.* 28, *Cat. Min.* 47; Suet. *Div. Jul.* 26.

9. Dio 40.54. Cicero later sent Milo a copy of the speech he had been too afraid to deliver at the trial because so many soldiers were present. Milo sarcastically replied that he was glad Cicero had not had the fortitude to use this speech or he, Milo, would not now be enjoying the wonderful seafood of Massilia.

10. Cic. *Balb.* 65, *Att.* 4.5, *Fam.* 1.9.

11. Plu. *Cras.* 31–33. Plutarch used Crassus's death to illustrate the folly of ambition. Despite being one of the wealthiest and most powerful men in Rome, Crassus was dissatisfied due to his lack of military renown, and his dissatisfaction led to his demise.

12. Plu. *Pomp.* 51; Cic. *Q.Fr.* 3.1.

13. Plu. *Pomp.* 51; Ap. *B.C.* 2.17.

14. Suet. *Div. Jul.* 27.

15. Suet. *Div. Jul.* 29; Ap. *B.C.* 2.26.

16. Val. Max. 9.1.6; Vel. 2.48; Suet. *Div. Jul.* 29; Plu. *Pomp.* 58, *Caes.* 29, *Ant.* 5; Ap. *B.C.* 2.26–27; Dio 40.60.

17. Plu. *Pomp.* 57.

18. Plu. *Pomp.* 57.

19. Plu. *Pomp.* 57.

20. Plu. *Pomp.* 59, *Cic.* 37.

21. Smith 1964: 303.

22. Plu. *Caes.* 66. According to legend Caesar fell at the foot of Pompey's statue; many Romans believed Pompey was watching, finally getting his revenge.

23. The will left nothing for either Caesarion or Cleopatra; they returned to Egypt almost immediately after Caesar's assassination.

24. Cic. *Att.* 2.19, 21, *Q.F.* 1.2.

APPENDIX D: The Ancient Evidence

1. The Loeb Classical Library, published by Harvard University Press (www.hup.harvard.edu/collection/php?cpk=1031), provides translations of all the relevant primary sources alongside the original Greek or Latin texts. Penguin Classics (www.penguinclassics.com) offers accessible translations of most of the texts as well. Translations of most ancient literary sources can also be found online: Perseus Digital Library-Tufts University (www.perseus.tufts.edu).

2. Cic. *Att.* 2.4–25, *Q.F.* 1.2. The last letter of 59 was written to Cicero's brother Quintus. For modern commentaries on Cicero's letters see: D. R. Shackleton Bailey, 1965, *Cicero's Letters to Atticus, Volume I,* Cambridge; A. Lintott, 2008, *Cicero as Evidence: A Historian's Companion*, Oxford.

3. Smith 1964: 303.

4. Hor. *Odes* 2.1.1.

5. L. Morgan, 2000, "The Autopsy of C. Asinius Pollio," *JRS* 90: 58–59. Suetonius records that Pollio criticized Caesar's writing for sometimes being careless and inaccurate (*Div. Jul.* 56).

6. Ap. *B.C.* 2.40, 45–46, 5.64; Plu. *Caes.* 32, 46, *Cato Min.* 53, *Pomp.* 72; Suet. *Div. Jul.* 30, 56; V.P. 2.63; Morgan 2000: 51. Pollio's work "formed the basis for all future accounts of the period, upon which non-contemporaries, from Livy to Dio, all similarly drew" (T. Rising, 2013, "Senatorial Opposition to Pompey's Eastern Settlement. A Storm in a Teacup?" *Historia* 62: 217). Pollio was Appian's "principal source" (E. Badian, 1958, "Review Article: Appian and Asinius Pollio," *CR* 8: 159). Pollio "influenced Dio" (A. W. Lintott, 1994, "The Crisis of the Republic: Sources and Source-Problems," in *The Cambridge Ancient History volume IX*: 3). Plutarch's "ultimate source" was "surely Asinius Pollio" (C. B. R. Pelling, 1979, "Plutarch's Method of Work in the Roman Lives," *JRS* 69: 84, 91).

7. Dio 38.1; Suet. *Div. Jul.* 20; Plu. *Pomp.* 47, *Caes.* 14, *Cat. Min.* 31; Ap. *B.C.* 2.10; Livy *Per.* 103.

8. Dio 38.2; Suet. *Div. Jul.* 20; Plu. *Pomp.* 47.

9. Dio 38.3; Suet. *Div. Jul.* 20; Plu. *Cat. Min.* 33.

10. Dio 38.3; Ap. *B.C.* 2.10; Plu. *Caes.* 14.

11. Dio 38.4–5; Ap. *B.C.* 2.10; Plu. *Pomp.* 47, *Caes.* 14.

12. Dio 38.1–12; Suet. *Div. Jul.* 19–20, 45; Ap. *B.C.* 2.10–14; Plu. *Pomp.* 47–48, *Caes.* 14, *Cat. Min.* 31–33; Livy *Per.* 103; V.P. 2.44.

13. Dio 38.6; Ap. *B.C.* 2.11; Plu. *Pomp.* 48, *Cat. Min.* 32.

14. Dio 38.6; Suet. *Div. Jul.* 20; Plu. *Caes.* 14.

15. Dio 38.6; Suet. *Div. Jul.* 20; Plu. *Caes.* 14, *Pomp.* 48; V.P. 2.44.

16. Dio 38.7; Suet. *Div. Jul.* 20; Plu. *Cat. Min.* 33; Livy *Per.* 103; V.P. 2.44.

17. Dio 38.7; Suet. *Div. Jul.* 20; Ap. *B.C.* 2.13.

18. Dio 38.8; Suet. *Div. Jul.* 22; Ap. *B.C.* 2.13; Plu. *Cat. Min.* 33, *Caes.* 14, *Pomp.* 48; V.P. 2.44.

19. Dio 38.9; Suet. *Div. Jul.* 20; Ap. *B.C.* 2.12; Plu. *Luc.* 42.

20. Taylor 1968: 175, 177.

21. Dio 38.9–11.

22. Lintott 1994: 3; Morgan 2000: 51.

23. Taylor 1968: 175.

24. Plu. *Al.* 1.

25. Plu. *Al.* 1.

26. Plu. *Aem. Paul.* 1, *Tim.* 1.

27. Pelling 1979: 75.

28. Cic. *Pro Arch.* 21.

29. Plu. *Luc.* 33.

30. Plu. *Cat. Min.* 27.

31. Plu. *Cat. Min.* 30.

32. Plu. *Cat. Min.* 9, 27, 45.

33. Suet. *Div. Jul.* 4–18.

34. C. Begbie, 1967, "The Epitome of Livy," *CQ* 17: 337–338.

35. Livy *Per.* 103.

36. Pelling 1979: 85, 91.

37. Ap. *B.C.* 2.35, 46, 82, 3.77, 4.110.

38. Livy 39.52, for example.

39. Dio 41.27.

40. Ap. *B.C.* 2.10.

41. Plu. *Caes.* 14.

42. Livy *Per.* 103.

APPENDIX E: Dating of Events of the Year 59

1. Cic. *Att.* 2.4–9, 12. Unfortunately no letters survive from earlier in the year.

2. Cic. *Att.* 2.12.

3. Cic. *Att.* 2.8–9.

4. Cic. *Att.* 2.4–7.

5. Cic. *Att.* 2.6–7. This can only be the first land law; according to later letters of Cicero (*Att.* 2.16–17), Caesar's second land law regarding Campania would not even be proposed until late April.

6. Cic. *Att.* 2.6.

7. Goldsworthy 2006: 170; Scullard 1982: 426 n.17; Taylor 1951: 254–268, 1968: 173–193; Lintott 1968: 192; Gelzer 1968: 74. Many historians who cover Caesar's consulship avoid discussing this problem altogether; for example, Mackay 2004: 143–144.

8. A. J. Marshall, 1984, "Symbols and Showmanship in Roman Public Life: The *Fasces*," *Phoenix* 38: 131–132.

9. Suet. *Div. Jul.* 20.

10. L. R. Taylor, and T. R. S. Broughton, 1949, "The Order of the Two Consuls' Names in the Yearly Lists." *Memoirs of the American Academy in Rome* 19: 6; Taylor 1968: 173. For an argument against this interpretation see Linderski 1965: 423–442, who contends unconvincingly that the names were for various reasons reversed in the *fasti*.

11. Dio 38.6; Plu. *Cat. Min.* 32, *Pomp.* 48; Ap. *B.C.* 2.11.

12. Dio 38.6; Suet. *Div. Jul.* 20.

13. Plu. *Pomp.* 48. It is known the Plutarch made use of Pollio's history elsewhere in the *Pompey* (*Pomp.* 72).

14. V.P. 2.44. Velleius adds that Bibulus remained at home for the "greater" part of the year.

15. For example, see Taylor and Broughton 1949: 1–14; Taylor 1968: 173.

16. Plu. *Caes.* 35, 45; Pelling 1979: 76–77, 83.

17. Plu. *Cat. Min.* 31–33, *Caes.* 14.

18. Pelling 1979: 77 n. 21. As he often did, Plutarch here "conflates" events to keep the narrative moving.

19. Michels 1967: 40.

20. Dio 38.6; Suet. *Div. Jul.* 20; Ryan 1996.

21. Hadzsits 1930: 165–174.

22. Taylor 1950, 1951, 1968.

23. Michels 1967: 41.

24. Cic. *Cael.* 1. Manilius's law was later annulled because he had not waited the full *trinundinum* between the proposal and the vote.

25. Taylor 1950, 1951, 1968.

26. This may have been one of the many reasons his opponents considered his legislation to be unlawful, providing them with a potential target for litigation in the years to come.

27. Suet. *Div. Aug.* 4; Cic. *Att.* 2.12; Plin. *N.H.* 7.176; Varro *RR* 1.2.10, 2.4.1; Dio 38.1.

28. Taylor 1968: 181.

29. Cic. *Att.* 1.18–19, 2.1.

SELECTED FURTHER READING

Here is a brief look at a few of the books and journal articles used in the writing of this volume.* Some of these secondary sources have already been cited in the pertinent locations in the main text, while others have not been previously noted; each played a role in the completion of this work. This section seeks to provide the reader not only with the scholarly context in which this book was written but also with a handy catalog of further readings concerning Roman Republican history in general and the year 59 in particular.

There are many valuable introductions to Roman history. Christopher Mackay provides a general overview in *Ancient Rome: A Political and Military History* (Cambridge 2004). For the late republic there is H. H. Scullard's (relatively) brief but engaging narrative *From the Gracchi to Nero: A History of Rome from 133 BC to AD 68* (London 1982). For a more detailed look there is volume IX of the *Cambridge Ancient History*, *The Last Age of the Roman Republic, 146–43 BC* (Cambridge 1994), edited by J. A. Crook, Andrew Lintott, and Elizabeth Rawson. It provides both a historical narrative of the period and detailed thematic chapters on almost every aspect of Roman government and society. Similarly, Erich Gruen's *The Last Generation of the Roman Republic* (Berkeley 1974), Peter Brunt's *The Fall of the Roman Republic and Related Essays* (Oxford 1988), *The Cambridge Companion to the Roman Republic* (Cambridge 2004), edited by Harriet Flower, and *A Companion to the Roman Republic* (Chichester 2010), edited by Nathan Rosenstein and Robert Morstein-Marx, all offer narratives along with chapters on specific political, military, legal, and social topics.

For an in-depth discussion of Rome's government see Andrew Lintott's *The Constitution of the Roman Republic* (Oxford 1999). Other informative books focus on specific aspects of that constitution: *Consuls and Res Publica: Holding*

*Most scholarly articles can now be accessed online through JSTOR at www.jstor.org and Project MUSE at www.muse.jhu.edu. The primary sources used in this book are discussed in appendix D.

High Office in the Roman Republic (Cambridge 2011), edited by Hans Beck; Francisco Pina Polo's *The Consul at Rome: The Civil Functions of the Consuls in the Roman Republic* (Cambridge 2011); and T. Corey Brennan's *The Praetorship in the Roman Republic, volumes I and II* (Oxford 2001).

There are many great books and articles on republican politics. Ronald Syme's *The Roman Revolution* (Oxford 1939) remains a classic; covering the republic's fall and the rise of empire, it was in many ways influenced by world events of the 1930s, in particular the failure of European democracies and the rise of totalitarian states. Fergus Millar changed the modern perception of Roman politics with three seminal works: "The Political Character of the Classical Roman Republic, 200–151 BC," *Journal of Roman Studies* 74 (1984): 1–19, "Politics, Persuasion and the People before the Social War (150–90 BC)," *Journal of Roman Studies* 76 (1986): 1–11, and *The Crowd in Rome in the Late Republic* (Ann Arbor 1998), which covers Caesar's consulship. Before these appeared, historians generally agreed that the republican government was a narrow oligarchy consisting of wealthy senators who controlled the state through various legal and social means. Millar argued that in fact the republic was in many ways a democracy, especially in the late republic, when the people often played a direct role in the course of political history. Numerous studies followed, many in favor of Millar's thesis: Alexander Yakobson's "Secret Ballot and Its Effect in the Late Roman Republic," *Hermes* 123 (1995): 426–442, and *Elections and Electioneering in Rome, A Study in the Political System of the Late Republic* (Stuttgart 1999); Morstein-Marx's *Mass Oratory and Political Power in the Late Roman Republic* (Cambridge 2004); James Tan's "*Contiones* in the Age of Cicero," *Classical Antiquity* 27 (2008): 163–201; and *Community and Communication: Oratory and Politics in the Roman Republic* (Oxford 2013), edited by C. Steel and H. van der Blom. Henrik Mouritsen's *Plebs and Politics in the Late Republic* (Cambridge 2001) argues against Millar's findings.

There are many other enlightening works on politics in the late republic, such as David Epstein's *Personal Enmity in Roman Politics, 218–43 BC* (London 1987). Other works discuss the continuing prominent role of the nobility, such as Brunt's "*Nobilitas* and *Novitas*," *Journal of Roman Studies* 72 (1982): 1–17, and John North's "Politics and Aristocracy in the Roman Republic," *Classical Philology* 85 (1990): 277–287. For a study of the equestrians and in particular the publicans and their part in Roman politics see Ernst Badian's *Publicans and Sinners* (Ithaca 1972). Bribery was an important part of the political process and has been analyzed in studies by Lintott, "Electoral Bribery in the Roman Republic," *Journal of Roman Studies* 80 (1990): 1–16, and in Yakobson's "*Petitio et Largitio*: Popular Participation in the Centuriate Assembly of the Late Republic," *Journal of Roman Studies* 82 (1992): 32–52. There have been numerous analyses of Roman law and the courts, and especially their connection to political competition—for example, A. H. M. Jones's *The Criminal Courts of Roman Republic and Principate* (Oxford 1972), and Michael Alexander's *Trials in the Late Roman Republic, 149–50 BC* (Toronto 1990). For a study of the calendar and its impact on Roman politics see A. K. Michels's *The Calendar of the Roman Republic* (Princeton 1967). Claude Nicolet provides a detailed study of the civic, political, and military duties of the Roman citizen in *The World of the Citizen in Republican Rome* (Berkeley 1980). Many studies have been done on the city of Rome as the stage upon which all Roman politics played out. Some useful books and articles on the subject include: J. E. Stambaugh, *The Ancient Roman City* (Baltimore 1988); S. M. Cerutti, "The Location of the Houses of Cicero and Clodius in the *Porticus Catuli* on the Palatine Hill in Rome," *American Journal of Philology* 118 (1997): 417–426; Peter Aicher, *Rome Alive, A Source-Guide to the Ancient City* (Wauconda, IL 2004); and John Patterson, "The City of Rome Revisited: From Mid-Republic to Mid-Empire," *Journal of Roman Studies* 100 (2010): 210–232. For a general study of one of the major problems that plagued the political process see Lintott's *Violence in Republican Rome* (Oxford 1968). As the title implies, *The Roman Triumph* (Cambridge 2007), by Mary Beard, provides a detailed account of the great parades held to celebrate Rome's military victories and their role in Roman politics. Numerous books and articles have covered the important link between politics and empire. One good example is A. N. Sherwin-White's *Roman Foreign Policy in the East, 168 BC to AD 1* (Norman, OK 1984), which in part focuses on Pompey's eastern conquests and their aftermath. The Roman army played an enormous role in the history of the late republic and in its eventual transformation. Still a valuable study remains Brunt's "The Army and the Land in the Roman Revolution," *Journal of Roman Studies* 52 (1962): 69–86, which discusses the backgrounds of Rome's soldiers and their willingness to follow their generals even against Rome itself. Lastly, a unique reference source is T. R. S. Broughton's *The Magistrates of the Roman Republic, Volume I* (New York 1951), and *The Magistrates of the Roman Republic, Volume II* (New York 1952). These books provide a list of (almost) every known Roman magistrate for each year beginning in 509, after the expulsion of the last king, and continuing down to the republic's fall in 31.

Because the stage of the late republic was graced by so many colorful characters it should not be a surprise that the list of biographies is almost limitless. The most popular subject of all is Caesar. Two old standards are Mattias

Gelzer's *Caesar: Politician and Statesman* (Cambridge, translated by Peter Needham, 1968), and Christian Meier's *Caesar* (New York, translated by David McLintock, 1995). Two recent and informative entries into the Caesarian corpus include Adrian Goldsworthy's *Caesar: Life of a Colossus* (New Haven 2006), and W. Jeffrey Tatum's *Always I Am Caesar* (Malden, MA 2008). Pompey (Robin Seager, *Pompey: A Political Biography*, Berkeley 1979), Crassus (F. E. Adcock, *Marcus Crassus Millionaire*, Cambridge 1966; B. A. Marshall, *Crassus, A Political Biography*, Amsterdam 1976; A. M. Ward, *Marcus Crassus and the Late Roman Republic*, Columbia, MO 1977), Cicero (T. N. Mitchell, *Cicero: The Senior Statesman*, New Haven 1991), Clodius (W. J. Tatum, *The Patrician Tribune, Publius Clodius Pulcher*, Chapel Hill 1999), and even Lucullus (Arthur Keaveney, *Lucullus, A Life*, London 1992) have also been the subjects of extended and informative profiles.

Journal articles generally provide the most meticulous investigations of the important episodes of the year 59. A partial list includes analyses of the order of events: Lily Ross Taylor, "On the Chronology of Caesar's First Consulship," *American Journal of Philology* 72 (1951): 254–268, "The Dating of Major Legislation and Elections in Caesar's First Consulship," *Historia* 17 (1968): 173–193; and Lintott, "*Nundinae* and the Chronology of the Late Republic," *Classical Quarterly* 18 (1968): 189–194. Other articles focus on the elections: W. C. Grummel, "The Consular Elections of 59 BC," *Classical Journal* 49 (1954): 351–354; and J. Linderski, "Constitutional Aspects of the Consular Elections in 59 BC," *Historia* 14 (1965): 423–442. Many scholars discuss the various political figures and the alliances they formed in 59: R. J. Rowland, "Crassus, Clodius, and Curio in the Year 59 BC," *Historia* 15 (1966): 217–223; G. R. Stanton and B. A. Marshall, "The Coalition between Pompeius and Crassus 60–59 BC," *Historia* 24 (1975): 205–219; F. X. Ryan, "Bibulus as President of the Senate," *Latomus* 55 (1996): 384–388. There are many in-depth discussions of individual episodes—for example, Gruen's "The Trial of C. Antonius," *Latomus* 32 (1973): 301–310; W. Allen's "The 'Vettius Affair' Once More," *Transactions of the American Philological Association* 81 (1950): 153–163; and Taylor's "The Date and Meaning of the Vettius Affair," *Historia* 1 (1950): 45–51. Lastly there is R. E. Smith's attempt to assess the overall importance of the year in "The Significance of Caesar's Consulship in 59 BC," *Phoenix* 18 (1964): 303–313.

Journal articles are also important for 58. Some examples include: Mitchell, "The *Leges Clodiae* and *obnuntiatio*," *Classical Quarterly* 36 (1986): 172–176; Badian, "The Attempt to Try Caesar," *In Polis and imperium: Studies in Honor of Edward Togo Salmon*, edited by J. A. S. Evans (Toronto 1974); Seager, "Clodius,

Pompeius and the Exile of Cicero," *Latomus* 24 (1965): 519–531; S. I. Oost, "Cato Uticensis and the Annexation of Cyprus," *Classical Philology* 50 (1955): 98–112; Badian, "M. Porcius Cato and the Annexation and Early Administration of Cyprus," *Journal of Roman Studies* 55 (1965): 110–121.

For those who enjoy historical fiction there are numerous items to choose from. The most comprehensive, and entertaining, is Colleen McCullough's Masters of Rome series. Comprising seven books altogether, the series follows Roman history from the year 110 BC down to Octavian's assumption of the title Augustus in 27. Caesar is a major character in books two through six, and the fourth book, *Caesar's Women*, covers his consulship in 59.

INDEX